Discover Your True North

Expanded and Updated Edition

Bill George

WILEY

Cover image: Compass © iStock.com/LdF
Cover design: Wiley

Published by John Wiley & Sons, Inc., Hoboken, New Jersey.
Published simultaneously in Canada.

Limit of Liability/Disclaimer of Warranty: While the publisher and author have used their best efforts in preparing this book, they make no representations or warranties with respect to the accuracy or completeness of the contents of this book and specifically disclaim any implied warranties of merchantability or fitness for a particular purpose. No warranty may be created or extended by sales representatives or written sales materials. The advice and strategies contained herein may not be suitable for your situation. You should consult with a professional where appropriate. Neither the publisher nor author shall be liable for any loss of profit or any other commercial damages, including but not limited to special, incidental, consequential, or other damages.

For general information on our other products and services or for technical support, please contact our Customer Care Department within the United States at (800) 762–2974, outside the United States at (317) 572–3993 or fax (317) 572–4002.

Wiley publishes in a variety of print and electronic formats and by print-on-demand. Some material included with standard print versions of this book may not be included in e-books or in print-on-demand. If this book refers to media such as a CD or DVD that is not included in the version you purchased, you may download this material at http://booksupport.wiley.com. For more information about Wiley products, visit www.wiley.com.

Library of Congress Cataloging-in-Publication Data:

George, Bill (William W.)
[Finding your true north.]
    Discover your true north/Bill George.-Second edition, Expanded and Updated Edition.
       pages cm
    Revised edition of the author's Finding your true north, 2008.
    Includes index.
    ISBN 978–1–119–08294–1 (hardback); ISBN 978–1–119–08297–2 (ePDF); ISBN 978–1–119–08295–8 (ePub)
    1. Leadership. 2. Organizational effectiveness. I.   Title.
    HD57.7.G45814 2015
    658.4'092-dc23   2015013574

Printed in the United States of America

10 9 8 7 6 5

This book is dedicated to my family. First to my wife, Penny, whose love, passion for life, and counsel have enabled all the Georges to discover our True North. And to our sons, Jeff and Jon, and our daughters-in-law, Renee and Jeannette, who are making important contributions to the world as authentic leaders.

BEST-SELLING BOOKS BY BILL GEORGE

Authentic Leadership: Rediscovering the Secrets to Creating Lasting Value (2003)

True North: Discover Your Authentic Leadership (2007) (with Peter Sims)

Finding Your True North: A Personal Guide (2008) (with Nick Craig and Andrew McLean)

7 Lessons for Leading in Crisis (2009)

Contents

Preface

The Remarkable Legacy of
Warren Bennis

Warren Bennis was one of the great pioneers in the field of leadership. Small in physical stature, he was a giant in his intellect, his heart, and his spirit. Just as Peter Drucker was the father of management, Bennis was the father of leadership.

Bennis transformed our understanding of what it means to be a leader. He was the first scholar who said leadership is not a set of genetic characteristics, but the result of a lifelong process of self-discovery. Rejecting the notion that leaders are born with certain traits, he opened the door to the real source of leadership: *within you.* He wrote:

> *The most dangerous leadership myth is that leaders are born—that there is a genetic factor to leadership. This myth asserts that people simply either have certain charismatic qualities or not. That's nonsense; in fact, the opposite is true. Leaders are made rather than born.*

He showed how leaders develop through their life experiences, are shaped by their crucibles, and emerge ever stronger to take on responsibilities of leadership. He said unequivocally, "Leadership is character," adding,

> *It is not just a superficial question of style, but has to do with who we are as human beings, and with the forces that have shaped us. The process of becoming a leader is much the same as the process of becoming an integrated human being.*

Bennis's early life was deeply influenced by his association at Antioch College and later at the Massachusetts Institute of Technology with Douglas McGregor, author of *The Human Side of Enterprise*. While in Cambridge, he connected with Abraham Maslow (creator of Maslow's Hierarchy of Needs), Peter Drucker, Paul Samuelson, and Erik Erikson, whose theories on the eight stages of human development influenced Bennis's own *generativity* in his later years. He went on to write 30 books. Many of today's influential leadership authors, such as Tom Peters, Nitin Nohria, David Gergen, Jim O'Toole, Bob Sutton, Jeff Sonnenfeld, and Doug Conant are indebted to Bennis for their ideas.

As president of the University of Cincinnati, he realized his personal truth, "I was never going to be able to be happy with *positional power*. What I really wanted was *personal power*: having influence based on my voice. My real gift is what I can do in the classroom and as a mentor." Following a heart attack in 1979, he found his home at the University of Southern California.

Bennis's influence on business leaders was widespread and profound. Thousands of leaders who never knew him were inspired by his writings and adopted his approach to leadership. Many chief executive officers (CEOs) have told me personally what a profound influence he had on their leadership.

I first encountered his writing in 1989 when I read *On Becoming a Leader*. It was a revelation: Finally, I had found a philosophy of leadership I could resonate with. Throughout my years at Medtronic and Harvard Business School (HBS), I have built on his philosophies in my work and teaching.

We first met at the World Economic Forum in the late 1990s. He suffered from heart problems, and had recently had a Medtronic defibrillator implanted. In December of 2000 I invited him as a guest patient to an annual Medtronic event, where he graciously thanked the employees who designed and manufactured his defibrillator in front of 10,000 people.

He was fond of saying he had Medtronic "in his heart" and then describing how his defibrillator saved his life half a dozen times. I once witnessed this in person in Cambridge. While he was speaking, his defibrillator went off, and he slumped to the ground, dropping his papers. Ever the gracious soul, he picked up his papers, apologized for the disruption, and continued his talk. When it went off a second time 10 minutes later, the Cambridge Fire Department escorted him to safety.

In 2002, my wife, Penny, and I attended a seminar Bennis and David Gergen led at the Aspen Institute. At the time I was eager to write a book on my experiences at Medtronic but was struggling to find a publisher. My intent was to offer practical approaches to leading and develop leaders that enabled people to be their authentic selves, rather than emulating others. With Bennis's encouragement, Jossey-Bass published *Authentic Leadership* as part of the Warren Bennis Signature Series. Bennis served as executive editor and wrote in the foreword, "Timeless leadership is always about character, and it is always about authenticity."

He became my mentor, friend, and intellectual colleague, and gave me the courage to become a writer. As executive editor for my four books in the Warren Bennis Signature Series, he generously shared his time and his insights. In the midst of writing *True North*, Peter Sims and I spent five days with him going over the conceptual ideas and stories used in the book. Unlike many great scholars who protect their ideas, Bennis genuinely wanted me to expand on his and make them fully accessible to the new generation of leaders, which he later called "the crucible generation." We shared a common aim to influence the next generation to lead with clear purpose to serve others and make the world a better place.

Two months before he died, Bennis asked my wife and me to discuss leadership in the next-to-last class he ever taught. Although Bennis was beset with bodily ills, his mind and humanity were as sharp as ever. What other professors have you known who were still teaching at age 89? Over dinner that evening Penny asked what he would like on his tombstone. He replied, "Generous Friend." A generous friend is just what Bennis was to thousands of friends, students, scholars, and mentees whom he influenced with kindness, buoyancy of spirit, and wisdom.

Bennis's last book, *Still Surprised*, has a photo of him walking barefoot on the beach with his pant legs rolled up, leaving behind large footprints in the sand. These footprints serve as a calling to incorporate his ideas in our leadership. Ultimately, this will become Bennis's greatest legacy. They bring to mind a stanza from Henry Wadsworth Longfellow's *A Psalm of Life*:

> *Lives of great men all remind us*
> *We can make our lives sublime,*
> *And, departing, leave behind us*
> *Footprints on the sands of time.*

Foreword

When Peter Drucker was in his prime, CEOs often traveled across the country to California to seek his counsel on how to lead and manage their companies. He was an iconic figure in the business world, the father of management studies, whose 30 books were highly influential in shaping modern global companies. As I found in conversation late in his life, he had a wisdom about him that was spellbinding.

Upon his death 10 years ago, people naturally asked, "Who will carry on Peter's work?" Soon it became apparent that the most obvious candidate was Warren Bennis, and once again, CEOs made the trek to California to meet quietly with one of the sweetest, wisest men I have been blessed to know. Warren was the father of leadership studies in American universities, the man who gave them academic legitimacy through his two dozen books, and the best mentor and friend one could possibly have.

Upon his death a year ago, the question naturally arose again: "Well, who will now carry on Warren's work?" With the publication of his sixth and most important book, *Discover Your True North*, we may well have our candidate: Bill George. There are obvious differences: Bill himself would modestly point out that both Drucker and Bennis were lifelong scholars deeply schooled in theory; by contrast, Bill first made his mark as a highly successful CEO of a large company before becoming a major thought leader. Yet all three have been at the forefront in shaping leadership and management practices of successive generations.

By chance, Warren introduced me to Bill along with Dan Vasella of Novartis at a dinner in Davos, Switzerland, where we were all attending the World Economic Forum in 2001. Bill was coming off his years as CEO of Medtronic and was beginning to pull together his thoughts and experiences about leadership so that he could share them with younger business leaders.

Soon Bill published his first book, essentially a memoir, titled *Authentic Leadership*, and it was quickly a best seller. Without realizing it, he had launched an entirely new career, one with even greater impact than his first. In reading *Discover Your True North*, you will find not only a distillation of his ideas about leadership but also revealing portraits of a galaxy of more diverse leaders and what they have learned on their own journeys toward a True North. This book bids to be a classic, standing alongside *The Effective Executive* by Peter Drucker and *On Becoming a Leader* by Warren Bennis. I am proud to call Bill a friend and trusted adviser—and to salute him on the completion of his best book.

Here's what is essential for a reader to understand: Experience shows that Bill's ideas not only work well in practice but *also* apply across the board, helping not only business leaders but those in the civic and public sectors as well. Most books that come from the academy are intended for a small audience of specialized scholars. That is the way advances in knowledge are often made. But non-scholars wonder how this progress applies to them.

Bill George's work—like Warren's and Peter's—intentionally crosses the bridge between the academy and practice. Through writing, teaching, and mentoring, he is helping leaders become better at leading themselves and, in turn, their organizations. At present more than two dozen CEOs of major global companies are calling on him regularly for counsel and advice.

The evidence shows that leaders from across the world are hungry to discover their True North and to make it their polar star. After initial teaching stints at the International Institute for Management Development (IMD) in Europe and at Yale School of Management, Bill came to the Harvard Business School (HBS) as a professor of management. There in 2005, he introduced his course, Authentic Leadership Development, as a second-year elective. Students embraced it with growing enthusiasm, such that it has become one of the most popular courses at HBS and attracts a growing number in executive education.

Bill no longer teaches the master of business administration course but instead is focusing on executive education, where CEOs and senior executives focus on their leadership, including three courses each year for CEOs. Now there is a cadre of other faculty members who are devotees, led by Scott Snook (a retired army officer) and Tom DeLong and blessed by Dean Nitin Nohria.

Fortunately, Bill's course has migrated to the Harvard Kennedy School (HKS), where I am a professor of practice and codirector of our Center for Public Leadership. Dana Born, a retired air force general and the first woman in any military branch to gain flag rank while at a military academy, has just started teaching the course, and once again students are responding with gusto. Moreover, Bill has introduced True North to an annual training program at the HKS for Young Global Leaders chosen by the World Economic Forum. Attendees love what the program offers, especially the deep-dive, small-group conversations every morning over breakfast.

Altogether, some 6,000 men and women have now been trained at Harvard alone in Bill's ideas about authentic leadership. Longitudinal studies are not yet possible on how much he may have shaped lives and leadership, but anecdotal evidence points to encouraging results.

One group that has had lots of exposure to Bill and his work is students who have pursued joint degrees at HBS and HKS and in their third year have received scholarships from Bill and Penny George. These George Fellows, typically in their late twenties, have a home at our Center for Public Leadership and meet frequently, often with Bill and Penny. Bill generously mentors a number of them and remains close long after they have graduated. Altogether, the George Fellowship now has 100 alumni.

To be sure, many had transformative experiences that strengthened their leadership before they became George Fellows. Even so, their recent achievements have been impressive. Here are a few whom Bill continues to mentor: Seth Moulton won an upset victory in his campaign for Congress and has attracted a national following. Maura Sullivan is now serving as an assistant secretary at the Department of Veterans Administration. Nate Fick is CEO of Endgame as well as former CEO of the Center for a New American Security and author of *One Bullet Away*. Brian Elliott founded Friendfactor, a lesbian, gay, bisexual, and transgender (LGBT) nonprofit for straight people that has been pivotal in winning battles for gay rights. Rye Barcott is running a venture fund for solar installations in North Carolina; was selected as a Young Global Leader at Davos; and is author of *It Happened on the Way to War*. John Coleman is a principal of Invesco in Atlanta and coauthored *How to Argue Like Jesus*. Stephen Chan is chief of staff for the Boston Foundation. Peter Brooks works for a water technology company and directs the Warrior-Scholar Project. Jonathan Kelly runs a private equity company based in Singapore. And Claude Burton is directing marketing for a rapidly growing information technology firm in Brazil. Can there be any doubt that the ideas here apply to emerging leaders from every sector of life and across national boundaries?

As this book is being published, the world is slipping ever more deeply into a leadership crisis. For people everywhere, life is becoming ever more volatile and unpredictable. Instead of putting a firm hand on the wheel, many leaders seem unable to steer toward safe ports in the storm. A survey of global opinion the World Economic Forum published in 2015 found that 76 percent believe we have had a serious loss of leadership. Business leaders have recovered some of their ground lost since 2008–2009, but they rank only modestly above political leaders.

This book can perhaps help us find our way. If individual leaders can recognize when they have drifted away from True North and make successful course corrections, as Bill George argues, nations can as well. Surely, authentic leadership beats what we have now.

David Gergen

Introduction

Have you discovered *your* True North? Do you know what your life and your leadership are all about?

Leadership starts with being authentic, the genuine you. The purpose of *Discover Your True North* is to enable you to become the leader you want to be. In the process you will discover your True North—the internal compass that guides you successfully through life.

Your True North

True North is your orienting point—your fixed point in a spinning world—that helps you stay on track as a leader. It is derived from your most deeply held beliefs, your values, and the principles you lead by. It is your internal compass, unique to you, that represents who you are at your deepest level.

Just as a compass needle points toward a magnetic pole, your True North pulls you toward the purpose of your leadership. When you follow your internal compass, your leadership will be authentic, and people will naturally want to associate with you. Although others may guide or influence you, your truth is derived from your life story. As Warren Bennis said, "You are the author of your life."

Discovering your True North takes a lifetime of commitment and learning. As you are tested in the world, you yearn to look at yourself in the mirror and respect the person you see and the life you are leading. Some days will be better than others, but as long as you are true to who you are, you can cope with the most difficult circumstances life presents.

The world may have very different expectations for you than you have for yourself. Whether you are leading a small team or at the top of an organization, you will be pressured by external forces to respond to their needs and seduced by rewards for fulfilling those needs. These pressures and seductions may cause you to detour from your True North. When you get too far off course, your internal compass tells you something is wrong and you need to reorient yourself. It requires courage and resolve to resist the constant pressures and expectations confronting you and to take corrective action when necessary.

As CEO of Sara Lee Brenda Barnes said, "The most important thing about leadership is your character and the values that guide your life." She added:

> If you are guided by an internal compass that represents your character and values, you're going to be fine. Let your values guide your actions and don't ever lose your internal compass. Everything isn't black or white. There are a lot of gray areas in business.

When you discover your True North, you find coherence between your life story and your leadership. A century ago psychologist William James wrote:

> I have often thought that the best way to define a man's character would be to seek out the particular mental or moral attitude in which . . . he felt himself most deeply and intensely active and alive. At such moments there is a voice inside which speaks and says: "This is the real me!"

Can you recall a time when you felt most intensely alive and could say with confidence, "*This is the real me*"? Professionally, I had that feeling from the first time I walked into Medtronic in 1989 and joined a group of talented people dedicated to the mission to "alleviate pain, restore health, and extend life." I felt I could be myself and be appreciated for who I was and what I could contribute.

I sensed immediately that my values aligned with the organization's values.

The Rise of Authentic Leaders

When I wrote *Authentic Leadership* in 2003, the most common question I received was "What do you mean by *authenticity?*" To me, being authentic was the natural way of leading, but many people in that era of charismatic leaders considered leading authentically a new idea.

Today *authenticity is seen as the gold standard for leadership*. No longer is leadership about developing charisma, emulating other leaders, looking good externally, and acting in one's self-interest, as was so often the case in the late twentieth century. Nor should leadership be conflated with your leadership style, managerial skills, or competencies. These capabilities are very important, but they are the outward manifestation of who you are as a person. You cannot fake it to make it, because people sense intuitively whether you are genuine.

The hierarchical, directive leadership style so prevalent in the past century is fading fast in favor of today's collaborative leaders, who believe in distributed leadership at all levels. The old notion of leaders as the smartest guys in the room—as Enron CEO Jeff Skilling typified—has been replaced by leaders with high levels of emotional intelligence (EQ).

Because of this move toward greater authenticity, we are blessed with much higher caliber leaders today. In discovering their True North, they have committed to leading with purpose to make a difference in the world and leave behind lasting legacies. The quality of today's leaders is reflected in the lasting results they are achieving within their organizations.

For this all-new edition, my colleague Zach Clayton and I interviewed and studied 47 authentic leaders that represent the diversity of the new generation of global leaders—among them, Unilever's Paul Polman, PepsiCo's Indra Nooyi, Alibaba's Jack Ma, the *Huffington Post*'s Arianna Huffington, Merck's Ken Frazier, and Sojourners' Jim Wallis.

Before writing *True North* in 2007, our research team of Peter Sims, Diana Mayer, Andrew McLean, and I set out to get definitive answers to the question of *how* to develop authentic leaders. We interviewed 125 authentic leaders to learn the secrets of their leadership. This research constitutes the largest in-depth study ever undertaken on how business leaders develop.

We circled back to most of the leaders interviewed for the first edition to get updated on their progress as leaders. Much to our pleasure, we found that the vast majority of them are doing exceptionally well. Some have moved to new positions, some have retired from their organizations and taken on new challenges, but almost all of them continue to make vital contributions to business and society. Only a handful have failed.

In *Discover Your True North*, we retain the structure of the first edition, but go much deeper into what we have learned about leadership in the past decade. It includes many insights that my Harvard Business School colleagues and I, as well as practitioners and scholars around the world, have learned about leaders: how they discovered their True North, developed as authentic leaders, became global leaders, and stayed on the course of their True North throughout their lifetimes.

Although the 47 new leaders included in *Discover Your True North* are more international and more diverse than the first group, their stories and beliefs about leadership showed a high level of congruence with the earlier interviewees. (The back of the book contains the list of interviewees for this updated edition.)

Rather than waiting to get to the top to become leaders, they looked for every opportunity to lead and to develop themselves. Every one of them faced trials, some of them severe. Many cited these experiences, along with the people who helped them develop, as primary reasons for their success. Without exception, these leaders believed being authentic made them more effective and successful.

As the result of our research into these leaders, we have a clearer understanding of what constitutes an effective and authentic leader. We know that each leader is unique, just as each human being is. The reality is that *no one can be authentic by trying to be like someone else.* You can learn from others' experiences, but you cannot be successful trying to be *like* them. People will only trust you when you are genuine and authentic.

If you create a false persona or wear a mask, people will quickly see through you. As Reatha Clark King, chair of the National Association of Corporate Directors, said:

> *If you're aiming to be like somebody else, you're being a copycat because you think that's what people want you to do. You'll never be a star with that kind of thinking. But you might be a star—unreplicable—by following your passion.*

Amgen chairman and CEO Kevin Sharer, who gained priceless experience at the beginning of his career by working as Jack Welch's assistant, saw the downside of General Electric's cult of personality in those days. "Everyone wanted to be like Jack," he explained. "Leadership has many voices. You need to be who you are, not try to emulate somebody else."

The Leadership Transformation

What has caused this dramatic change in today's leaders?

As CEO of Medtronic in the 1990s, I witnessed firsthand many corporations choose the wrong people as CEO. Under pressure from Wall Street to maximize short-term earnings, boards of directors frequently selected leaders for their image, style, and charisma rather than their substance and character. Many of these leaders put their companies at risk by focusing on the trappings and spoils of leadership instead of building their organizations for the long term. When those who failed walked away with enormous financial settlements, confidence in business leaders further eroded.

These stock market pressures boomeranged in the fall of 2008 when many financial institutions became insolvent, forcing the U.S. government to intervene to save the economic system from complete collapse. In the deep recession that followed, millions of Americans depleted their savings and unemployment rose above 10 percent. The root cause of this crisis was not financial instruments, such as subprime mortgages, but *failed leaders*, just as it was in the early 2000s.

As a result, public trust in business leaders fell to its lowest level in 50 years. In business, trust is the coin of the realm. The success of any organization depends upon customers' trust in the products they buy, employees' trust in their leaders, investors' trust in those who steward their funds, and public trust in capitalism as a fair and equitable means of creating wealth for all. More than seven years after the global financial crisis, the public still has low trust in business leaders.

The positive side of these crises is the high quality of leaders who have emerged in the new generation and how well they have learned the lessons of these debacles. These leaders lived through the corporate governance debacle of 2003, when Enron and WorldCom went bankrupt, and survived the global financial collapse of 2008.

From these negative experiences when many leaders went awry, today's leaders learned what *not* to do. They saw many of their predecessors get caught in the trap of chasing money, fame, and power, and lose sight of their True North. They learned the perils of putting self-interest ahead of the institutions they were chosen to lead. Most important, they learned that being authentic is the most effective and sustainable way to lead.

As we will see through their stories, today's leaders have discovered their True North and are pursuing it to the best of their abilities. And yet, leading an organization today is much more difficult than when I was CEO. Today's leaders have to cope with vastly increased pressures for short-term results and far greater legal and regulatory compliance, all of which can pull them off the course of their True North.

In reading *Discover Your True North*, you may wonder why we focus so much on your life story and on developing yourself, as opposed to leading others. As we have learned from working with many leaders, *the hardest person you will ever have to lead is yourself.* Once you are fully comfortable with who you are—and feel good in your own skin—leading others authentically becomes much easier.

Authentic leaders who follow their True North have learned from their crucibles and setbacks. They have the resilience to resist pressures and seductions. They know they must be authentic to gain legitimacy with those with whom they work and the multiple stakeholders who have vested interests in their organizations. They are committed to building sustainable value for their institutions, while producing near-term results.

The fact that business today is far more global than it was a decade ago has significant implications for leadership throughout the world. As World Economic Forum USA chair Jean-Pierre Rosso reflected, "Today's leaders are more global, more open, and more concerned about societal issues than their predecessors."

The new generation of leaders introduced here are much more diverse than their predecessors, more global in their outlook and national origin, and more likely to be promoted from within. Many more women, people of color, and leaders who live and work outside their country of origin are among today's authentic leaders. They have global visions and a desire to make lasting contributions. As a result, authentic global leaders who understand today's global business world are rising to the top of organizations around the world.

As *Fortune*'s Manager of the Century, Jack Welch has long been thought of as the prototypical leader of the twentieth century. Unilever's Paul Polman is emerging as such a leader in this new century. Figure I.1 shows some of the ways this generation of leaders differs from its predecessors.

Characteristics	Twentieth-Century Leaders	Twenty-First-Century Leaders
Image	Charismatic	Purpose-driven
Focus	U.S.-centric	Global vision
Motivation	Self-interest	Institution's best interests
Experience	Perfect resume	Learning through crucibles
Time frame	Short-term	Long-term
Organizational approach	Hierarchal leadership	Distributed leadership
Greatest strength	IQ	EQ
Personal measurement	External validation	Intrinsic contribution

Figure I.1   Differences in Twentieth-Century and Twenty-First-Century Leaders

What is an authentic leader? *Authentic leaders have discovered their True North, align people around a shared purpose and values, and empower them to lead authentically to create value for all stakeholders.*

Authentic leaders are true to themselves and to what they believe in. They engender trust and develop genuine connections with others. Because people trust them, authentic leaders are able to motivate them to achieve high levels of performance. Rather than letting the expectations of others guide them, they are their own persons and go their own ways. As servant leaders, they are more concerned about serving people than about their own success or recognition.

This is not to say that authentic leaders are perfect. Far from it. All leaders have weaknesses and are subject to human frailties and mistakes. Yet by acknowledging their shortcomings and admitting their errors, their humanity and vulnerability come through, and they are able to connect with people and inspire them.

Discover Your True North is written for anyone who wants to be an authentic leader and discover his or her True North. It is for leaders at all stages of their lives, from students aspiring to lead to those at the top of organizations. You are never too young, or too old, to take on leadership challenges and lead authentically. *Discover Your True North* is grounded in the hundreds of years of experience of the authentic leaders we interviewed as well as my own 50 years in leadership roles. For you, the reader, it is an opportunity to learn from authentic leaders and to create your own development plan to become an authentic leader.

The bottom line is this: *You can discover your True North right now.*

- You do not have to be born with the characteristics or traits of a leader.
- You do not have to be at the top of an organization.
- You can step up and lead at any point in your life.

As CEO of Young & Rubicam Ann Fudge said:

All of us have the spark of leadership in us, whether it is in business, government, or as a nonprofit volunteer. The challenge is to understand ourselves well enough to discover where we can use our leadership gifts to serve others. We're here for something. Life is about giving and living fully.

Discover Your True North

Discovering your True North is hard work. You may take many years to find it, as was the case for me.

This book does not contain six easy steps to discover your True North or other simple formulas. It takes the opposite approach. Discovering your True North requires you to maintain your individuality and retain your authenticity. This requires introspection, support, and feedback of friends and colleagues. Ultimately, *you must take responsibility for your own development.* Like musicians or athletes born with great abilities, you must devote yourself to a lifetime of development to realize your potential.

Part I of *Discover Your True North* examines the journey to authentic leadership. It begins with the leaders' life stories, which are unique to them and more powerful than any set of characteristics or leadership skills they possess. Next, the three phases of the leader's journey are dissected, looking at key steps in each phase of the journey. During their journeys, many leaders lose their way. To understand how derailment happens, we analyze five types of leaders who see themselves as heroes of their own journeys. Finally, by exploring the crucibles and life-changing experiences leaders have had, we see how they overcame setbacks and built the resilience to become authentic leaders.

Part II offers five elements of your internal compass that help you develop as a leader and get back on track when you are at risk of losing your way. This section provides you the insights to stay true to who you are as you confront challenges in the world around you. It includes five key areas of your development as a leader: self-awareness, at the center of your compass, and at the four points, your values and principles, sweet spot, support team, and integrated life (see Figure I.2).

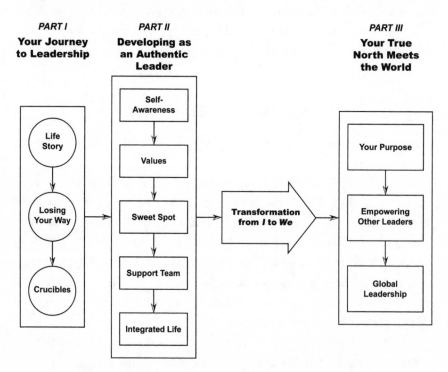

Figure I.2   Book Map: Part I, Part II, and Part III

Part III describes your transformation from an *I* leader focused on yourself to a *We* leader focused on serving others. Only when you make this transformation will you be ready to discover the purpose of your leadership and empower people around a shared purpose. Finally, as the world becomes truly global, you can develop the special qualities required to be an authentic global leader. In the afterword, we challenge leaders to serve society by making capitalism a force for solving the world's most challenging problems.

After each chapter, you will find a series of exercises that you can use to build your leadership development plan. Better yet, purchase the companion workbook, *The Discover Your True North Fieldbook: A Personal Guide to Finding Your Authentic Leadership*, written with my colleagues Nick Craig and Scott Snook, which contains in-depth exercises corresponding to each chapter in this book.

By dedicating yourself to discovering your True North, you *will* become an authentic leader who can make a positive difference in the world and leave a legacy for others to follow.

Part One

Your Journey to Leadership

In our interviews with leaders about their development, the most striking commonality was the way their life stories influenced their leadership. Your life story is your foundation. It shapes how you, as a human being, see the world. And in leadership, the most human of all endeavors, it can propel you forward or hold you back.

In Part I we examine three topics:

1. *How you frame your life story.* Your journey through life will take you through many peaks and valleys as you face the world's trials, rewards, and seductions. Reflection and introspection will help you understand your life experiences, and in some cases reframe them.

2. *The risk of losing your way.* Everyone experiences pressures and difficulties in life, and all of us have to deal with fears and uncertainties. In your life journey, you will be confronted with seductions that threaten to pull you off course from your True North. We will examine five archetypes that can cause you to lose your way.

3. *The role crucibles play in shaping your leadership.* The way you deal with your greatest adversities will shape your character far more than the adversities themselves. Much like iron is forged by heat, your most significant challenges and your most painful experiences present the greatest opportunities for your personal growth.

As you gain greater clarity and insight about your life's journey, you will discover the focus of your True North.

1

YOUR LIFE STORY

The reservoir of all my life experiences shaped me as a
person and a leader.
—*Howard Schultz, CEO, Starbucks*

The journey to authentic leadership begins with understanding
yourself: your life stories, crucibles, and setbacks. This knowledge
gives you the self-awareness to discover your True North.

Howard Schultz's Leadership Journey

In the winter of 1961, 7-year-old Howard Schultz was throwing
snowballs with friends outside his family's apartment building in the
federally subsidized Bayview Housing Projects in Brooklyn, New
York. His mother yelled down from their seventh-floor apartment,
"Howard, come inside. Dad had an accident." What followed has
shaped Schultz throughout his life.

He found his father in a full-leg cast, sprawled on the living room
couch. While working as a delivery driver, Schultz's father had fallen
on a sheet of ice and broken his ankle. As a result, he lost his job—
and the family's health care benefits. Schultz's mother could not go
to work because she was seven months pregnant. His family had
nothing to fall back on. Many evenings, Schultz listened as his
parents argued at the dinner table about how much money they
needed to borrow. If the telephone rang, his mother asked him to tell
the bill collectors his parents were not at home.

Schultz vowed he would do things differently. He dreamed of building "a company my father would be proud to work at" that treated its employees well and provided health care benefits. Little did he realize that one day he would be responsible for 191,000 employees working in 21,000 stores worldwide. Schultz's life experiences provided the motivation to build Starbucks into the world's leading coffeehouse.

"My inspiration comes from seeing my father broken from the 30 terrible blue-collar jobs he had over his life, where an uneducated person just did not have a shot," Schultz said. These memories led Schultz to provide Starbucks employees access to health coverage, even for part-time workers.

> That event is directly linked to the culture and the values of Starbucks. I wanted to build the kind of company my father never had a chance to work for, where you would be valued and respected, no matter where you came from, the color of your skin, or your level of education. Offering health care was a transforming event in the equity of the Starbucks brand that created unbelievable trust with our people. We wanted to build a company that linked shareholder value to the cultural values we create with our people.

Unlike some who rise from humble beginnings, Schultz is proud of his roots. He credits his life story with giving him the motivation to create one of the great business successes of the last 25 years. But understanding the meaning of his story took deep thought because, like nearly everyone, he had to confront fears and ghosts from his past.

Brooklyn is burned into Schultz. When he took his daughter to the housing projects where he grew up, she surveyed the blight and said with amazement, "I don't know how you are normal." Yet his experience growing up in Brooklyn is what enables Schultz to connect with practically anyone. He speaks with a slight Brooklyn accent, relishes an Italian meal, dresses comfortably in jeans, and respects all types of people. He has not forgotten where he came from or let his wealth go to his head: "I was surrounded by people who were working hand-to-mouth trying to pay the bills, felt there was no hope, and just couldn't get a break. That's something that never leaves you—never.

"From my earliest memories, I remember my mother saying that I could do anything I wanted in America. It was her mantra." His father had the opposite effect. As a truck driver, cab driver, and factory worker, he never earned more than $20,000 a year. Schultz watched his father break down while complaining bitterly about not having opportunities or respect from others.

As a teenager, Schultz clashed often with his father, as he felt the stigma of his father's failures. "I was bitter about his underachievement and lack of responsibility," he recalled. "I thought he could have accomplished so much more if he had tried." Schultz was determined to escape that fate. "Part of what has always driven me is fear of failure. I know all too well the face of self-defeat."

Feeling like an underdog, Schultz developed a deep determination to succeed. Sports became his early calling, because "I wasn't labeled a poor kid on the playing field." As star quarterback of his high school football team, he received a scholarship to Northern Michigan University, becoming the first in his family to earn a college degree. His fierce competitiveness never faded; it just shifted from football to business.

Working in sales at Xerox, Schultz felt stifled by the bureaucratic environment. While others thrived in Xerox's culture, Schultz yearned to go his own way. "I had to find a place where I could be myself," he said.

> I could not settle for anything less. You must have the courage to follow an unconventional path. You can't value or measure your life experience in the moment, because you never know when you're going to find the true path that enables you to find your voice. The reservoir of all my life experiences shaped me as a person and a leader.

Schultz encountered Starbucks Coffee during a sales call at Pike Place Market in Seattle. "I felt I had discovered a whole new continent," he said. He actively campaigned to join the company, becoming its director of operations and marketing. On a buying trip to Italy, Schultz noticed the Milanese espresso bars that created unique communities in their customers' daily lives. He dreamed of creating similar communities in America, focusing on creating coffee breaks, not just selling coffee.

When he learned he could acquire Starbucks from its founders, Schultz rounded up financing from private investors. As he was finalizing the purchase, he faced his greatest challenge when his largest investor proposed to buy the company himself. "I feared all my influential backers would defect to this investor," he recalled, "so I asked Bill Gates Sr., father of Microsoft's founder, to help me stand up to one of the titans of Seattle because I needed his stature and confidence."

Schultz had a searing meeting with the investor, who told him, "If you don't go along with my deal, you'll never work in this town again. You'll never raise another dollar. You'll be dog meat." Leaving the meeting, Schultz broke into tears. For two frenzied weeks, he prepared an alternative plan that met his $3.8 million financing goal and staved off the investor.

> If I had agreed to the terms the investor demanded, he would have taken away my dream. He could have fired me at whim and dictated the atmosphere and values of Starbucks. The passion, commitment, and dedication would have all disappeared.

The saddest day of Schultz's life came when his father died. Schultz shared with a friend the conflicts he has had with his father, and his friend remarked, "If he had been successful, you wouldn't have the drive you have now." After his father's death, Schultz reframed his image of his father, recognizing strengths such as honesty and commitment to family. Instead of seeing him as a failure, he realized his father had been crushed by the system. "After he died, I realized I had judged him unfairly. He never had the opportunity to find fulfillment and dignity from meaningful work."

Schultz channeled his drive into building a company where his father would have been proud to work. By paying more than minimum wage, offering substantial benefits, and granting stock options to all its workers, Starbucks offered employees what Schultz's father had never received and used these incentives to attract people whose values are consistent with the company's values. As a result, the employee turnover at Starbucks is less than half that at other retailers.

Among Schultz's greatest talents is his ability to connect with people from diverse backgrounds. He tells his story and the Starbucks story at special events and visits two dozen Starbucks stores per week. Each day he gets up at 5:30 AM to call Starbucks employees around the world. He said, "Starbucks gave me the canvas to paint on."

> Starbucks is the quintessential people-based business, where everything we do is about humanity. The culture and values of the company are its signature and its competitive difference. We have created worldwide appeal for our customers because people are hungry for human connection and authenticity. Whether you're Chinese, Japanese, Spanish, or Greek, coffee is just the catalyst for that connection. I don't know if I was drawn to this business because of my background, or whether it gave me the opportunity to connect the dots, but it has come full circle for me.

In 2000, Schultz turned the reins over to a new CEO, Jim Donald, but remained as board chair. In 2007, a controversial e-mail he wrote to Donald and Starbucks' executive committee expressing his concerns that the Starbucks experience was becoming *commoditized* was leaked to the press. This created a firestorm in the media and among Starbucks' customers and employees. In January 2008, Schultz returned to Starbucks as CEO. One of his first moves was to shut down all U.S. stores for a half day of employee training to emphasize Starbucks' need to restore its original culture. Starbucks' spectacular results since then have validated the effectiveness of Schultz's leadership.

Howard Schultz is one of dozens of authentic leaders who traced their inspiration and success directly to their life stories. Like most leaders, Schultz deals with both positive and negative thoughts that compete in his mind. I call this phenomenon "dueling narratives," a phenomenon that influences even the most successful leaders.

Schultz's positive narrative keeps him focused on his dream. Yet he retains a deep fear of failure emanating from his father's experiences. Rather than let his negative narrative drag him down, he uses it in conjunction with his positive narrative to keep Starbucks focused on succeeding.

Your Life Story Defines Your Leadership

The leaders we interviewed discovered their True North by understanding their life stories. Their stories cover the full spectrum of experiences, including the impact of parents, teachers, coaches, and mentors; the support of their communities; and leadership in team sports, scouting, student government, and early employment. Many leaders were influenced by difficult experiences, such as personal illness or illness of a family member; death of a loved one; or feelings of being excluded, discriminated against, or rejected by peers.

These leaders found their passion to lead through the uniqueness of their life stories.

Not by being born as leaders.

Not by believing they had the characteristics, traits, or style of a leader.

Not by trying to emulate great leaders.

Simply by being their authentic selves, they became great leaders, using their gifts to help others. Some outstanding leaders, such as Regeneron chair Roy Vagelos, did not see themselves as leaders at all. Instead, they wanted to make a difference and inspire others to join with them in pursuing common goals. If that isn't leadership, what is?

As former secretary of Health and Human Services John Gardner once said, "I guess I had certain leadership qualities that life was just waiting to pull out of me." Have you examined what leadership qualities life wants to pull out of you? Let's focus on the life stories of two more leaders. As you read these stories, think about the ways your life story inspires you and defines your leadership.

Dick Kovacevich: From Grocery Store Clerk to Premier Banker

For 20 years as chairman and CEO of Wells Fargo, Dick Kovacevich compiled the most successful track record of any commercial banker. In his interview for this book, however, he did not focus on his professional success but talked instead about how his experiences growing up in a small town in western Washington shaped his leadership philosophy.

Kovacevich was raised in a working-class family and interacted with people of all incomes and education levels. The dairy farmers, loggers, and workers that he knew at the local Weyerhaeuser sawmill were intelligent people who worked hard and had high ethical standards but lacked college educations. His teachers had a tremendous influence on him, encouraging him to do well academically and go to college.

From the age of 11, Kovacevich worked in a local grocery store, which stimulated his interest in business. After school he played sports, then rushed home so that he could eat before heading to work from 6 to 9 PM. In the summers, he ran the produce department when the manager went on vacation, handling displays, pricing, and ordering. Those experiences taught Kovacevich the importance of customer relations. He noted, "There I developed the intuition and leadership skills, more than in business school, where there weren't any leadership courses."

Athletics had a significant impact on Kovacevich's development as a leader. He played a team sport several hours every day, becoming team captain in baseball and football. "On the athletic field I learned people can perform so much better as a team than the sum of their individual talents. By trial and error, I learned skills I could apply in business."

If you had 11 quarterbacks on the field, you would lose every game. Just as quarterbacks are overrated, CEOs are too. You can't be an all-star quarterback unless you have some great linemen, outstanding receivers, and good running backs. Diversity of skills is an important element of any effective team. There is no way that leaders who surround themselves with people just like them can be effective. We need to recognize our weaknesses, but not amplify them, and then surround ourselves with people whose strengths complement our weaknesses.

Kovacevich used that principle at Wells Fargo, surrounding himself with talented executives who built the bank's individual businesses. He gave them authority to lead in their own way, while acting as quarterback of the team.

His life experience growing up in a small town profoundly influenced his banking philosophy. While other banks were using computers to eliminate customer service personnel, Kovacevich endeavored to make Wells Fargo the most client-friendly bank in every community. The primary concern of its employees is helping clients meet their financial needs. Because Kovacevich and his handpicked successor, John Stumpf, surrounded themselves with highly talented executives, Wells Fargo navigated the 2008 financial crisis better than any commercial bank.

Reatha Clark King: From Cotton Fields to the Boardroom

Reatha Clark King's roots trace to a rural community, where many encouraged her to become a leader. King acknowledged, "I didn't get here on my own. I am standing on the shoulders of the giants who helped me get launched."

King grew up in Georgia in the 1940s, the daughter of farm laborers. Her father left the family when she was young, so her mother worked as a maid to support her three children. Her family was so poor that she often had to leave school to work in the cotton fields for $3 per day so that her mother could pay the bills. "Those were bitter moments in my experience, because white children didn't have to leave school," she recalled. "That contrast was so clear and so wrong."

Her church was a haven amid constant poverty and discrimination. "I have fond memories of going to church every Sunday morning. I can still close my eyes and see my grandmother praying." The older women of the church identified King's special abilities, noticing her intellectual potential, initiative, work ethic, and dependability. "The sisters, teachers, and people in the community kept an eye on me, and encouraged me to overcome unjust barriers against black people."

King credited her grade school teacher and the school librarian with influencing her development. They encouraged her to go to Clark University in Atlanta, where she won a scholarship and worked in the library for 35 cents an hour to pay for room and board. While King studied at Clark, the chair of the chemistry department mentored her, stimulating her interest in becoming a research chemist.

She applied to the University of Chicago's doctoral program, a bold step for a poor woman from Georgia. After earning her PhD in physical chemistry, she worked at the National Bureau of Standards and taught at York College in New York City. Even there, things were not easy. "One black faculty member called me an Uncle Tom for trying to resolve issues," she recalled. "That was one of the most hurtful moments of my life."

She got her first opportunity to lead when she became president of Metropolitan State University in Minneapolis. Even then she did not see herself as a leader.

Others thought of me as a leader, but I saw myself as someone doing what needed to be done. My reasons for leading were not centered on my needs but on the needs of women, my people, and my community. I saw compelling challenges to be met. If no one else is willing or capable of leading, then it is my

obligation to step up to the challenge. My inspiration comes from the sisters and
teachers who had such great influence on my life.

While at Metro State, King was recruited by the CEO of General Mills to be president of its foundation. Using this platform, she pioneered programs to help young people of color. Since retiring from General Mills, she has devoted her energies to corporate boards. Her reputation grew as she was elected a director of Exxon-Mobil, Wells Fargo, and other companies. An advocate for strong corporate governance, King currently chairs the National Association of Corporate Directors, which named her director of the year in 2004. "I enjoy serving on corporate boards because diversity should be at that table," she said.

Throughout her life, King has used the inspiration of her life story to stay on course to her True North. She reaches out and helps others as she quietly walks past barriers of racial and gender discrimination, without ever succumbing to anger. As comfortable in the boardrooms of the world's largest corporations as she is in creating opportunities for the poor, King still worries whether she is doing enough. "I'm leading toward a cause: to get more opportunities for people. It is in my blood to remove unjust barriers and help people appreciate themselves and be who they are."

What Is Your Life Story?

What can you learn from the stories of Howard Schultz, Dick Kovacevich, and Reatha Clark King? All of them, like the other leaders interviewed, found the inspiration to lead in their own life stories. By understanding the formative experiences of their early lives, they have been able to reframe their understanding of their life stories and shape their leadership around fulfilling their passions and following their True North.

At this point, you may be asking, Doesn't everyone have a life story? What makes leaders' stories different? Many people with painful stories see themselves as victims, feeling the world has dealt them a bad hand. Some get so caught up in chasing the world's esteem that they never become genuine leaders. Or they lack the introspection to connect the dots between their life experiences and the goals they are pursuing now. Often this causes them to repeat the mistakes that led to earlier problems.

The difference with authentic leaders lies in the way they *frame* their stories. Their life stories provide the context for their lives, and through them, they find the passion to make an impact in the world. Novelist John Barth once said, "The story of your life is not your life. It is your story." In other words, it is how you understand yourself through your story that matters, not the facts of your life. Leaders who have reflected on their stories understand how important events and interactions with people have shaped their approach to the world.

Reframing our stories enables us to recognize that we are not victims at all but people shaped by experiences that provide the impetus to become leaders. Our life stories evolve constantly as we shape the meaning of our past, present, and future.

Can you connect the dots between your past and your future to find your inspiration to lead authentically? What people or experiences have shaped you? What have been the key turning points in your life? Where in your story do you find your passion to lead?

Having considered how our life stories provide the basis for our leadership, we are ready to embark on the journey to authentic leadership.

The Journey to Authentic Leadership

When I graduated from college, I had the naive notion that the journey to leadership was a straight line to the top. I learned the hard way that leadership is not a singular destination but a marathon journey that progresses through many stages until you reach your peak. I was not alone. Of all the senior leaders we interviewed, none wound up where they thought they would.

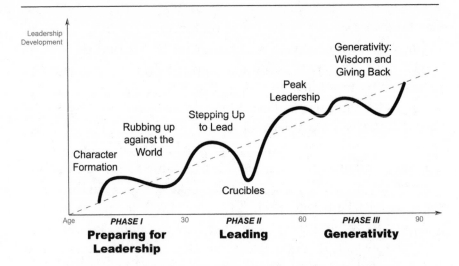

Figure 1.1   The Journey to Authentic Leadership

Former Vanguard CEO Jack Brennan believes that the worst thing people can do is to manage their careers with a career map: "The dissatisfied people I have known and those who experienced ethical or legal failures all had a clear career plan." Brennan recommended being flexible and venturesome in stepping up to unexpected opportunities. "If you're only interested in advancing your career, you'll wind up dissatisfied," he said.

The idea of a career ladder places tremendous pressure on leaders to keep climbing ever higher. Instead, Sheryl Sandberg, chief operating officer (COO) of Facebook, favors the idea of a career "jungle gym" where you can move up, down, or across. Realistically, your development as a leader is a journey filled with many ups and downs as you progress to your peak leadership and continue leading through the final stage (see Figure 1.1).

The leader's journey follows the new span of life, which often runs into the nineties. Individuals move through three periods of leadership with different types of leadership opportunities unfolding in each. There will be differences in the pace at which leaders navigate the timeline, but there are many commonalities among their experiences.

Phase I is "Preparing for Leadership," where leaders develop through education and studying, as well as extracurricular experiences and early work as individual contributors. Phase II, "Leading," begins as individuals take on more responsibility for leading others and culminates in their peak leadership experience. Phase III is "Generativity," a stage of human development psychologist Erik Erikson identified. It begins when leaders have completed their principal career leadership roles, and it continues for the rest of their lives. In this phase, authentic leaders look for opportunities to spread their knowledge and wisdom across many people and organizations, even as they continue an active learning process.

Phase I: Preparing for Leadership

Phase I is preparing for leadership, when character forms and people act as individual contributors or lead teams for the first time. Today, very few leaders make career commitments in their twenties. Increasingly, they use the time following college to gain valuable work experience, oftentimes changing jobs every 18 to 24 months to diversify their experience. Many young leaders are interested in going to graduate school in business, law, or government. Even some who complete their master's degrees prefer individual contributor roles in consulting or finance before committing to a specific company or industry.

There is a natural amount of self-absorption in this phase. Measures of success in your teens and twenties are based primarily on what you accomplish as an individual. Your performance determines what schools you are admitted to and how well you do in your work. Here's how Kleiner Perkins Caufield & Byers's Randy Komisar described it:

> We begin life on a linear path where success is based on clear targets. Life gets complicated when the targets aren't clear, and you have to set your own. By rubbing up against the world, you get to know yourself. Either do that, or you're going to spend your life serving the interests and expectations of others.

He acknowledged that the start of the journey is particularly hard for young people. "They look at me and say, 'Hey, man. All I want to do is to get a good job, buy a house, get married, and have kids.'" Komisar said he wished life were so simple. Instead, he tells them:

> Let me just plant this seed. Keep it alive and come back to it in 10 years, but don't flush it. Ask yourself the question "What do you want out of your life?" I want to empower you for that time when it's relevant to you.

Wendy Kopp: Stepping Up at 21

As a student at Princeton, Wendy Kopp developed a passion to transform K–12 education. Growing up in a middle-class family in an affluent Dallas suburb, she lived in a community that was "extraordinarily isolated from reality and the disparities in educational opportunity." Kopp was influenced by her freshman roommate at Princeton, who was from inner-city New York. Kopp described her roommate as brilliant but unable to keep up with her studies because her high school had not prepared her for the rigors of Princeton. Ultimately, her roommate dropped out of school.

As a senior, Kopp burned with desire to transform education but didn't know how to get there. Not wanting to pursue the typical corporate-training track, she went into "a deep funk." As she explored teaching, she realized many others also believed that depriving kids of an excellent education was a national tragedy.

So she organized a conference of students and business leaders to examine ways to improve K–12 education. During the conference, an idea came to her: "Why doesn't this country have a national teacher corps of recent college graduates who commit two years to teach in public schools?" Her rhetorical question inspired her to found Teach For America (TFA), the most successful secondary educational program of the past 25 years.

Kopp's journey wasn't easy. Lacking management experience and permanent funding, Teach For America was constantly short of cash, lurching from one crisis to the next. Time and again, Kopp threw herself into fundraising as she restructured budgets and financing to cover deficits. After working 100 hours a week for five years to build TFA to 500 new teachers per year, Kopp felt overwhelmed by the financial pressures of raising money to keep the organization going.

When many initial funders decided not to continue funding the organization, losses mounted to a cumulative deficit of $2.5 million. A blistering critique of TFA in an influential educators' journal said, "TFA is bad policy and bad education. It is bad for the recruits. It is bad for the schools. It is bad for the children." Reflecting on the article, Kopp recalled, "It felt like a punch in the chest. I read it more as a personal attack than an academic analysis of our efforts." When some of her original team left TFA, Kopp thought about shutting it down. "Yet my passion for our cause and fear that we might let the children down kept me going," she said.

Kopp's experience at such a young age is the essence of authentic leadership: Find something you are passionate about, and inspire others to join the cause. TFA's crisis accelerated her development as a leader. Twenty years after founding TFA, Kopp's tireless efforts and passionate leadership have paid off. Today the program has 11,000 corps members who are teaching more than 750,000 students.

Ian Chan: Creating a Scientific Revolution

Ian Chan is another young leader who discovered his passion to lead at an early age. As his college graduation approached, he knew he wanted "an opportunity that would get me excited to jump out of bed every day and go to work." After uninspiring experiences in investment banking and private equity, he and his younger brother focused on the human genome revolution.

The Chan brothers founded U.S. Genomics to revolutionize medicine by delivering personalized genomics on a broad scale. They attracted noted advisers, such as scientist Craig Venter, who originally mapped the human genome, and Bob Langer, a renowned technologist. They began with a $100,000 credit card loan, and subsequently raised $52 million from venture capitalists, several of whom joined the board as the Chan brothers gave up more than half their ownership.

Over the next five years the company's work attracted attention in the scientific community and venture capital world as U.S. Genomics became a pioneer in its field. When the founders presented the company's exceptional performance in December 2001, the board gave them a standing ovation. Yet, as the full potential of U.S. Genomics became apparent to the venture capitalists, they decided they needed a more experienced executive to lead it. Four months later, Chan was shocked when his board told him he was being replaced as CEO. "To this day, I have no idea why this happened when things were going so well," he said.

> *I put my heart and soul into it for many years, and then boom, it's all gone. It was gut-wrenching to have something taken away that I created and believed in deeply. I still had some shares, but I wasn't part of the enterprise anymore with its mission I believe in. I wanted to continue fighting, but I felt helpless.*
>
> *In hindsight, it was a rich experience I can build on for the next journey. I had been working crazy hours and was very tired. I didn't have a personal life and needed more balance. To regroup, I spent two years getting my MBA. That provided time for self-reflection and opportunities to interact with some of the world's top business leaders.*
>
> *I realized I was still fortunate to have my health, family, and the privilege of living in a free country. These should never be taken for granted. My heart is still in entrepreneurship and biotechnology because there are so many untreatable diseases that provide opportunities to make broad impact.*

Chan was a victim of his own success. Yet for all the heartache and pain, he had an invaluable experience that has been formative on his leadership journey. He and his brother, Eugene, rejoined forces in 2007 to found Abpro, focusing on producing proteins used in life sciences. They raised $1.5 million in seed capital but have retained more than 50 percent ownership to avoid repeating the U.S. Genomics experience. Chan said he learned from these experiences "the importance of pursuing your passion to make scientific breakthroughs" but also "not to give up control to outsiders."

Unfortunately, fear of failure keeps many young leaders from jumping into opportunities like Kopp and Chan did. Ann Fudge offered a priceless point of view, noting, "Struggle and tough experiences ultimately fashion you."

> *Don't worry about the challenges. Embrace them. Go through them even if they hurt. Tell yourself, there is something to be learned from this experience. You may not fully understand it now, but you will later. It's all part of life, and life is a process of learning. Every challenging experience develops your core of inner strength, which gets you through those storms. Nothing worth doing in life is going to be easy.*

Phase II: Leading

The second phase of your leadership journey begins with a rapid accumulation of leadership experiences. As you take on greater responsibilities, you will likely face personal and professional setbacks that test you to your core. These periods transform your understanding of what leadership is all about and can dramatically accelerate your development. Typically, your successive leadership assignments will culminate in your peak leadership experience.

In Phase II, many leaders face experiences at work that dramatically test their sense of self, their values, or their assumptions about their careers. I call this "hitting the wall," because the experience resembles a fast-moving race car hitting the wall of the track, something most leaders experience at least once in their careers.

Jeff Immelt: Hitting the Wall

General Electric (GE) CEO Jeff Immelt was a rising star in his midthirties when he faced his toughest challenge. Asked to return to

GE's plastics business as head of worldwide sales and marketing, he had reservations about accepting the move because it was not a promotion. Jack Welch, the current CEO, told him, "I know this isn't what you want to do, but this is a time when you serve the company."

Facing stiff competition, the plastics division had entered into several long-term, fixed-price contracts with key customers, including U.S. automakers. When inflation spiked and his division's costs soared, Immelt's operation missed its profit target by $30 million, 30 percent of its budget. Welch did not hesitate to reach down by phone to pepper him with questions. Immelt tried to increase prices, but progress was slow, and his efforts negatively affected GE's relationship with General Motors (GM). This intensified the pressure on Immelt to produce results and required Welch to resolve issues directly with GM CEO Roger Smith.

For Immelt, the year was a remarkably difficult one. As he looked back at this experience, he noted, "Nobody wants to be around somebody going through a low period. In times like that you've got to be able to draw from within. Leadership is one of these great journeys into your own soul." Immelt lost the external validation that comes from success during this assignment, yet demonstrated the inner qualities—tenacity and resilience—necessary to lead through hard times.

He needed these qualities as he faced far greater challenges as Welch's successor. The September 11, 2001, attacks occurred during Immelt's first week as CEO, negatively affecting several GE businesses, including jet engines, insurance, and financial services. During the 2008 financial meltdown, GE's balance sheet became so precarious that Immelt telephoned President George W. Bush to ask for financial support.

More than a decade later, Immelt is reinventing GE with a clear focus on product innovation in health care, energy, and transportation. In those sectors, he is building on GE's traditional manufacturing and services strengths to include big data and advanced analytics solutions. He is further reshaping GE by divesting major businesses such as NBC Universal and parts of GE Capital that don't align with his strategy.

Hank Paulson: A Life of Service in All Sectors

Hank Paulson has contributed to the private, public, and philanthropic sectors with fervor and determination. I have known him since he worked as assistant to the assistant secretary of defense (comptroller), sitting at the same metal desk I'd sat in just two years before. After two years, he moved to the White House staff of President Richard Nixon as assistant to John Ehrlichman. In 1974, he joined Goldman Sachs in its Chicago office, eventually running its investment banking business before becoming COO in 1994. In 1998, he became CEO and led the company's first public offering the following year.

Paulson was in the midst of a highly successful era at Goldman Sachs when President George W. Bush asked him to become treasury secretary. Initially, he turned the position down, preferring to continue running Goldman, but Bush's chief of staff, Josh Bolton, was persistent in recruiting him. Torn between his options, Paulson asked former Goldman Sachs co-CEO Steve Friedman for advice. Friedman simply asked, "Hank, if you turn down this opportunity to serve your country, will you regret it later in life?" Paulson realized just how committed he was to public service and decided to accept the position.

For the sake of his country, it was a good thing Paulson accepted. When the financial crisis hit, Paulson aggressively took charge, working through the bankruptcy of Lehman Brothers; nationalizing Fannie Mae, Freddie Mac, and American International Group (AIG); bailing out Citibank; and finding new owners for Merrill Lynch, Bear Stearns, Wachovia, Washington Mutual, and Countrywide Financial. Throughout the crisis Paulson partnered with Federal Reserve Board Chair Ben Bernanke to reopen credit markets and capitalize the strong banks with the controversial Troubled Asset Relief Program (TARP).

This was a stressful time for Paulson. An extremely responsible leader, he foresaw the risk of a 1929-style financial collapse and resolved to do whatever was required to avoid it. Paulson is a dedicated Christian Scientist who does not drink or smoke, and was an Eagle Scout. At Dartmouth, he was Phi Beta Kappa and played offensive lineman on Dartmouth's football team, winning All-Ivy, All-East, and honorable mention All-American honors. His college nickname was "the Hammer." In person, he is aggressive, blunt, and physically intimidating. Nevertheless, in his book *On the Brink* he described four times he had to excuse himself during speeches or key meetings to go into the men's room because he had stress-induced dry heaves.

Throughout the financial crisis, Paulson made hundreds of telephone calls, trying to understand what was happening, negotiating solutions with private-sector leaders, and urging political leaders to stay calm in the midst of the presidential campaign. He told me he had full support from President Bush to take aggressive actions that normally Bush would have opposed and to hold regular calls with then Senator Barack Obama.

He became desperate while he was trying to persuade Congress to pass the $700 billion TARP authorization because both Democrats and Republicans had politicized the legislation. As Paulson described the chaotic meeting President Bush called on September 25, 2008, with Senators Obama and John McCain and Congressional leaders:

> *It got so ridiculous. I'd never seen anything like it before in politics or business—or in my fraternity days. Finally the president said, "I've clearly lost control of this meeting. It's over." Appalled and disheartened, I approached the Democrats gathered in the Roosevelt Room and urged moderation. They shouted at me to leave. I didn't know what to do. In an attempt at levity, I walked over to (House Speaker Nancy) Pelosi and dropped down to my knees. "Don't blow this up," I pleaded.*

Ultimately, Paulson was successful in pushing through the controversial TARP, which played a key role in averting a second

Great Depression. Despite criticism for being "bailed out," financial and automobile institutions in the end paid back the investments with interest, enabling the Treasury to earn a profit on its investment.

Concluding his government service in early 2009, Paulson could have retired, but that would have gone against his nature. After writing his memoir, he founded the Paulson Institute at the University of Chicago, funded with his own money, to strengthen relations between the United States and China. His new book, *Dealing with China*, provides unique insights into U.S.-China relationships. An avid birder, he continues to support the Nature Conservancy, an organization he chaired in 2004 when it was in crisis.

Few leaders would have had Paulson's tenacity and courage to take such bold actions, knowing he would be severely criticized. History may well credit him with saving the U.S. financial system.

Phase III: Generativity

The last phase of a leader's journey can be the most rewarding of all. These days many leaders are foregoing conventional retirement to share their leadership and wisdom with multiple organizations. They serve on for-profit or nonprofit boards, mentor young leaders, take up teaching, or coach leaders. Many of these leaders work across all three sectors: for-profit, nonprofit, and public service.

In *Geeks and Geezers*, Warren Bennis described his philosophy of the third phase of leadership with the little-known term *neoteny*, "the retention of all those wonderful qualities we associate with youth: curiosity, playfulness, eagerness, fearlessness, warmth, energy."

> *Undefined by time and age, older people with neoteny are open, willing to take risks, courageous, hungry for knowledge, and eager for each new day. Neoteny keeps older people focused on all the marvelous undiscovered things to come, rather than on past disappointments. Neoteny is a metaphor for all the youthful gifts the luckiest of us never lose.*

It is a philosophy worthy of consideration throughout our lifetimes, but especially in the final third. Let's look at how some leaders are using the third phase of their leadership journeys.

Erskine Bowles: Connecting Public Service and Private Sectors

Few leaders have moved as smoothly from the for-profit arena to the political and educational domains as has Erskine Bowles. Early in his career, Bowles built one of the first midmarket investment banks, which was sold for $300 million. Next he served as President Clinton's chief of staff, where he led negotiations to produce the first balanced federal budget in 40 years. Later he became president of the 16-institution University of North Carolina system.

Throughout his varied career, Bowles has exemplified authentic qualities of leadership. "I'm not a visionary," he said. "I'm about organization, structure, focus, and timeline." He uses his strengths to create high levels of employee engagement, setting high expectations, building teamwork, and ensuring intended outcomes.

In the last five years, Bowles emerged as the leading national voice on fiscal reform as cochair of President Obama's National Commission on Fiscal Responsibility and Reform with Senator Alan Simpson. Bowles worked closely with Democrats, including President Obama, and Republicans to forge consensus on fiscal recommendations. Meanwhile, he serves on important corporate boards, such as Facebook, Morgan Stanley, Norfolk Southern, and Belk, which strengthens his ability to influence public issues. "At 69, I want to stay relevant to what's going on in the economy and continue to learn," he said.

Michael Bloomberg: Going His Own Way

Mike Bloomberg is a leader who has always gone his own way. When I knew him in business school, he was so brilliant that he didn't need to study the cases like the rest of us. He tells the story of getting called on in class when he hadn't even bothered to glance at the case.

> *Called out for not being prepared, I suggested to the professor he should first get inputs from several students and then I would summarize and draw conclusions. With that, the professor dismissed the entire class and told us to come back prepared the next day. When he called on me the next day, I offered a radical solution that he and the rest of the class completely rejected. Years later, the company did exactly what I suggested and was highly successful.*

After graduation, Bloomberg went to work at Salomon Brothers. He was a rising star and head of equity trading at Wall Street's hottest firm 15 years later. When Salomon merged with Phibro, he was ushered into Chairman John Gutfreund's office and abruptly fired. He was surprised and hurt. "There I was, 39 years old, terminated from the only full-time job I'd ever known and the high-pressure life I loved. Was I sad? You bet, but as usual, I was much too macho to show it."

His firing still gives him something to prove 30 years later. He decided he no longer wanted to work for someone else, so he used $4 million of his $10 million termination settlement to found a company he named Bloomberg. There, he created the Bloomberg Terminal, still the most ubiquitous tool in the financial industry.

When we were in graduate school, I thought he was one of the least likely of my classmates to go into politics. Was I wrong about that. In 2001, he was elected mayor of New York, and became the most successful big-city mayor in the country. Direct, practical, and completely unafraid of confrontation, he took on tough issues and powerful groups, such as teachers' unions and the National Rifle Association. During his tenure, he improved K–12 education, reduced rates of obesity, and controlled guns. Now an independent after switching political parties twice, many believe he would be an excellent candidate for president. He says he couldn't win as an independent, joking that he's too short to be president.

After completing his third term as mayor, Bloomberg intended to focus on philanthropy and run his foundation, while giving away his entire $38 billion fortune. Within months, his passion for his business brought him back as CEO to the firm he founded. An entrepreneur at heart like Howard Schultz, Bloomberg realized the call of continuing to build this very successful company.

He told me recently he will continue to focus on the big public-sector issues: obesity, tobacco cessation, gun control, entrepreneurship, and the environment. He said, "At this stage what do I have to lose?" adding, "I intend to give it all away. The best financial planning ends with bouncing the check to the undertaker." In Bloomberg's third phase, he is blending together his philanthropic, public policy, and business passions to make an enormous difference in the world.

Exploring Leadership after Phase II

Early in life I adopted the philosophy of an old Schlitz beer commercial, *"You only go around once, and you've got to grab for all the gusto you can."* My goal was to lead a major organization doing important work, turn it over to my successor, and then move on to new and equally meaningful opportunities.

When I was elected CEO of Medtronic in 1991, I told the board I should not serve more than 10 years, because that was sufficient time to accomplish the organization's goals and develop a well-qualified successor, who turned out to be Art Collins. At the conclusion of my term, I was 58 and lacked a clear vision of what was next for me. I spent six months exploring wide-ranging opportunities in government, education, health care, and international relations. Each field was interesting, but none seemed just right.

Meanwhile, I stayed active in the business community by serving on the boards of Goldman Sachs, Novartis, and Target, and later ExxonMobil and the Mayo Clinic. Viewing these corporations from the board's vantage point has been a superb education into the challenges leaders face in such vital industries as financial services, health care, energy, and retail.

In 2002, Penny and I moved to Switzerland for a "working sabbatical," as I had appointments to teach leadership at two outstanding Swiss institutions. It was quite an adjustment to go from leading an organization of 26,000 people to being completely on my own: creating my own courses, developing syllabuses, learning how to teach—even getting my students to help me create PowerPoint charts.

I vividly recall my first day in the classroom, when I taught 90 MBA students from 35 countries. It was a scary feeling to stand in front of these very bright and demanding students. Talking about Medtronic was easy, but leading a case discussion on Intel that engaged all 90 students was a great challenge. I learned I loved teaching and enjoyed counseling students. Returning from Switzerland, I did a four-month stint at Yale School of Management, then joined the Harvard Business School (HBS) faculty as professor of management practice. At Harvard, I taught Leadership and Corporate Accountability and then created an elective called Authentic Leadership Development, based on the ideas I wrote about in *True North*.

Shedding the constant pressures of running a large organization gave me the opportunity to creatively explore how to develop a new generation of authentic leaders. At Medtronic, I often had 15 tightly scheduled meetings per day. As I transitioned to Phase III, I created room to think deeply. One product was my first book, *Authentic Leadership*. Through it, I discovered writing as a means of sharpening my own ideas and sharing them with others. I have since written five other books, including this one. My 12 years at HBS have been the most creative years of my life, replete with opportunities to integrate all my interests.

As someone who has led many organizations, the irony is that I have not led anything in the past decade. Instead, I have discovered a new purpose for my leadership: to develop authentic leaders following their True North who are dedicated to making a positive impact on society. During the past two years, I have focused on developing global leaders, a topic that is the focal point of Chapter 12.

Regardless of where you are in your journey—just getting started, looking for a new challenge, or reaching the top of your organization—each leadership experience enables you to grow and to discover your authentic leadership. As Amgen's Kevin Sharer said, "You are the mosaic of all your experiences." Just as you conclude one portion of your journey, another opportunity emerges, so you can take what you learned from previous experiences and apply it to new situations. If you embrace your life story and learn its lessons, your leadership journey will never end.

Exercise: Your Life Story and Journey to Authentic Leadership

After reading Chapter 1, it's important to examine your life story and leadership opportunities to this point.

1. Looking at patterns from your early life story, what people, events, and experiences have had the greatest impact on you and your life?

2. In which experiences did you find the greatest inspiration and passion for your leadership?

3. Do the failures or disappointments you experienced earlier in your life constrain you, even today, or have you been able to reframe them as learning experiences?

4. Do you think you need to make any adjustments to your personal and leadership development as a result? If so, what are they?

2

LOSING YOUR WAY

Money is very seductive . . . However much you say
that you will not fall into the trap of it, you do fall
into the trap of it.
—*Rajat Gupta, former worldwide managing director, McKinsey*

All of us have fears, anxiety, and confusion—these are an integral part of the human condition. By understanding our life stories, we begin to recognize and accept these qualities. Howard Schultz fully embraced his life story, learning respect for all people from his experience growing up in poverty. He also reframed his negative image of his father from a poor family provider to someone who never had the right opportunities. This ultimately motivated Schultz to build Starbucks into the type of company where people like his father would be proud to work.

Unfortunately, many leaders do not ground themselves in their life stories. Instead, they try to bury their past, and put on a new mask. Or they get caught up in chasing the world's esteem by trying to accumulate money, fame, and power, rather than pursuing their intrinsic motivations. Perhaps they fear vulnerability or lack close friends who can help them reflect on their experiences.

The consequences of denying or repressing your life stories, your crucibles, and your fears can be severe. It magnifies your shadow side that shapes your behavior but operates hidden from view. Many leaders with great potential lose their way because they do not face their shadow sides and wind up way off course from their True North.

The Tragedy of Rajat Gupta

Rajat Gupta was a close professional colleague of mine. We interacted in many professional settings and worked together on three boards—Goldman Sachs, World Economic Forum USA, and Harvard Business School (HBS) Board of Dean's Advisors. Gupta also served on the boards of Procter & Gamble and American Airlines. I considered him one of the world's most accomplished leaders, someone who was intelligent and savvy and demonstrated strong values. He was well connected with many of the world's most important people. Heads of state, CEOs, and billionaires all returned his calls.

At McKinsey, he was the first worldwide managing partner born outside the United States. He expanded the firm into a global powerhouse during his nine years at the helm, as McKinsey's revenues grew by 280 percent to $3.4 billion. Gupta was a philanthropic leader as well. He chaired the Global Fund to Fight AIDS, Tuberculosis and Malaria. Later he founded the Indian School of Business and served on an array of nonprofit boards. For the Indian community he was a role model of the American dream fulfilled, a symbol that an Indian immigrant could make it to the top in America.

Rajat Gupta is currently serving a two-year sentence in federal prison.

He was convicted in 2012 on four criminal counts for providing inside information to Galleon Fund founder Raj Rajaratnam. He shared privileged information that he learned at Goldman board meetings during the fall of 2008, which in turn Rajaratnam used to make insider trades. After Gupta's final appeal was turned down by the U.S. Supreme Court, he entered prison in June 2014.

How could such an exceptional leader at the peak of his success fall so far, so fast? Although we may never know the full story, perhaps we can discover some clues through his life story. Gupta was born in Calcutta, India. His father was a journalist and freedom fighter who had been jailed by the British when India was fighting for independence. Young Gupta faced a major crucible in his life when he was orphaned as a teenager. His father died when Gupta was 16, and his mother passed away just two years later. With no money to live on, he took responsibility for raising his two younger siblings. He gained admission to the famed Indian Institute of Technology in Delhi by finishing fifteenth in the nation on the entrance exam. After graduation, he immigrated to the United States to attend business school before joining McKinsey in 1973.

We may never know what caused him to cross the line to provide Rajaratnam inside information. Throughout the trial, Gupta maintained his innocence, suggesting he was a victim of Rajaratnam, who had already been convicted on multiple counts of insider trading and sentenced to 11 years in prison. Some have asserted it was simply greed, and speculated that Gupta resented the large sums of money his peers on Wall Street and in Silicon Valley were making.

Even as he accumulated a net worth of $120 million, he seemed to have an unquenchable thirst for more. A 2013 article in the *New York Times Magazine* speculated, "Teaming up with Rajaratnam seemed to be his plan for a spectacular career finale—a bid not only to stay vital after stepping down from McKinsey but also to establish himself in the elite circle of billionaires." In his 2005 speech at Columbia University, Gupta confirmed this weakness, saying, "When I look at myself, yeah, I am driven by money," adding:

> When I live in this society, you do get fairly materialistic. I am disappointed. I am probably more materialistic today than I was before. Money is very seductive. You have to watch out for it, because the more you have it, you get used to comforts, and big houses and vacation homes and doing whatever you want. However much you say that you will not fall into the trap of it, you do fall into the trap of it.

On paper, Gupta had it all. He had talent, having worked his way up to CEO of the most respected global consultancy. He had wealth and power. He was a board member of the most respected companies in the world. He had respect. People admired him and looked up to him. Apparently, none of this was enough.

For years, Gupta and I spoke with some frequency, and we sat together at board meetings. There were no outward signs of his inner struggle, yet he clearly faced demons that pulled him away from his True North. While he is paying an enormous price for his actions, his is not a simple case of greed. My intuition tells me that he was deeply scarred by his teenage crucible and the poverty that ensued and never resolved his need for financial security. Most likely, Gupta is a man who lost his way by not controlling his need for financial wealth.

Why Leaders Lose Their Way

All of us should ask ourselves, Could this happen to me? Am I vulnerable to being seduced by money, fame, or power? What personality weaknesses do I have that might cause me to lose sight of my True North? Under what circumstances could I fall into this trap?

Let's explore what causes people with excellent potential to lose their way. Why do they often derail just as they are hitting the peak of their leadership? Can they recover from failures and still become authentic leaders?

These questions trouble everyone who wants to lead.

People who lose their way are not necessarily bad people. They have the potential to become good leaders, even great leaders. However, somewhere along the way, they get pulled off course. Little by little, bit by bit, they get caught up in their own success. As leaders are acclaimed by the world and receive the rewards that come with achievement, they are at the greatest risk of deviating from their True North.

Leaders whose goal is having power over others, maximizing their wealth, or becoming famous tend to look to other people for fulfillment and acknowledgment of their status. In public and private, they often display a high degree of narcissism. As leaders of institutions, they ultimately believe the institution cannot survive without them because in their mind they *are* the institution.

Before you take on a leadership role, ask yourself: "What motivates me to lead this organization?" If the honest answers are simply power, prestige, and money, you are at risk of being trapped by external gratification as your source of fulfillment. There is nothing wrong with desiring these outward symbols *if, and only if, they are balanced by a deeper desire to serve something greater than yourself.* Extrinsic rewards exert a force that can pull you away from True North if not counterbalanced by a deeper purpose or calling that gives you a passion to lead.

Let's take a deeper look at the root causes of leaders losing their way.

Losing Touch with Reality

Leaders who focus on external gratification instead of inner satisfaction have trouble staying grounded. They reject the honest critic who holds up a mirror and speaks the truth. Instead, they surround themselves with sycophants—supporters telling them what they want to hear. Over time, they lose perspective and capacity for honest dialogue, and people learn not to confront them. Late in the career of CBS's Bill Paley, people knew that he would kill the messenger who brought him bad news. Not surprisingly, he got a filtered view of reality from his subordinates.

Fearing Failure . . .

Underlying these tendencies may be a fear of failure. Many leaders advance by imposing their will on others. By the time they reach the top, they may be paranoid that someone is waiting in the wings to knock them off their pedestal. Underneath their bravado lies the fear that they are not qualified for such powerful leadership roles, and any day someone is going to unmask them.

To overcome their fears, some leaders drive so hard for results that they lose touch with reality and become incapable of acknowledging their failures or weaknesses. When confronted with their failures, they may try to cover them up or to create a rationale that convinces others these problems are not their fault. Often they look for scapegoats to blame, either within their organization or outside. By combining power, charisma, and charm, they convince others to accept these distortions, causing their organizations to lose touch with reality. In the end, their organizations suffer the greatest harm.

. . . and Craving Success

The other side of the fear of failure is an insatiable craving for success. Most leaders want to do a good job for their organizations, be recognized, and rewarded accordingly. When they achieve success, they receive added power and enjoy the prestige that goes with it. That success can go to their heads, and they develop a sense of entitlement. At the height of some leaders' power, success itself creates a deep desire to keep it going, so they are prone to pushing the limits, thinking they can get away with it.

Novartis CEO Daniel Vasella described this process in a *Fortune* magazine interview:

> *Once you get under the domination of making the quarter—even unwittingly . . . you'll begin to sacrifice things that may be vital for your company over the long term. The culprit that drives this cycle isn't the fear of failure so much as it is the craving for success . . . For many of us the idea of being successful is intoxicating. It is a pattern of celebration leading to belief, leading to distortion. When you achieve good results, you are celebrated, and you begin to believe that the figure at the center of all that champagne toasting is yourself. You are idealized by the outside world, and there is a natural tendency to believe what is written is true.*

The Loneliness Within

It is lonely at the top. Leaders know they are ultimately responsible for their company's performance, and the well-being of many rests in their hands. If they fail, many people will be harmed. To ignore mounting pressures, some leaders simply run faster. Whom can they share their worries with? It can be difficult to talk with subordinates or their boards about their biggest problems and deepest fears. Friends outside the organization may not understand their challenges. Sharing their doubts openly may set off rumors. Sometimes it is even difficult to share these concerns with spouses or mentors.

Because of this loneliness, many leaders deny their fears. They shut down their inner voice because it is too uncomfortable to hear. Instead, they try to respond to the external voices pressuring them, thinking all will be well if they can satisfy them. Because the advice of outsiders is often conflicting or too painful to face, some leaders choose to listen only to people who reinforce their views. As Apple founder Steve Jobs advised, "Don't let the noise of others' opinions drown out your own inner voice."

Meanwhile, leaders' work lives and personal lives grow more unbalanced. Fearing failure, they favor their work life, even saying, "My work *is* my life." Eventually, they lose touch with those closest to them—their spouses, children, and best friends—or they co-opt them to their point of view. Over time, little mistakes turn into major ones. No amount of hard work can correct them. Instead of seeking wise counsel at this point, they dig a deeper hole. When the collapse comes, there is no avoiding it.

Who are *they*? They could be one of those executives facing prosecution for their actions. Or a CEO forced to resign for personal reasons. *But* they *could also be you, me, or any one of us.* We may not face a plight as severe as these leaders face, but we can all lose our way.

Derailing: Losing Sight of Your True North

In observing leaders who have derailed, we identified five types who lose sight of their True North. Their shortcomings link directly to the failure to develop themselves: *Imposters*, who lack self-awareness and self-esteem; *Rationalizers*, who deviate from their values; *Glory Seekers*, who are motivated by seeking the world's acclaim; *Loners*, who fail to build personal support structures; and *Shooting Stars*, who lack the grounding of an integrated life.

Can you see yourself in any of the following archetypes? Could these characteristics cause you to derail?

Imposters

Imposters rise through the organizational ranks with a combination of cunning and aggression. They understand the politics of getting ahead and let no one stand in their way. They are often unabashed students of Machiavelli, determining every angle to advance as they execute their game plan. They are the ultimate political animals, adept at figuring out who their competitors are and then eliminating them one by one. They have little appetite for self-refection or developing self-awareness.

Abraham Lincoln once said, "If you want to test a man's character, give him power." Having acquired power, Imposters may not be confident about how to use it. They are beset with doubts about the responsibilities of leadership. Because their greatest strength is besting internal opponents, they are often paranoid that underlings are out to get them.

Richard Grasso's Fall from Grace

A tragic example of an Impostor was Richard Grasso in his closing days as CEO of the New York Stock Exchange (NYSE). Grasso, who never went to college, started at the exchange earning $80 per week as a clerk. He rose to the top of one of the world's most powerful institutions by building strong relationships with everyone engaged with the exchange. He was also not someone to be crossed, because he had ways to get revenge. Grasso was bitter when he was passed over for CEO in favor of Bill Donaldson, an establishment candidate who came from investment banking. "I'm going to keep my mouth shut," Grasso confided to a friend, "and when the time comes, I'm going to take his job."

When Donaldson retired in 1995, Grasso was the obvious choice for CEO. Yet beneath his charm, he seemed to carry deep feelings of resentment for having been unfairly treated over the years and a wariness of the investment bankers on his board, many of whom had attended Ivy League schools. With the success of the NYSE, he felt entitled to earn as much as his board members without having the risks of their businesses.

When two airplanes flew into the World Trade Center's twin towers on September 11, 2001, Grasso immediately stepped up, getting the NYSE back online by September 17, much sooner than anyone believed was possible. He instantly became a symbol of America's courage in the face of tragedy. For his actions he was handsomely rewarded by his board's compensation committee, an order of magnitude greater than other regulators or government officials.

Two years later, Grasso was forced to resign by his board in a 13–7 split vote. What happened? It seems he got so caught up in his power and celebrity that he lost touch with the public's negative reaction to a regulator receiving a $140 million compensation package. Yet Grasso could justifiably argue that he had only accepted the compensation the board awarded him. Sadly, America lost a highly competent government official in a messy departure at a time when the country sorely needed great public leaders.

Rationalizers

To people outside their organizations, Rationalizers always appear on top of the issues. When things don't go their way, they blame external forces or subordinates. Masters of denial, they rarely take responsibility themselves. As they advance and face greater challenges, they transmit pressure to their subordinates instead of modulating it. When pressuring subordinates fails to produce the numbers, they cut funding for research, growth initiatives, or organization-building to hit financial expectations. Eventually, these short-term actions catch up with them. Then they borrow from the future to make today's numbers look good, or stretch accounting rules, rationalizing that they can make up the deficit in the future.

Unfortunately, their actions only make the future worse. So they turn to more aggressive schemes, such as reporting future revenue streams in quarterly sales or filling customer warehouses with inventory. When these short-term actions fail to stem the tide, they resort to even more desperate measures. Ultimately, they become victims of their rationalizations, as do their depleted organizations.

The misdeeds of Rationalizers have become all too apparent in recent years. Pressures from shareholders caused many executives to play the game of meeting stock market expectations while sacrificing the long-term value of their companies. Even years later, many Rationalizers cling to denial, unwilling to take responsibility for problems they caused. As Warren Bennis said, "Denial and projection are the enemies of reality."

The Collapse of Mike Baker

Mike Baker joined Medtronic in 1989, the same year I did. A graduate of West Point, he served five years in the military, worked in the banking industry, and received his MBA from the University of Chicago. In his eight years at Medtronic, he progressed rapidly through staff roles into line positions. My colleagues and I saw him as someone who had the potential to become CEO one day. He was a superb leader who was intelligent and had solid values. In 1997, he had his first unsuccessful assignment and was moved to a new position. Much to my dismay, that triggered his decision to leave the company.

In 1999, he became chief executive of the fledgling orthopedic company Arthrocare. Under Baker's leadership, Arthrocare achieved great success for nine years, as revenues and profits grew rapidly and its stock price skyrocketed. Baker was viewed as a rising star in the medical technology industry. On July 21, 2008, it all blew up. Arthrocare's auditors announced a restatement of its revenues and earnings for the prior seven quarters, dating back to 2006, acknowledging the company recognized revenues inappropriately. This was far more than a technical audit adjustment. Arthrocare's stock price dropped 40 percent, causing shareholders losses of $758 million.

In the trial that ensued, Baker and chief financial officer (CFO) Michael Gluk were charged with inflating sales and earnings through end-of-quarter transactions from 2005 to 2009. In June 2014, a court found them guilty of fraud and of lying under oath to the Securities and Exchange Commission (SEC) and the court. Two months later, Baker was sentenced to 20 years in prison. He and Gluk had to repay $22 million in compensation they had received.

Baker's case still gnaws at me. Here is a seemingly high-caliber leader with deeply held values and a solid family life who will spend much of his life in jail. How could this have happened? Ironically, in his 2006 *True North* interview, he spoke of the importance of learning from failure. "I'm suspicious of somebody who's never failed, because you don't know how they're going to react when they do," he said. "Everyone is born to fail. Everyone is going to break down. What matters is not how often you have been on the canvas, but whether you get up, how you get up, and what you learn from it."

I suspect that Mike Baker got too caught up in his success. Maybe he started to define himself by his net worth instead of his self-worth. This contortion led him to rationalize these inappropriate accounting practices in order not to acknowledge publicly that revenue growth wasn't there, which would have triggered a sharp drop in Arthrocare's stock price and Baker's wealth. So he kept the scheme going until it blew up in 2009. He is paying an enormous price for his misdeeds, from which he may never recover.

Knowing Baker as I did, I can't see him simply as greedy or evil, but rather a leader who lost his way. I feel sorry for him but acknowledge we all must be held to account under the law. This could happen to any one of us if we rationalize our mistakes rather than openly acknowledge them and accept the consequences.

Glory Seekers

Glory Seekers define themselves by the acclaim of the external world. Money, fame, and power are their goals. Often it seems more important to appear on lists of the most powerful business leaders than it does to build organizations of lasting value. Glory Seekers' thirst for fame is unquenchable. No achievement is sufficient because there are always people with more money, more accolades, and more power. Inside, Glory Seekers feel empty and envy those who have more. Outsiders struggle to understand this emptiness because Glory Seekers seem to have it all.

Lance Armstrong's Ruthless Quest for Glory

Lance Armstrong captivated the world with his cycling successes. He called his story of surviving cancer and winning the Tour de France seven times a "miracle." The U.S. Olympic Committee named him Sportsman of the Year four separate times. Armstrong's renown transcended sport, as he became a best-selling author and motivational speaker, and launched one of the most successful charities of its time, the Livestrong Foundation.

Yet in January of 2013, he confessed to Oprah Winfrey that he had cheated for 20 years. He told her, "This story was so perfect for so long. It's this mythic perfect story, and it wasn't true." Armstrong admitted to using performance-enhancing drugs and banned substances. He told Winfrey he tried to control every outcome of his life.

> I was always a fighter. When I was diagnosed and being treated, I said, "I will do anything to survive." And that's good. I took that attitude—that ruthless and relentless and win-at-all-costs attitude right into cycling. And that's bad.

We now know Armstrong led a systematic doping program and repeatedly lied about it. He ruthlessly attacked people, such as Tour de France winner Greg LeMond, who questioned his performance.

Before his fall, I met Armstrong as we cycled together in a fun outing. Looking back, I see that he had positive qualities and made important humanitarian contributions. Yet his need for recognition, money, and success overtook his sense of morality and ethics. His extreme focus on winning contributed to his competitive success, but it also undermined his character. In his own words he was "a guy who . . . truly believed he was invincible." As it turns out, he was not—nor is any of the rest of us.

Loners

Loners avoid forming close relationships, seeking out mentors, or creating support networks. They believe they can and must make it on their own. Not to be confused with introverts, Loners often have myriad superficial friends and acolytes but do not actually listen to them. They reject honest feedback, even from those who care about them.

Without wise counsel, Loners are prone to make major mistakes. When results elude them and criticism of their leadership grows, they circle the wagons. They become rigid in pursuing their objectives, not recognizing their behavior makes it impossible for them to reach their goals. Meanwhile, their organizations unravel.

Richard Fuld Leads Lehman into Bankruptcy

This is precisely what happened to Richard Fuld Jr. as CEO of Lehman Brothers. From March to September 2008, close associates inside and outside the company warned Fuld that the firm was overleveraged, lacked liquidity, and was inadequately capitalized, making it vulnerable to volatility in the market. Treasury Secretary Hank Paulson had nearly 50 discussions with Fuld in that period, telling him Lehman had "to recognize its losses, raise equity and strengthen its liquidity positions." In his book Paulson wrote, "My conversations with Dick were becoming very frustrating. Although I pressed him to accept reality and operate with a greater sense of urgency, I was beginning to suspect that despite my blunt style, I wasn't getting through."

As Lehman teetered on the brink of bankruptcy, Paulson called the heads of all the big investment banks to a meeting on Friday, September 12, 2008, to address the implications of Lehman's pending bankruptcy. Fuld was not present, choosing to stay in his office behind closed doors, perhaps hoping for a government bailout. He was still waiting at 8 PM on Sunday evening when SEC Commissioner Chris Cox called to tell him again there would be no bailout. In the early hours of September 15, Lehman filed for bankruptcy, putting Fuld and most of his employees out of work, making their Lehman stock worthless, and triggering the greatest financial crisis since the Great Depression.

Shooting Stars

The lives of Shooting Stars center entirely on their careers. To observers, these individuals are perpetual motion machines, always on the go, traveling incessantly to get ahead. They rarely make time for family, friendships, their communities, or even themselves. Much-needed sleep and exercise routines are expendable. As they run ever faster, their stress mounts.

They move up so rapidly in their careers that they never have time to learn from their mistakes. A year or two into any job, they are ready to move on, before they have had to confront the results of their decisions. When they see problems of their making coming back to haunt them, their anxiety rises, and so does the urgency to move to a new position. If their employer doesn't promote them, they are off to another organization. One day they find themselves at the top, overwhelmed by an intractable set of problems. At this point, they are prone to irrational decisions.

A Tale of Two Tech Entrepreneurs

In Silicon Valley, where momentum is a currency to venture capitalists, entrepreneurs can focus too much on managing impressions instead of managing their businesses.

During the past decade, YouSendIt, a Silicon Valley–based software company, raised multiple rounds of venture capital alongside other file-sharing companies, such as Dropbox and Box.com. CEO Brad Garlinghouse was a darling of the media. He shared his ideas for building culture and talked at length about the impact of the cloud on the economy. He even rebranded the company Hightail, explaining to *Fortune*, "We wanted to choose a name that captured this larger vision of where the world was going." Hightail always sought quick wins, public relations, and easy solutions—at least until it ran low on cash. Garlinghouse departed in 2014, and the incoming CEO immediately fired half the company's workforce in an effort to restore profitability.

Contrast Hightail with ShareFile, a company started two years later by Raleigh-based entrepreneur Jes Lipson, who made sustainable growth one of ShareFile's core values. Without relying on venture capital funds, he built the company to profitability with 85 employees and sold it to Citrix for $93 million. Following the acquisition, he grew the ShareFile business to 600 employees. Today ShareFile has eclipsed Hightail, the former market leader that had raised $83 million from venture capitalists. Lipson said, "I didn't focus on media coverage, investors, or the analysts. I just listened to what customers wanted."

Lipson and his wife, also an entrepreneur, both served as president of their local Entrepreneur's Organization chapter. Together, they created a 15,000-square-foot incubator called HQ Raleigh, where the next generation of entrepreneurs can launch their ideas. The entrepreneur-turned-corporate executive no longer needs to work for money, but he's as committed as ever—motivated by his company's mission and continuing to serve.

Heroes of Their Own Journeys

All five archetypal leaders described here—Imposters, Rationalizers, Glory Seekers, Loners, and Shooting Stars—frame their life stories in the model of an all-conquering hero. This approach may work well for musicians, actors, or athletes who excel as solo performers. It fails utterly when one leads a team, however, precisely because being a hero is *not* empowering to teammates or subordinates.

The role of leaders is *not* to get other people to follow them but to empower other people to lead. They cannot elicit the best performance from their teams if they are in the game primarily for themselves. In the end, poor leaders' self-centeredness keeps other people from leading. Why should others try to excel when their efforts are for the leader's glory and not the team's success?

Before going on to Chapter 3, think carefully about whether you see yourself in any of the five archetypes of leaders who lose their way and become derailed by challenging yourself in the exercise below.

Exercise: Why Leaders Lose Their Way

1. Have you seen leaders lose their way or worked with someone who fits any of the archetypes? Which of the qualities of the five archetypes do you see in yourself?

2. Can you envision a situation in which you could lose your way in the future?

3. Do you have a fear of failing? Do you fear what other people would think about you if you did? Are you avoiding situations in which there is a risk of failing? How could the experience of failing help you achieve your ultimate goals?

4. In what ways do you crave success? How is this affecting your decisions about leadership and your career? Do you choose only situations that give you a high probability of success?

5. What steps can you take to prevent being derailed during your career?

3

CRUCIBLES

> The crucible is an essential element in the process of
> becoming a leader.
> —*Warren Bennis*, On Becoming a Leader

Most of the leaders we interviewed were shaped by severe trials in their lives, which we call crucibles. Psychologist Abraham Maslow found that tragedy and trauma were the most important human learning experiences leading to self-actualization. Crucibles enable people to learn life is uncertain, and they have limited control. This new reality empowers individuals to challenge old assumptions and understand they must demonstrate personal agency to deal with their world.

Crucibles often launch leaders into despair, crisis, and doubt. In the midst of a crucible, pain and suffering may overwhelm leaders. With sufficient resilience, leaders emerge from despair and become open to introspection that can catalyze major breakthroughs in their development.

Daniel Vasella's Long Journey

Novartis chairman and CEO Daniel Vasella followed a path to leadership that was one of the most difficult and unusual of all our interviewees. Vasella's emergence from extreme challenges in his youth to reach the pinnacle of the global pharmaceutical industry vividly illustrates the transformation many leaders undergo on their journeys.

Vasella was born in 1953 to a modest family in Fribourg, Switzerland. His early years were filled with medical problems that stoked his passion to become a physician. Suffering from asthma at age 5, he was sent alone to the mountains of eastern Switzerland for two summers. There he lived on a farm with three brothers and their niece.

At age 8, he had tuberculosis followed by meningitis and spent a full year in a sanatorium. He suffered not only from illness but also from isolation. His parents never visited him that year, and his two sisters came only once. Young Vasella was lonely and homesick. He still remembers the pain and fear of the lumbar punctures as the nurses held him down "like an animal" so that he couldn't move.

One day a new physician arrived and took time to explain each step of the procedure to the 8-year-old. Rather than being held down, Vasella asked the physician whether he could hold the nurse's hand. "This time the procedure didn't hurt, so I reached up and gave him a big hug," Vasella recalled. "These human gestures of forgiveness, caring, and compassion made a deep impression on the kind of person I wanted to become."

Even after Vasella recovered, his life did not stabilize. When he was 10, his older sister passed away from cancer. The following year, his other sister died in an automobile accident. Two years later, his father died in surgery. To support the family, his mother went to work in a distant town and came home only once every three weeks. Left alone, 14-year-old Vasella rebelled and joined a motorcycle gang that drank a lot and got into frequent fights. This lasted for several years until he met his first girlfriend, whose affection changed his attitude.

At 20, Vasella entered medical school at the University of Fribourg. "I decided to become a physician so I could understand health, and gain more control over my own life after disease had impacted my family so much," he explained. "The compassionate physician at the sanatorium became the role model for the kind of doctor I wanted to be."

During medical school, Vasella sought out psychoanalysis so that he could come to terms with his early experiences. "I wanted to understand myself and not feel like a victim," he said. "I learned I did not have to be in control all the time." Graduating with honors from medical school, Vasella did his residency at the Universities of Bern and Zürich, eventually becoming chief resident.

It was during this time that Vasella realized he wanted to affect the lives of many more people by running an organization that restored people to health. Completing his residency, he applied to become chief physician at the University Hospital Zürich and was disappointed when the search committee considered him too young for the position. So he talked to his wife's uncle, Marc Moret, who was CEO of Sandoz, one of Switzerland's leading chemical and pharmaceutical companies, about his interest in getting into business. Moret advised him, "Believe me, I know how unpleasant it can be leading a firm. You don't want to go into business."

Moret's discouraging words only piqued Vasella's interest. Eventually he was offered a sales position in Sandoz's U.S. affiliate and later a product manager role. Vasella hesitated, but his wife, Anne-Laurence, told him, "Daniel, do it. Otherwise, you will turn 50, look back in regret, and be unhappy." He flourished in his five years in America, advancing rapidly through the Sandoz marketing organization.

Returning to Switzerland as assistant to the COO of Sandoz's pharmaceutical business, Vasella was forced to take a step back. Frustrated, he languished without responsibilities in a cubicle outside his boss's office. "My pay was cut by 40 percent, and I wrote minutes and did my boss's mail."

Soon he was asked to lead a team to redesign the research and development process, giving him intimate knowledge of drug discovery and development. He was promoted to head of marketing and then global drug development. When both his bosses left in a political battle, he became CEO of the pharmaceutical division. Vasella loved his new position because he had full responsibility for moving the business forward.

Within two years, he got involved with negotiations to merge Sandoz with Ciba-Geigy, its crosstown rival in Basel. It was a natural fit, facilitated because neither company had a successor to its powerful CEO. In spite of Vasella's youth, Moret nominated him to be CEO of the merged companies, to be called Novartis. Ciba-Geigy leadership agreed, as its CEO became board chairman.

As CEO, Vasella blossomed as a leader. He envisioned building a great global health care company that could help people by creating lifesaving drugs. Drawing on the physician role models of his youth, he created an entirely new Novartis culture built on compassion, competence, and competition. He used the integration of the two companies to empower new leaders throughout the new organization.

One success came from the drug Gleevec, which Vasella found languishing in Novartis's research labs. Stunned by positive results in preliminary clinical trials in patients with chronic myelogenous leukemia, Vasella was upset to learn the drug was given low priority because of modest market projections. He convinced his team to get the drug to market within two years, breaking all records for U.S. Food and Drug Administration approval. Characteristic of his passion for helping patients, Vasella had personal contact with many Gleevec users.

Gleevec is just one of a continuing stream of lifesaving drugs emerging from Novartis research labs. Vasella's commitment to improving patients' lives motivated decisions to expand the company's research budget and move its research headquarters to Massachusetts. These decisions established Novartis as a global health care giant and Vasella as a compassionate leader in the industry. Today Novartis has a pipeline full of new, lifesaving drugs emerging from its research labs.

Vasella said his greatest satisfaction comes when his organization is fulfilling its mission.

My childhood illnesses, the deaths of my father and my sisters, and the experience of patients dying all had a powerful impact on my life. As CEO, I have the leverage to impact the lives of many more people and do what is right, based on my moral compass. Ultimately, the only thing that matters is what we do for other people.

Crucibles of Leadership

Arthur Miller popularized the term *crucible* in his 1953 play, *The Crucible*, about the Salem Witch Trials, in which John Procter's fidelity to his beliefs is tested by the threat of being hanged for practicing witchcraft.

Crucibles will test us to our limits, just as Vasella's life-threatening diseases did. All of us have had crucibles, whether they were as painful as Vasella's or as basic as being rejected by our social group in high school. These experiences affect our lives and our self-perceptions. Warren Bennis discussed crucibles in *On Becoming a Leader*. "The crucible is an essential element in the process of becoming a leader," he wrote.

> *Some magic takes place in the crucible of leadership, whether a transformational experience like Mandela's years in prison, or a relatively painless experience such as being mentored. Whatever is thrown at them, leaders emerge from their crucibles stronger and unbroken.*

Crucibles may come early in your life, such as the death of a loved one, illness, divorce of your parents, growing up in poverty, discrimination, rejection by peers, or early failures. Left unaddressed, they can leave you feeling like a victim or even become incapacitating. Unresolved anger, grief, or shame may cause you to deny your experiences, shut down your deepest feelings, avoid pain in confronting difficult issues, or experience difficulties in intimate relationships.

Later in life, crucibles can be triggered by events such as difficult situations at work, critical feedback, or loss of your job. Or they may result from painful personal experiences, such as divorce, illness, or the death of a loved one. Quite often, crucibles occur when you least expect them. As my wife, Penny, explained about her breast cancer diagnosis in 1996, "Life is what happens when you're expecting something else."

It is hardest to cope with crucibles when you're in the midst of them, as you may feel so much pain that you cannot see the lessons that come from the experience. To navigate through a crucible, you need to believe in yourself and your purpose in life and summon the inner strength and courage to endure. These difficult times also require the affirmation and support of those closest to you.

No one goes through life without experiencing severe challenges. Some are dramatic and life changing whereas others seem insignificant until you reflect on the influence they have had in your life. Crucibles are the real test of your character and can be transformative experiences that empower you to reframe your life's meaning. Eventually, you will look back at your experiences and draw strength from them.

Oprah Winfrey: Reframing Her Story at 36

When she was 36, Oprah Winfrey interviewed a woman named Truddi Chase, who had been sexually abused as a child. Hearing Chase's story, Winfrey was overcome with emotion. "I thought I was going to have a breakdown on television. And I said, 'Stop! Stop! You've got to stop rolling cameras!'" But the cameras kept rolling as feelings roiled inside her.

Chase's story triggered many traumatic memories from Winfrey's own childhood. "I think it was on that day that, for the first time, I recognized that I was not to blame," she said. Her demons had haunted her without explanation to that point of her life.

> I became a sexually promiscuous teenager and as a result of that got myself into a lot of trouble, and believed that I was responsible for it. It wasn't until I was 36 years old, 36 that I connected the fact, "Oh, that's why I was that way." I always blamed myself.

Born out of wedlock, Winfrey grew up in poverty in rural Mississippi. When she was very young, her mother moved north to find work. "I came to live with my grandmother . . . It actually probably saved my life," she said. Yet even as a young child, she had a vision that she could make something of her life. She recalled standing outside on the back porch when she was four, watching her grandmother boiling the laundry in a large cauldron. "I remember thinking, 'My life won't be like this. It will be better,'" she said. "It wasn't from arrogance. It was just a place of knowing that things could be different for me somehow."

Winfrey credited her grandmother for teaching her to read. "That opened the door to all kinds of possibilities for me . . . I loved books so much as a child. They were my outlet to the world." She recited biblical verses in church from age three, which endowed her with a reservoir of self-confidence.

> All the sisters sitting in the front row would fan themselves and turn to my grandmother and say, "Hattie Mae, this child is gifted." And I heard that enough that I started to believe it . . . I didn't even know what "gifted" meant. I just thought it meant I was special.

Winfrey recalled the trauma of being raped by her cousin after she relocated to Milwaukee to be with her mother when she was nine. She was molested several more times by family members and a family friend during the five years she lived with her mother. "It was an ongoing, continuous thing. So much so, that I started to think, 'This is the way life is.'" At age 14, she gave birth prematurely to a child who lived only two weeks.

Winfrey started out trying to make it in the world as an individual contributor. She went to college and had her first opportunity in broadcasting. "It was very uncomfortable for me at first . . . pretending to be Barbara Walters, looking nothing like her." She said she had to take the heat from her college classmates, who called her a token. "I used to say, 'Yeah, but I'm a *paid* token.'"

Today Winfrey has built a media empire that is one of the most respected in the world, but not until the Truddi Chase interview did she realize her broader mission. Ever since the traumatic experiences of her youth, she had felt the need to please people and could never say no. That day she finally understood why.

Since then, her mission has gone far beyond pursuing personal success to empowering people all around the world, especially young women.

> *I was . . . always searching for love and affection and attention, and somebody to say, to look at me and say, 'Yes, you are worthy.' . . . And that, to me, has been the greatest lesson of my life: is to recognize that I am solely responsible for it, and not . . . living to please other people, but doing what my heart says.*

Asked about her show's theme, Winfrey replied, "The message has always been the same: You are responsible for your life. I hope my show and my speeches can help young people get the lesson sooner than I did."

Like many others, I saw Winfrey as a celebrity and missed her greater calling. As we spoke for three hours at the Nobel Peace Prize dinner in Oslo, Norway, I realized the real impact of her leadership and its effect on the lives of her viewers. She described how passionate she is about influencing millions of people and emboldening them to take responsibility for their lives. From Oslo, Winfrey was on her way to Africa with a planeload of books and supplies to launch a new school to empower young women, where she has personally invested $30 million.

Although perhaps not as dramatic as Winfrey's or Vasella's experiences, all of us encounter crucibles in our lives. It is naive to think that you can go through life without difficulties, or spend your entire life trying to avoid them. Life is not always fair. The important thing is how you frame and use your crucibles.

Given the abuse and poverty she experienced earlier in her life, it would have been easy for Winfrey to feel like a victim. Yet she rose above her difficulties by reframing her story in positive terms: first by taking responsibility for her life, then in recognizing her mission to empower others to take responsibility for theirs. Her transformation did not occur until her midthirties. Often the gestation period takes that long because we need to gain real experiences to help us see where we fit in the world and help us understand the meaning of difficult times in our personal missions. That's what happened to Pedro Algorta.

Pedro Algorta: Turning Wounds into Pearls

Shortly after *True North* was published in 2007, I received this amazing letter:

> *Dear Bill,*
>
> *35 years ago, I lived an extreme life experience. The plane I was flying with other 45 friends crashed over the Andes Mountains. 72 days later, after surviving in the mountains at 14,000 feet without food or clothing and no preparation, and even going into cannibalism to feed ourselves, 16 of us were finally rescued.*
>
> *During this ordeal, I had a clear True North: it was to survive one more day, each day. I also found out that we are not strange people, and there were no heroes. The ones that survived were no better than the ones that died. Almost any person in our place, given similar conditions, would have done the same.*
>
> *For 35 years this has not been an issue for me. I even went through my MBA at Stanford without saying a word about my ordeal. Now, I am starting to think about it, and to relate it to my business career. I am reading True North and would like to share my experience with you. That might help me draw more learnings that might help others in their careers.*
>
> *Cordially,*
>
> *Pedro Algorta*

After receiving Algorta's letter, I invited him to share his experience with my MBA class. His story and the pictures he showed mesmerized the students. He returned to my class in 2013, having had five more years to process his crucible, and described three ways to deal with crucibles:

- Focus on the event, and live your life looking backward, often an angry life of blaming others.
- Live your life as if nothing happened, while the memories and the pain remain deep inside you.
- Use the event to transform your wound into a pearl.

He shared the metaphor of the oyster pearl: When sand grates against the oyster shell, its natural reaction is to cover up the irritant to protect itself with a substance called nacre (mother-of-pearl), which eventually forms the pearl itself. Are you turning your wounds into pearls? To do so, you will have to process your crucible, discern its meaning, and reframe it as an opportunity for personal growth.

Taylor Carol: Terminal Cancer Survivor

When you meet Taylor Carol, he seems like the All-American college student: ingenuous, hardworking, engaged in sports, and popular. Then he tells his story of being diagnosed with terminal cancer at age 11.

Taylor was a typical 11-year-old boy when he was hit by a pitch in a baseball game. But his injury did not heal, and at the same time he was feeling lethargic. Concerned about his condition, his parents took him to a hospital near his home in Orange Country, California, for blood tests. When his white cell counts came back off the charts, his parents raced him to the Children's Hospital of Orange County. After several days of tests, the results were stark. Taylor had a rare form of leukemia that does not respond to normal treatment. Taylor and his parents were told he had only two weeks to live.

Not willing to accept that diagnosis, his parents moved to Seattle so that he could be treated at Seattle Children's Hospital under the care of Dr. Brian Drucker, inventor of the Novartis drug Gleevec, and Dr. Paul Carpenter, leading specialist in graft-versus-host disease at the Fred Hutchinson Cancer Research Center. The next two years of Taylor's life were as difficult as anyone can imagine: bone marrow transplant from a 27-year-old German donor; struggling with graft-versus-host disease; weeks in complete isolation; inability to eat, walk, or speak for extended periods; and severe pain treated with extreme painkillers.

The most difficult of all was watching his best friend, Christian, die after two years. As Taylor describes his feelings at that time, "I was broken by Christian's death. Why did he die and I lived? I was furious with God for letting Christian die. I was lost." But Taylor learned that using his voice and singing brought him back. He wrote a song with Matthew Messina called "True Courage" that he sang at the one hundredth anniversary of Seattle Children's.

Over time, Taylor recovered and his body returned to normal, but by then, he had missed four years of school. His counselors suggested that he skip high school and get a graduate equivalent degree. Instead, Taylor decided he wanted to go to Harvard College, knowing nothing about the school except its name. With this as his goal, he made up for lost time, was admitted, and is currently an engaged, successful student. Today he is a national spokesperson for the Leukemia & Lymphoma Society, traveling the country to raise funds for cancer research by singing and speaking.

How did his battle with terminal cancer affect his life? Taylor said:

> After beating cancer, I resolved to use my singing, my words, and every ounce of [my] life force to glorify God and help beat this horrific illness. Over the past seven years I've been lucky enough to help raise over $10,000,000 in these pursuits, but I know it's only the beginning. I aspire to change the world with my words and voice by pursuing my career as a singer/songwriter.

Taylor has dealt with his incredible crucible by transforming his wound into a pearl, using it as an opportunity for post-traumatic growth.

Post-Traumatic Growth

If you follow either of the first two approaches Algorta described—being angry about your crucible or burying it—you may experience post-traumatic stress disorder (PTSD). With PTSD, the traumatic event is commonly relived through recurrent recollections, nightmares, and flashbacks. Many people refuse to address or even acknowledge their crucible, saying, "That's in the past; I don't want to dig it up." The problem is that you cannot bury your crucible, because the memories are always with you. If you avoid all thoughts and discussions about it, as Algorta did, you may find yourself reliving your crucible in a different form later in life or avoiding highly stressful situations that incapacitate you.

New research shows that traumatic experiences can result in post-traumatic growth (PTG) as often as PTSD. Similar to Algorta's metaphor of the oyster pearl, PTG starts by recognizing the uncertainties in life and embracing them as fundamental tenets of human existence. It also requires self-awareness and a desire to undertake personal change. Finally, PTG requires acknowledging your personal responsibility for the choices you make in life. Nick Craig, founder of the Authentic Leadership Institute, describes the path to PTG in his classes on crucibles. He encourages participants to move from seeing themselves as victims to seeing themselves as survivors, then using their learning to elevate themselves into thrivers.

Let's look at some examples of leaders who pursued post-traumatic growth.

Philip McCrea: Learning from Failure

For his first 35 years, charming and likeable Philip McCrea had a great life: wonderful family, lots of friends, and success in school, sports, and work. In high school, he garnered the name "Mr. Perfect," a teasing reference to the sense that he always had things going his way. In his early thirties, he founded Vitesse Learning, a spin-off from his former company, C3I, to focus on automated software education for pharmaceutical companies. Its sales crossed the $10 million mark, but profit margins were razor thin.

Although many leaders have a deep-seated fear of failure, the irony is they learn the most from their failures. Asked in 2004 if he had ever failed, McCrea replied, "Certainly, I have not faced disaster. I haven't had a company that's blown up, or been terminated for not performing." He added:

> However, I need to move from being "ever the optimist" to become more of a realist and look at a balanced picture of each decision as opposed to the rosy picture. I get too aggressive in making decisions about the results we will achieve, and tend to absorb challenges, believing I can work through any issue on my own. I need to realize I don't have the answers, and have discussions with others to help me get there.

Because McCrea's family and friends funded Vitesse, it was often short of capital, especially when the business experienced cost overruns in software development. In the fall of 2005, McCrea realized Vitesse had run out of funding resources, so he merged with a Canadian firm that promised 35 percent lower software development costs. McCrea retained 30 percent ownership of the merged company.

The merger did not go well. Costs rose instead of declining while client relationships deteriorated. After the owner of the Canadian firm rebuffed him, McCrea realized the problems were not going to be resolved and resigned in 2006. Six months later, the firm declared bankruptcy and McCrea's equity was worthless. He explained:

> This was the first time I experienced significant personal failure. It led to my greatest growth, as I had to look myself in the mirror and accept personally that I had failed. I learned people still loved me, and lots of business opportunities and dreams were still achievable.

McCrea also described the impact his professional problems had on his marriage:

> I was intolerable during that period. Although I wouldn't admit it, I was depressed. I got angry easily and lashed out at people, especially my wife. She was there to support me, but I chose instead to use her as a lightning rod. Fortunately, it did not permanently impair our relationship.

After resigning, McCrea took a six-month sabbatical to reflect on his experience and decide what came next. Realizing he was an entrepreneur at heart, he began working with ClearPoint, a competitor in health care training systems, soon becoming its CEO. Since that time, McCrea has used what he learned from his failure to build his new organization. He has teamed with a strong operations partner and maintained a more conservative balance sheet. He reflected, "While I hated every minute of the Vitesse experience, I'm a more balanced person and more seasoned executive as a result."

Mike Sweeney: Dealing with Personal Illness

Mike Sweeney, CEO of piano maker Steinway, was only 28 when he discovered he had testicular cancer. "That was the first time I realized I wasn't immortal," he said. "In some ways I'd recommend it to everyone. If you're going to get cancer, testicular cancer is the one to get because it is usually curable. Cancer caused me to think differently about my life."

Sweeney described an experience he had *after* all the treatments were done:

> *I woke up one morning and literally couldn't get up off the sofa. I got hit by a wave of depression I had never experienced before. It wasn't a matter of will; I just could not get up. While I was fighting cancer, my work was to heal. When that stopped, the room got really quiet, and all of a sudden I realized, holy cow, I could die. At that age the thought of death never occurs to you.*

The experience changed the way Sweeney thought and propelled him on a path of understanding himself and rethinking his life and career.

> *The shock of not being able to get off that sofa scared me. I spent time thinking about what I want to do, what is meaningful in my life, and who do I want to do it with. I saw a psychiatrist and talked about having cancer not as a physical matter, but an emotional one. Cancer gave me clarity about those things.*

His father told him that now that his cancer problem was solved, he should shake it off and get back to work. "I thought there was more involved than that," Sweeney said. "I started asking myself what is important to me in business and in life. I wasn't less ambitious; I just wanted different things out of life. I wanted to build businesses where everyone involved did as well as I did." Just as Algorta did, Sweeney used this crucible to transform his life.

Sweeney had a second awakening when he turned 50. After a highly successful decade as managing partner of a midsized private equity firm, he noted, "Fifty was the first birthday that actually mattered."

> *I realized I only want to work for companies whose products or services make a difference. Unlike private equity where we were always one step removed from the action, I'd rather be on the front lines. I became chair of the Star Tribune newspapers because I believe dissemination of news and information is essential in the life of the community. Restoring the newspaper to profitability required a new business model and new content that rebuilt subscription sales. We also found a new owner committed to the community in Minnesota Timberwolves owner Glen Taylor. In retrospect, working with a team of talented people on a mission we pursued with passion was one of the best experiences of my career.*

After retiring from the *Star Tribune*, Sweeney became CEO of Steinway. He observed, "Here was a jewel of a company being managed for cash that was at risk of losing the essence of what made it great." Before he could rebuild Steinway, Sweeney had to restructure its dysfunctional board of directors, whose members had conflicting purposes. To do so, he gained agreement to sell the company to hedge fund investor John Paulson.

> *Paulson recognized that Steinway is an essential part of the cultural community as well as an important financial asset, so I agreed to stay as CEO. Now we are growing Steinway as a global business, while retaining the great craftspeople who are so committed to making the highest-quality pianos. For me it's a unique opportunity to make a contribution.*

When Sweeney was a young man facing his own mortality, his True North became clear. He continued to hold on to that thread in his life and had the wisdom to make other career changes that kept him aligned with his True North as his career continued.

Marilyn Carlson Nelson: Losing a Loved One

When you meet Marilyn Carlson Nelson of the hospitality conglomerate Carlson, you are struck by her warmth, zest for life, and optimism that any problem can be solved by inspiring people to lead. Yet hers is a more complex story. As if it were yesterday, she vividly recalled learning the news of her daughter's death. "My husband and I heard one morning that our beautiful 19-year-old Juliet had been killed in an automobile accident."

> *That's the most profound test we've ever had, a test of our faith and our personal relationship. I lost my faith at the time and felt angry with God, but God didn't abandon me and didn't let me go. I discovered how valuable every day is and how valuable each person is. I decided to make whatever time I had left meaningful so that the time Juliet didn't have would be well spent. My husband and I vowed to use every tool at hand as an opportunity to give back and make life better for people. We are all human beings with one short time on Earth.*

Soon after her daughter's death, Nelson joined Carlson full-time as vice chair and later became CEO. At Carlson, she devoted herself to empowering the organization's 150,000 employees to serve its customers in a highly personalized manner. Looking back at her time at the helm, Nelson said she is proudest of the culture she built.

Nelson used the trauma of her daughter's death to rethink what her life and leadership were about. By reframing this tragedy with a newfound sense of mission, she transformed her leadership into building strong institutions that serve others and address difficult issues facing society. She concluded, "Business well run is a force for good in the world."

My Crucibles Came Early

On my journey, I experienced several crucibles as I developed into a leader. In my early years, I was hardly recognized by my peers as a leader. I was not the one chosen to head organizations, elected to the student council, or made captain of the tennis team. There was a simple reason for this. I was so ambitious and self-centered that I never took the time to develop close relationships.

In my desire to become a leader, I studied the biographies of world leaders and the great business leaders of my era, attempting to develop the leadership characteristics of these successful people. It didn't work. No wonder my early attempts at leadership failed: I was more a persona than an authentic leader. In high school, I ran for president of the senior class but lost by a two-to-one margin. I was devastated. I had not yet learned what it takes to have people want to follow you. Looking back on those years, I never felt good about myself or secure in my relationships and thus came across as self-centered.

Discouraged, I went off to Georgia Tech so that I could have a fresh start where no one knew me. I hadn't yet learned the lessons of mindfulness meditation from expert Jon Kabat-Zinn's book, *Wherever You Go, There You Are*. Eager for a fresh start, I joined many organizations at Georgia Tech and ran for election six times. I lost each one.

At this point, a group of seniors gave me some sound advice. "Bill, you have a lot of ability, but you seem more interested in getting ahead than you are in helping other people. No wonder no one wants to follow your lead." Devastated by this feedback, I took their advice to heart. In the ensuing months, I asked for help from friends about how I could change. I came to grips with my shortcomings and began to focus on others instead of myself. As I gradually became more self-aware, I was chosen to lead many organizations. Most rewarding of all was being selected as fraternity president by the same people who had rejected me earlier. I learned the hard way I couldn't escape my past unless I changed myself in the present.

Coping with Tragedy

Bad things happen in life that we cannot anticipate. In my mid-twenties, I faced two more crucibles for which I was wholly unprepared. They brought me face-to-face with the meaning of life, its pain, and its injustices.

After graduating from Harvard Business School, I went to work in the Department of Defense. Feeling on top of the world, I loved my work, friends, and new environment. Just four months later, I received an emergency telephone call from my father. He could barely speak as he told me my mother had died that morning of a sudden heart attack. As my role model, my supporter, my ally, and the person from whom I learned unconditional love, my mother was the person the closest to me in the world. Arriving home that afternoon, I will never forget my father's face. Looking into his eyes, I saw he couldn't cope with Mother's death. I had to become my father's father. In a real sense, I lost two parents in one day.

Not long after Mother's death, I fell in love and got engaged. Weeks before the wedding, my fiancée started to experience severe headaches, double vision, and loss of sense of balance. I was so worried that I took her to a leading neurosurgeon, who put her into the hospital for a week of neurological tests. All her exams were negative, but the severe headaches continued. The neurosurgeon told us rather coldly that my fiancée was emotionally disturbed about getting married, recommending she see a psychologist.

Intuitively, I knew this was a misdiagnosis. Something was seriously wrong with my fiancée, but it was definitely not psychological. I was desperate but didn't know where to turn for help. The wedding was three weeks away, and we had still not sent out the invitations. We talked by telephone on a Saturday night but were paralyzed about what to do next. The following morning I returned home from church, where I'd been praying for my fiancée's recovery. Our large Georgetown house was dark, and the curtains were pulled, which seemed odd for a sunny August morning.

One of my roommates met me at the door and asked me to sit down in the living room. I immediately sensed the worst, exclaiming, "She's not dead, is she?" I felt shock and searing pain as he nodded affirmatively. She had died that morning in her father's arms from a malignant brain tumor. Once again I tumbled into the well of grief, alone in the world and unable to comprehend the deeper meaning of what had happened. Thankfully, my friends gathered around me that day and in the weeks that followed and provided the love and support I so desperately needed. I will be forever grateful to them.

This was a crucial time in my life when I could have easily become bitter and depressed and even lost my faith. In times of personal crisis, the grace of God and the power of faith can provide the basis for healing. So can the support of friends. I was blessed to have both. Together they gave me hope for the future and enabled me not to feel sorry for myself, just for my fiancée and her family.

Tragic as these events were, they opened my heart to the deeper meaning of life and got me thinking more profoundly about what I could contribute to others during my lifetime. I came to the realization that there are many things in life we may never be able to explain. The words of St. Paul in 1 Corinthians 13:12 provided the greatest comfort: "Now we see through a glass, darkly; but then face to face."

Sometimes in life when one door closes, another one opens. In the months that followed my fiancée's death, I had the blessing of meeting my future wife, Penny, who supported me in my grief. We fell in love, and a year later we were married. The support of Penny and my friends enabled me to turn my crucibles into post-traumatic growth. Penny is the best thing that has ever happened to me. She is an amazing wife, mother, grandmother, leader, and counselor to me. We recently celebrated our forty-sixth wedding anniversary, a source of great joy for both of us.

Exercise: Your Greatest Crucible

After reading Chapter 3, think back over your life and recall the experience that involved the greatest pressure, stress, or adversity.

1. Write freely about your greatest crucible, and describe:
   a. How you felt at the time
   b. The resources you called upon to get through it
   c. How you resolved the issues, if you have
   d. How this experience shaped you and your views about the world

2. How can you use these experiences to reframe your life story and understand yourself and your life more fully?

3. Are there ways in which these experiences are holding you back today?

Part Two

Developing as an Authentic Leader

True North

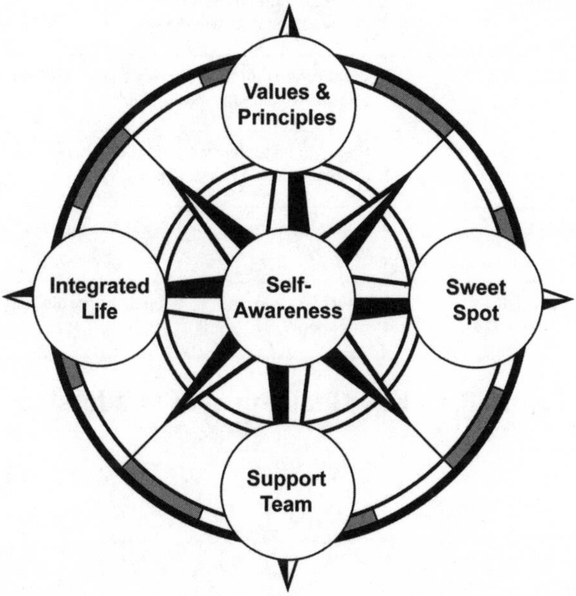

Values &
Principles

Integrated
Life

Self-
Awareness

Sweet
Spot

Support
Team

A Compass for the Journey

Having examined your life story in detail, you are prepared to pursue your development as an authentic leader. In our interviews, we learned that there are five essential elements in your personal development: self-awareness, values, sweet spot, support team, and integrated life. With one chapter devoted to each area, Part II challenges you to engage in continuous personal growth as you become an authentic leader.

Taken together, these five elements form the compass that guides you to your True North. After each experience, you need to calibrate your compass to ensure the steps you are taking on your leadership journey are consistent with your True North and the way you want to lead your life. Because your circumstances, your opportunities, and the world around you are constantly changing, this is a never-ending process.

As you consider each of these areas, ask yourself the fundamental questions listed in Figure II.1.

Leadership Element	Key Challenge
Self-Awareness	How can I increase my self-awareness through introspection and feedback?
Values	What are my most deeply held values? What principles guide my leadership?
Sweet Spot	How can I find my sweet spot that integrates my motivations and greatest capabilities?
Support Team	Whom can I count on to guide and support me along the way?
Integrated Life	How can I integrate all aspects of my life and find fulfillment?

Figure II.1   Key Challenges of Leadership

4

SELF-AWARENESS

Know Thyself.
—*Inscribed at the temple wall at Delphi in Greece
during the sixth century BC*

Self-awareness is the foundation of authenticity, and thus it is at the center of your compass. You develop it by exploring your life story and then understanding the meaning of your crucibles. As you do this, you need to understand who you are at a deeper level. This is hard work but an essential step in your development as a leader. A foundation of self-awareness leads to self-acceptance and ultimately self-actualization so that you can fulfill your greatest potential.

Arianna Huffington: Redefining Success

In 2007, Arianna Huffington's career was on a rapid upward trajectory. Several years after starting the *Huffington Post*, her celebrity was rising, and she was featured on magazine covers. *Time* chose her as one of the world's 100 Most Influential People.

Then she had a wake-up call. One day she found herself lying on the floor of her home office in a pool of blood, having collapsed from exhaustion. She explained:

> *On my fall, my head hit the corner of my desk, cutting my eye and breaking my cheekbone. I went from doctor to doctor, from brain MRI (magnetic resonance imaging) to CAT (computed axial tomography) scan to ECG (electrocardiogram), to find out if there was any underlying medical problem beyond*

exhaustion. There wasn't, but doctors' waiting rooms proved to be good places to ask myself deeper questions about the kind of life I was living.

The gravity of the collapse forced Huffington to confront reality about her life.

I was working 18 hours a day, seven days a week, trying to build a business, expand our coverage, and bring in investors. My life was out of control. By traditional measures of money and power, I was highly successful, but by any sane definition I was not living a successful life. Something had to change radically, as I knew I couldn't go on that way.

Huffington's life did not begin on a fast track. She was raised in a one-room apartment in Athens, Greece, where she lived with her mother and sister. Her parents separated when she was 11 but never divorced. Looking back, she credits her parents for shaping her. "My mother was an incredible person who was self-taught," she said.

She always made us see we were not limited by our circumstances. We could pursue our dreams and if we failed, she wouldn't love us any less. She told us, "Failure is not the opposite of success. It's a stepping stone to success." My father was a brilliant journalist who kept starting newspapers, all of which failed. He started an underground newspaper during Germany's occupation of Greece, was arrested, and spent the war in a concentration camp.

At 19, Huffington went to Cambridge University, eventually becoming president of Cambridge Union, the campus debating society. After an English publisher watched a debate Huffington organized on the changing roles of women, she received her first book contract and produced *The Female Woman*. Continuing her writing, she moved first to London and then to New York.

In 2005, she founded the *Huffington Post*. "Facilitating interesting conversations has always been part of my Greek DNA," she said.

The point of the Huffington Post was to take conversations found at water coolers and around dinner tables—about politics and art and books and food and sex—open them up and bring them online. The site was created as a unique combination of three things: news aggregation with an attitude, opinion, and community. Our secret ingredient is our willingness to innovate.

The instant success of the *Huffington Post* had one victim—its founder. Notoriety brought opportunities, and with opportunities came an increasing workload. Huffington's 2007 fall catalyzed her to ask: "Is this what success looks like? Is this the life I want?"

As she prepared the 2013 commencement address for Smith College, she conceived ideas for a *Third Metric*. "I ask you to redefine success," she told the graduates. "Don't just take your place at the top of the world, as so many Smith graduates do, but change the world." The Third Metric does not supplant the first two—money and power—but it balances them. In her book *Thrive*, Huffington noted eulogies rarely celebrate the first two metrics. It is our capacity for well-being that truly enriches our lives.

Huffington was overwhelmed by the response to her speech. "Society has a widespread longing to redefine success and what it means to lead the good life," she said. "This question has been asked by philosophers since the ancient Greeks."

> *Somewhere along the line we shifted our attention to how much money we can make, how big a house we can buy, and how high we can climb the career ladder. As I discovered painfully, these are far from the only questions that matter in creating a successful life. I want to see millions more people around the world embrace the recognition that a good life must go beyond the first two metrics of money and power, and include well-being, wisdom, wonder, and giving.*

Like many of us, Huffington's journey to self-awareness took many turns. Money, fame, and power did not imperil Huffington to the extent they did Rajat Gupta and Mike Baker, but they distracted her from her True North. How could the same thoughtful woman who frequently discussed her yearning for wisdom sacrifice her health and well-being?

This is actually a common occurrence for high performers, who constantly walk a tightrope between the drive that makes them successful and the perspective that keeps them grounded. For tightrope walkers who balance intensity and reflection, self-awareness acts like an internal ballast. In Huffington's case, she recognized the need to change her behavior well before something more dramatic occurred, such as a heart attack. That ability to step back and understand the alignment (or misalignment) of her actual behavior and her vision for herself is part of what makes her a remarkable leader.

Becoming Self-Aware

The charge to "Know Thyself" may be thousands of years old, but following this advice is not easy to do. As human beings, we have many aspects to our character. We are constantly evolving, as we test ourselves in the world, are influenced by it, and adapt to our environment—all to find our unique place. But you must be true to yourself and follow your True North. If you know who you are, you can achieve what you seek from life and overcome the obstacles you face.

Discovering your authentic self becomes more complicated when you face myriad options. These options either provide opportunities to develop yourself or become seductions that take you away from your authentic self. Without self-awareness, it is easy to get caught up in chasing celebrity and the external symbols of success as Arianna Huffington did, rather than becoming the person you want to be.

In life, you will be confronted by people who threaten you, do not like you, or reject you. When you feel threatened or rejected, it is difficult to regulate your emotions, control your fears, and avoid impulsive outbursts. To protect yourself from harm, you may develop a false self by building protective layers. In so doing, you become less authentic. Without being aware of your vulnerabilities, fears, and longings, it is easy to go off the track of your True North, and others can take advantage of you.

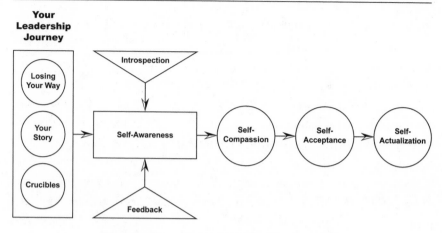

Figure 4.1   Gaining Self-Awareness

Gaining self-awareness begins with understanding your life story and framing your crucibles (see Figure 4.1). Then you need to reflect on your experiences through introspection and get feedback from those who know you best. Early in their careers, many leaders try so hard to establish themselves that they never take time for self-exploration. As they age, they may find something is missing in their lives or realize something is holding them back from being the person they want to be. They may encounter a life-changing event that causes them to reflect deeply on what they want from life.

For other leaders, memories of childhood are so painful that they shut themselves off from their feelings. Anxious to bury these memories altogether, they drive extremely hard to achieve success in the tangible ways that are recognized in the external world—money, fame, power, status, or a rising stock price. Often their drive enables them to be successful, at least for a while, but it leaves them vulnerable to derailment, because their lack of self-awareness can lead to major mistakes and errors in judgment.

The Importance of Emotional Intelligence

Although intellectual intelligence, or IQ, has long been thought of as an essential characteristic for managers, new research is demonstrating that emotional intelligence (EQ) is more important for authentic leaders. Psychologist Daniel Goleman, author of *Emotional Intelligence*, outlines five areas essential to a high EQ: self-awareness, self-regulation, social skill, empathy, and motivation. Through his research, Goleman has found that above an IQ of 120, EQ becomes the more important factor in predicting leaders' success. Leadership, interpersonal skills, and teamwork are worth far more than a few extra IQ points.

Many leaders believe by being the smartest person in the room, their intellect will carry the day. Leaders who lead only with their intellect tend to dismiss the opinions of others and dominate decision making. As a result, they overpower less forceful voices that have vital ideas, insights, and answers needed for sound decision making. Leaders with exceptionally high IQs often get too intellectually involved and may be intolerant of others with less raw intellect. Wells Fargo's Dick Kovacevich argues high IQ can be an impediment to leadership. "Above the ninety-ninth percentile of intelligence, there is an inverse correlation between leadership and intelligence."

Former Procter & Gamble (P&G) CEO Durk Jager is an example of someone who failed because he tried to impose his intellect on others. Jager was a brilliant strategist; however, his abrasive style threatened the essence of P&G's culture. As a result, his management team rebelled, and the board asked him to step down in less than two years. In taking his place, longtime P&G executive A. G. Lafley used his deep understanding of P&G's culture to successfully build a leadership team that grew P&G and transformed it into a global company.

Self-awareness should be the starting point in every leader's development. The leaders we interviewed said gaining self-awareness was central to becoming authentic leaders. When Stanford Graduate School of Business asked its advisory council the most important capability for leaders to develop, their answer was nearly unanimous: self-awareness. It is at the center of your inner compass and an essential component of knowing yourself, discerning your passions, and discovering the purpose of your leadership.

David Pottruck: Journey to Self-Awareness

Of all the leaders we interviewed, David Pottruck, co-CEO of Charles Schwab, had one of the most courageous journeys to discovering his authentic self. He grew up in modest circumstances: His father was a Grumman Aircraft machinist and his mother was a nurse. He was an all-league high school football player and earned a scholarship to the University of Pennsylvania.

Disappointed not to be recruited for professional football, Pottruck went to the Wharton School for his MBA, joined Citigroup, and later moved to San Francisco, to become head of marketing at Charles Schwab. He worked extremely hard but couldn't understand why his colleagues resented his long hours and aggressiveness in pushing for results. "I thought my accomplishments spoke for themselves," he recalled. "It never occurred to me that my level of energy intimidated and offended other people."

The most difficult thing in becoming self-aware is to see ourselves as others see us. Leaders need accurate feedback to identify their blind spots. Pottruck was shocked when his boss rated him poorly, telling him, "Dave, your colleagues don't trust you." He recalled, "That feedback was like a dagger to my heart. I was in denial, as I didn't see myself as others saw me."

> I had no idea how self-serving I looked to other people, but somewhere in my inner core the feedback resonated as true. I thought about finding another job, but Chuck Schwab asked me to stay and work out the differences with my team. I had to confront my reality that I had to change.

Pottruck found changing was a very hard process.

> The more stress you are under, the more you revert to your old patterns. Much like Alcoholics Anonymous, I went and said to my colleagues, "I'm Dave Pottruck, and I have some broken leadership skills. I'm going to try to be a different person. I need your help, and ask you to be open to the possibility that I can change."

Pottruck worked with a coach and developed a cadre of advisers to use as a sounding board. His coach taught him about authenticity and the power of storytelling. In speeches, he began telling stories that revealed his life, fears, ambitions, and failures. Pottruck found that people were inspired.

After his second divorce, Pottruck realized he still had large blind spots. "When my first marriage ended, I was convinced it was all her fault. After my second marriage fell apart, I thought I had a wife selection problem." Then he worked with a counselor, who told him, "I have good news and bad news. The good news is you don't have a wife selection problem; the bad news is you have a husband behavior problem."

Yet Pottruck still struggled with denial.

I was like a guy who has had three heart attacks and finally realizes he has to quit smoking and lose some weight. Denial is our biggest challenge we face. To overcome, you must be honest with yourself and not make up excuses. This has helped me accept criticism and take it seriously, even if it's painful.

These days Pottruck is happily remarried and listens to his wife's constructive feedback, yet he still falls into his old habits, particularly during moments of high stress. "We all want to be stroked, admired, and complimented, but we have to listen to feedback we don't want to hear," he noted.

Pottruck's hard work in becoming self-aware paid off. He won the support of his colleagues, and his dynamic leadership produced outstanding results for the firm. As a result, Schwab promoted him to be his co-CEO. During his 14 years at the helm of Schwab, Pottruck substantially broadened Schwab's business base while it became one of the most admired companies in America and was named to *Fortune*'s 100 Best Companies to Work For list. He concluded, "All of us have an innate ability to become better."

None of us is born perfect. We all have things we do wrong. Either you let them get in your way your whole life, or you fix them. If I can help people believe they can improve, they too can make this journey of discovery, honest self-appraisal, and hard work toward fundamental change.

David Pottruck readily acknowledges his imperfections—even while admitting that it is hard to see them all. His experience of discovering "blind spots" is instructive and humbling. He relishes the opportunity to learn from every experience: "You don't have to be perfect," he said. "You can start off on a bad path and recover. You can turn most failures into successes if you ask yourself, What can I learn from this so that I can do better the next time?"

Pottruck believes that the key is to avoid denial and be honest with yourself. "If you're open, you can learn a lot more from failure than success," he said.

When you're successful, you take it for granted and move on to the next thing. Failure forces you to reflect. What went wrong? How could I have done this better? It's an opportunity for you to take responsibility. The path of least resistance is to blame it on someone else. I failed many times but learned from each experience and managed to come back stronger.

Perfection is not the goal of authentic leadership; rather, it is important to understand yourself at the deepest level. This process takes introspection, feedback, and support. Credit Pottruck for always learning and trying to improve his leadership. He did not want to come across as untrustworthy, but he found that his aggressive behavior fostered that perception among his Schwab colleagues. To be successful, Pottruck did not mask his natural self. Rather, he sought to bring forth deeper elements of himself that he had previously cloaked and share stories that showed his vulnerabilities. As a result, his colleagues connected with him more authentically.

Peeling Back the Onion

As you search for your true self, you are peeling back the layers of an onion (see Figure 4.2). The outer layers of the onion are the visible

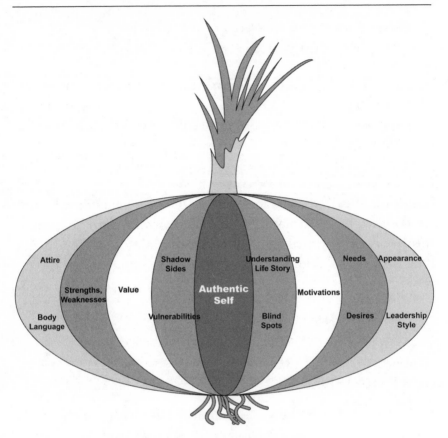

Figure 4.2   Peeling Your Onion

ways you present yourself to the world—how you look, your facial expressions, your body language, your attire, and your leadership style. Often these layers are rough and hardened to protect you from the assaults of the world around you. I once asked a teenage mentee why he spent so much time in front of the mirror. His reply was telling: "I need to look good on the outside, because I feel so rotten on the inside."

Understanding your outer layers is a necessary first step to going deeper into what lies beneath, because these layers provide access to your inner core. Peeling the onion further, you gain a deeper understanding of your strengths, weaknesses, values, and motivations. Underneath the layers of your metaphorical onion lies your understanding of your life story. There your experiences create a mosaic of your life. As you approach the deepest layers surrounding your inner core, you find your blind spots and your vulnerabilities. At the core of your being is your True North: what you believe and how you envision your place on Earth.

As you explore who you are, you peel back one layer only to discover a deeper and often more interesting layer underneath it. As you get nearer to your core, you find that the inner layers feel quite tender and vulnerable because they have not been exposed to the assaults of the outside world. When you're not in a safe place, you cover your core self to protect it from exposure and harm. Too often, this leads people to develop a false self or a persona. This persona interferes with your ability to form genuine connections with other people. Most important, it can obscure your acceptance of yourself.

Vulnerability Is Power

What would it mean if we were willing to be vulnerable and expose our full selves to the world by just being our authentic selves? No more false layers of protection. At first, it might be scary, but as we realize that people accept and love us for who we really are, it would be liberating: *I can be who I am.*

Yet many of us fear people will reject us if we show our vulnerabilities, admit our weaknesses, and acknowledge our mistakes. Will they think less of us? Will they try to take advantage of our weaknesses? As hard as we try to deny them, these questions nag us when we are feeling most vulnerable.

For many years of my career, I felt I had to do things perfectly and have all the answers. I lacked the confidence to share my weaknesses, fears, and vulnerabilities. When I finally learned to do so, things went much better for me, and my relationships with colleagues improved. Most important, I felt more comfortable in my skin and had a stronger sense of well-being.

In his book *Love Leadership*, John Hope Bryant, who was homeless for six months in his teens, proclaims, "Vulnerability is power." When I share this idea with executives in my classrooms, a look of fear comes over some of them. Yet Bryant backs it up with his life story and personal experiences of being vulnerable. He grew up poor in the rough neighborhood of South Central Los Angeles. He recalled, "When I was five, my parents divorced over money, the number one cause of divorce in America."

Bryant's life was a roller coaster. He had a strong work ethic and an entrepreneurial spark that resulted in some early business successes. However, by his late teens, he was struggling. "I didn't know my True North, and didn't have any role models to help me figure it out," he explained.

> So I faked it, acting like a big cheese, wearing sunglasses at night to feel important. It was just low self-esteem. Then I came up short one too many times, lost an investor's money and couldn't pay him back, and wound up homeless. I went from having a beach house in Malibu to living in my leased Jeep behind a restaurant. Everybody knew I lost everything because I was so arrogant. People were literally cheering for my failure.
>
> Life is 10 percent what happens to you and 90 percent how you respond. I had gotten into that mess, and had to work my way out of it. It grew resilience in me. You cannot go to the highest mountain unless you go to the depths of the valleys. The key to success in life is navigating your pain.

In 1992, when the Los Angeles Police Department officers who had been videotaped beating Rodney King were found not guilty at trial for assault and use of excessive force, people rioted in Bryant's neighborhood. "I remember asking Reverend Jesse Jackson what I could do to help," he said. "He told me, 'We need businesspeople with investment to rebuild this community. Take your business skills and put them to work.'" With that, 19-year-old Bryant sprang into action. The next day he organized a group of bankers to take a bus tour through South Central Los Angeles. That eventually led to the founding of Operation Hope, a social investment bank that aims to eradicate poverty and grow the U.S. economy. As CEO, he is now recognized for his efforts to enable low-income people to become financially literate and build their own businesses.

Reflecting on his experiences, Bryant said, "Vulnerability is the key to freedom."

If I've got nothing to hide and admit my faults before you can call them out, what are you going to do to me? Being self-aware without being vulnerable leads to depression and schizophrenia because there's no expression. We're looking for love in all the wrong places. Our addictions are caused by emotions we can't handle. So we medicate ourselves with drugs, alcohol, shopping, overworking, or sex. Tomorrow we need more of these seductions in order to give us the second buzz. Eventually our addictive response cocktails are filled up to the top, and we die inside.

He said the alternative is feeling good in our skin, which directly correlates with our willingness to be vulnerable. He observed:

If I don't feel comfortable in my own skin, there is no way I am willing to be vulnerable. So I live a lie by creating a false persona. People are smiling when they feel like crying. They're laughing, but they're miserable inside. The only path forward is healing: You've got to find your True North.

There are three ways to live—suicide: physically, mentally, spiritually, or emotionally; coping, which is what most of society is doing; and the last way to live is to heal. Healing is the only path forward, but it is the most courageous and most terrifying. To heal, you've got to get over the fear of just being yourself. Most adults we're dealing with are reliving pains of their childhood—a domineering mother, an abusive or absent father, or [experiences of] being ignored, chastised, molested, teased, or bullied. A lot of bullies today who walk around looking cool with tons of money are just trying to escape memories of being little kids in school with thick glasses on.

Bryant has not had an easy life but did have the resilience to bounce back from adversity. He also has had the courage to share his story and inspire others. In my classroom, he openly acknowledged the pain he experienced in being homeless. He comes across as being less than perfect, but this makes him more sympathetic, more believable, and more persuasive. Bryant's vulnerability is his power. Through his authenticity, others connect with him. Former president Bill Clinton, former ambassador Andrew Young, and Fortune 500 CEOs are now partnering with Bryant. His bold goal is to create 1,000 HOPE Inside locations as he scales Operation Hope to become the nation's private banker to low-income and struggling middle-class Americans.

Reflection and Introspection

How can we develop self-awareness and acceptance of ourselves? The best ways are having an introspective practice and getting honest feedback. In the über-busy, 24/7 world in which we are electronically connected virtually all the time, we need to have daily practices that enable us to pause and focus on ourselves, take stock of our actions and pressures, and go deeper inside ourselves. Reflecting on our life story and our crucibles helps us understand them at a deeper level. Then we can reframe our story in a coherent way so that our actions and decisions are congruent with understanding who we are.

Randy Komisar's Struggle to Find His Track

Randy Komisar went through a period of deep reflection to figure out what he wanted out of life. At LucasArts, he clashed frequently with legendary founder George Lucas, creator of *Star Wars*. Frustrated by his lack of independence, Komisar became CEO of LucasArts's rival Crystal Dynamics. It turned out to be the worst decision he ever made, as he realized the business did not stir his passions.

> *I couldn't find my reason for being there. The business floundered and ultimately succeeded, but I failed. First, I had to admit my mistakes. Then I had to face tough issues like, What do I want out of my life? I could have made Crystal work, but at what cost? I hadn't asked myself that question before.*

He resigned after a year and began practicing meditation to gain clarity, with a Buddhist monk as his teacher. "That was a point in my life when it was time to just *be*. My Buddhist practice was formative for the next phase of my life." After reflection, Komisar realized the conflicts inside him traced to his father and grandmother. His father craved material success and gambled constantly. "When he lost money, we feared we couldn't pay our college tuition. Insecurity about money was ingrained in me as a child," Komisar said. He was close to his grandmother, who died when he was 10. "We bonded in ways I never did with anyone else," he said. "Her death devastated me. She had incredible influence on my life. She was generous, interested in people, and had great character. She loved people and they loved her."

Komisar recognized he needed to release himself from his father's influence and to embrace his own desires. "I was on a fast track, but it wasn't my track," he said.

> *There was a war inside me between my need for fulfillment versus being successful in my father's eyes. I had to let go of the notion I was climbing the ladder of success, and recognize I was on a long and winding journey. The ability to face reality and acknowledge that you can fail and still feel good about yourself is an important turning point in your self-awareness.*

Only when leaders accept who they are and release the need to be on someone else's fast track can they be comfortable in their own skin. There are several introspective practices that leaders find effective in enabling them to focus their attention and their energies. The most powerful of these is meditation. Meditation has recently come of age as a mainstream practice. In 2014, *Time* put the ideas of meditation teacher Jon Kabat-Zinn on its cover. He has taught secular programs in mindfulness-based stress reduction for more than 45 years.

Arianna Huffington started meditating when she was 13 but had difficulties maintaining her practice. Since her 2007 fall, she starts every morning with 20 minutes of meditation. She noted:

> *I respect the principles of Buddhism and have incorporated them into my daily life. My conversations with the Dalai Lama have been hugely influential. I'm in awe*

of the way he looks to neuroscience to convince our skeptical and secular society of the power of contemplation and compassion to change our lives and our world.

In 1975, at my wife's insistence I went to a four-hour program on Transcendental Meditation. At the time I was going nonstop from dawn until evening, having late dinners, and then coming home exhausted. I even got denied for life insurance because of high blood pressure. So I started meditating twice a day—not as a spiritual practice, but for health reasons. Forty years later, I am still practicing regularly.

Meditation is the best thing I have ever done to calm myself and separate from the 24/7, connected world. By centering into myself, I am able to focus my attention on what's really important, and develop an inner sense of well-being. Through meditation, I am able to gain clarity about important issues. My most creative ideas come from meditating. Most important, meditation has enabled me to build resilience to deal with difficult times. I have no doubt it has helped me become a better leader.

Chade-Meng Tan, Google's Jolly Good Fellow

Leading companies, such as General Mills, Aetna, Black Rock, and Goldman Sachs, are encouraging their employees to establish meditation practices. At Google, perhaps the world's most innovative company, meditation has taken off. Chade-Meng Tan, who is known as Google's Jolly Good Fellow, has taught thousands of employees how to meditate.

Tan was born in Singapore, a child of Chinese immigrant parents. He was exceptionally bright, becoming the national programming champion at 17. In spite of his accomplishments, Tan said, "I was deeply unhappy as a child because I didn't fit in. I had the perpetual feeling I didn't deserve to be loved. After I completed my master's degree at the University of California at Santa Barbara, I joined Google as employee #107."

My breakthrough came in 1991 when I discovered meditation. It was a moment of great insight where suddenly everything in my life made sense. Before I was a meditator, I was very depressed. Since meditating regularly, I have become very happy. It was a huge change. Through meditation I learned the ability to calm my mind on demand and stay in a state of clarity and calmness as long as I want to. A key part of my practice is kindness and compassion. You cannot be genuinely compassionate toward others if you have no compassion for yourself.

Tan described the creation of Google's meditation program:

In 2003, I had an epiphany that we could create the conditions for world peace through scaling inner peace, joy, and compassion worldwide by aligning them with success and profits. The solution was emotional intelligence (EQ). I engaged some of the world's top experts, and together we created Search Inside Yourself. In addition to teaching 2,000 Googlers per year to meditate, we also founded the non-profit Search Inside Yourself Leadership Institute, which has been training clients like SAP and Kaiser.

Meditation isn't for everyone. There are many other introspective practices that leaders find effective: saying a centering prayer, taking a long walk, or having deep discussions with a loved one. The important thing is to have an introspective practice you do daily.

The Importance of Feedback

One of the most important skills leaders need to develop is the ability to see themselves as others see them. Honest feedback is often hard to get, because far too many people tell leaders what they want to hear. For this reason, authentic leaders have to seek out feedback from their peers and subordinates. One of the best ways to do this is through anonymous, 360-degree feedback.

Feedback is an essential tool to use to get outside our egos and listen to constructive criticism we may not want to hear. Verizon's Judy Haberkorn explained:

> They called me the feedback queen. The best thing you can get in this world is honest feedback from someone who cares about your success and well-being. Some are more self-aware than others, but few of us see the world as it sees us.

Kroger CEO David Dillon discovered the value of feedback during college after he lost an important election. His first reaction was to get defensive and think, "I'm better than that guy. Why didn't they choose me?" Following introspection, he realized, "My point of view wasn't relevant. The important one was what others thought." Through feedback, he learned he had a number of traits that needed improvement. As a result, he went on to become president of the student body at the University of Kansas and of his fraternity, the first steps in a life of successful leadership. Dillon said, "Feedback helps you take the blinders off, face reality, and see yourself as you really are."

Dillon regularly asks his colleagues at Kroger for feedback. Occasionally, it hits too close to home.

> When I get defensive, I go back and apologize, saying, "My reaction was against me, not you. My defensiveness is a mechanism to cope with unpleasant personal news. I assure you I hold you in higher regard because you shared that with me."

In Chapter 7, we describe the importance of having a support team—spouses, friends, mentors, and small groups—who will give you honest feedback.

Opening up Hidden Areas

The Johari Window, designed in 1955, is a means of gaining self-awareness and becoming more open.

For many of us, the upper left quadrant—known to ourselves and others—is far too small (see Figure 4.3). Opening up this quadrant is

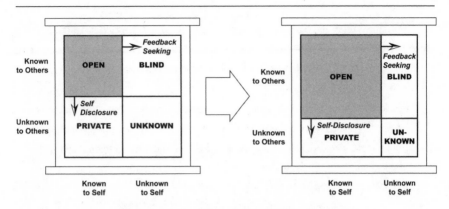

Figure 4.3   The Johari Window

crucial to becoming more authentic. The easiest way to do so is to share more of our hidden areas—known to ourselves but not to others—with other people. This requires sharing your life story and difficult times, along with exposing your weaknesses. When we do, we are validated by other people, not rejected as many fear, and this enables us to truly be ourselves.

In the upper right quadrants are blind spots—known to others but unknown to us. This is undoubtedly the most difficult area to address. Nearly all of us have traits, habits, and tendencies that others see in us but we are unable to see in ourselves. The only way to open our blind spots is to get honest feedback from others and take it to heart. Seeing our blind spots and opening up our hidden areas enables us to be fully open, transparent, and authentic as leaders.

Lord John Browne and Tim Cook: Emerging from the Closet

For five years, I sat next to Lord John Browne, then chief executive of British Petroleum (BP), as we served together on the Goldman Sachs board. Browne has a brilliant financial mind and was a superb chair of Goldman's audit committee. He was also gay, a subject we never discussed. In May 2007, he was forced to resign from BP for perjuring himself by giving false testimony about how he met a former lover.

As he writes in his poignant 2014 book, *The Glass Closet,* "My overwhelming desire to conceal my sexual orientation over four decades in the oil industry had culminated in this terrible juncture."

> My long-kept secret was about to be exposed and I was not going to hide any longer. My refusal to acknowledge my sexual orientation publicly stemmed from a lack of confidence. Inside I concealed deep unease and had to deal with inner turmoil almost daily. It is difficult to feel good about yourself when you are embarrassed to show who you actually are.
>
> Closeted people cannot fully grasp how much their secret weighs them down. But living a lie is too costly. One's life should not be built around pleasing the minority of people who may find your sexual orientation objectionable. It should be built around creating meaningful relationships with people who value you, not what you pretend to be.

Although legal barriers against gay people are falling rapidly, it remains a tragedy that old norms in our society have prevented so many people from being open about who they are. Remarkably, Browne was the first chief executive of a Fortune 500 company to publicly acknowledge he is gay. His openness has encouraged others to follow suit. In 2014, Apple CEO Tim Cook addressed his sexuality in an article, writing:

> While I have never denied my sexuality, I haven't publicly acknowledged it either, until now. So let me be clear: I'm proud to be gay. I consider being gay among the greatest gifts God has given me. Being gay has given me a deeper understanding of what it means to be in the minority and provided a window into the challenges that people in other minority groups deal with every day.
>
> It's made me more empathetic, which has led to a richer life. It's been tough and uncomfortable at times, but it has given me the confidence to be myself, to follow my own path, and to rise above adversity and bigotry. It's also given me the skin of a rhinoceros, which comes in handy when you're CEO of Apple.

Cook said he is not defined by his sexuality: "I'm an engineer, uncle, nature lover, fitness nut, son of the South, sports fanatic, and many other things." This letter gives us a window into his soul. Cook has not only accepted his sexuality; he has also accepted himself.

"The Civil Rights Issue of our Time"

When all banks were under great pressure in 2011, Goldman Sachs CEO Lloyd Blankfein had the courage to take on what he calls "the civil rights issue of our time"—equal treatment for gays and lesbians. Blankfein, a Harvard-trained lawyer who is happily married with three successful children, knew well the price of discrimination from encounters with anti-Semitism early in his life. While other CEOs were holding back from addressing these issues, Blankfein stepped up and became a national spokesperson for the lesbian, gay, bisexual, and transgender equality movement.

In Minnesota, when we were facing the threat of a constitutional amendment to ban same-sex marriage—what I term "legalized discrimination"—Blankfein came to the state at my request and gave a poignant speech that helped turn the tide against this onerous amendment. Not only was it defeated, but also six months later the Minnesota legislature legalized same-sex marriage.

All of us have hidden differences we are reluctant, even ashamed, to reveal to those closest to us. What closet are you hiding in? Wouldn't you feel better if you could reveal your secrets to others close to you? Opening up our hidden areas is an essential part of accepting ourselves as we are. Browne's wisdom applies to us all: Only by opening up ourselves to others can we find that deep sense of well-being.

Self-Compassion and Self-Acceptance

When we are self-aware, we can develop compassion for ourselves and the challenges we have faced in navigating life's difficulties. Only through self-compassion can we have genuine empathy for others and the difficulties they have faced. Respecting others' experiences requires you to love yourself unconditionally first.

In *The Poetry of Self Compassion*, poet David Whyte talks about dealing with your weaknesses and shadow sides so that you can accept the things you like least about yourself. That requires digging into experiences you have hidden for years. Whyte says you cannot wall yourself off from the pain of past experiences. Like David Pottruck did, you have to confront them directly, accept yourself unconditionally, and learn to love your weaknesses as much as you revel in your strengths. That level of self-compassion enables you to get to the source of your True North.

It is easy to love our strengths and bask in our successes. Even Narcissus could do that. To love ourselves unconditionally, we have to learn to accept ourselves as we are, with all our warts and our flaws, rather than wish we were different. Reatha Clark King captured this feeling when she said, "I feel good in my skin. I get along well with myself and have learned to accept myself race wise and gender wise."

Once armed with a high level of self-awareness and self-acceptance, it is much easier to regulate your emotions and your behavior. Your emotional outbursts usually result when someone penetrates to the core of what you do not like about yourself, or still cannot accept, as Dave Dillon described. By accepting yourself just as you are, you are no longer vulnerable to these hurts. You are prepared to interact authentically with others who come into your life—your family, friends, and coworkers, even complete strangers. Free of having to wear a mask, you can focus on pursuing your passions. That leads you on the path to self-actualization, which enables you to fulfill your greatest dreams.

Becoming a Mindful Leader

Given the pressures of today's world, and the failures of many leaders, there is rapidly growing interest in mindfulness. Mindfulness is the ability to focus your attention on your thoughts, emotions, and feelings in the present moment.

Psychologist Ellen Langer, often called "the mother of mindfulness," published her classic work *Mindfulness* in 1989, long before the practice was accepted in the mainstream culture. She sees mindfulness as the essence of leadership. She added:

Whatever you're doing, you're doing it mindfully or mindlessly. The consequences of being in one state of mind or the other are enormous. Virtually all of the ills individuals experience are the result of mindlessness. As the culture becomes more mindful, we increase our effectiveness, our health, and our overall well-being.

In 1979, I learned an important lesson from Buddhist monk Thích Nhất Hạnh: "The longest journey you will ever take is the 18 inches from your head to your heart." Our hearts are where such essential leadership qualities as passion, compassion, and courage reside. By practicing mindfulness, mindful leaders exhibit high levels of self-awareness and intentionality in their actions.

The key to effective leadership is the ability to integrate your head (IQ) with your heart (EQ). Jon Kabat-Zinn explained:

In Asian languages mind and heart are the same word. Mindfulness is not just about our minds but our whole beings. When we are all mind, things get rigid. When we are all heart, things get chaotic. Both lead to stress. When the mind and heart work together—the heart leading through empathy, the mind guiding us with focus and attention, we become harmonious human beings.

Exercise: Knowing Your Authentic Self

1. What are your vulnerabilities, blind spots, and shadow sides? To what extent do you use defensive armor as a shield to protect yourself from exposing your vulnerabilities with others?

2. When you face displeasing situations or receive critical feedback from others, how well are you able to take in the feedback and respond in a constructive manner without acting defensively?

3. How well do you understand the emotional makeup of others and their needs? How sensitive are you in relating to others' needs and helping others? How skillful are you in building lasting relationships?

4. How comfortable are you with who you are right now?

5

VALUES

Leaders with principles are less likely to get bullied or
pushed around because they can draw clear lines in the
sand . . . The softest pillow is a clear conscience.
—*Narayana Murthy, founder and CEO, Infosys*

In gaining self-awareness, it is important to identify the values and
principles that guide your leadership. The values that form the basis
for your True North are derived from your beliefs and convictions.
Staying centered on those values is not easy. The temptations and
pressures of the outside world often conspire to pull you away from
your True North.

David Gergen: Crisis Strengthened His Values

David Gergen wanted to lead a life consistent with values he learned
from his family and the Durham, North Carolina, community where
he grew up. He is the only person to serve as a senior White House
adviser to four U.S. presidents: Republicans Richard Nixon, Gerald
Ford, and Ronald Reagan and Democrat Bill Clinton.

Gergen was 28 when he was hired as a White House speechwriter
during Nixon's first term. He had a ringside seat for history as it was
being made. "When I first arrived, the power, glamour, and status
went to my head," he said. Years later, he realized how naive and
unprepared he was for the events of the next few years—particularly
the Watergate scandal.

Initially, his talent and ambition enabled him to become a rising star in the Nixon administration. He recalled, "I was grasping for the brass ring and was as ambitious as everybody else, probably more so." After Nixon's 1972 reelection, Gergen was named head of the president's speechwriting and research team, with the responsibility for supervising 50 people. "It was tempting to fall into the trap of thinking I was important, instead of recognizing that people think you're important only because of where you're standing. I had some of the arrogance that other people in that administration had," he reflected.

When stories about the Watergate cover-up began to emerge in early 1973, Gergen did not believe the allegations were true. "We were continuously reassured that neither Nixon nor anyone high up in the White House staff had done anything wrong," he explained. "Nixon told us that directly, and Bob [Nixon's chief of staff] and others confirmed it in the most adamant terms." As the public's focus on Watergate intensified throughout 1973 and 1974, an increasing number of staff members resigned, including some of Gergen's team. However, he did not feel he could leave. "My resignation would have made a public statement about my lack of belief in President Nixon's integrity. So I stayed and kept hoping against hope he was innocent."

Gergen learned of Nixon's guilt only two days before the news broke in August 1974. Even then, he did not feel he could leave, lest he be viewed as "a rat leaving the sinking ship," especially when Nixon asked him to write his resignation letter. As he watched Nixon leave the White House for the last time on the presidential helicopter *Marine One*, Gergen thought his career in public life was over. He recalled the infamous 1919 Chicago Black Sox World Series team, whose players were accused of cheating and banned from baseball for life. "I thought I'd never play again," he said. "Watergate was an epiphany for me. It shattered my notion that because you are in a position of power and glamour you can rise above being challenged. You can't."

Almost immediately, Gergen's phone stopped ringing. "Suddenly, you're not as glamorous as you were. You realize just how fast it all comes and goes." During the lonely and depressing days that followed, Gergen was most impressed by the people who stood by him—primarily his old friends from Durham and his college classmates. "When you're in trouble and all your defenses get stripped away, you realize what matters and who matters," he said.

> That's when you need to get back to your roots and to your values. The people who were innocent have come back to outstanding careers. Jon Huntsman, founder of Huntsman Corporation, was one who did that. Hank Paulson is another who came through it and had an extraordinary career as CEO of Goldman Sachs and secretary of the Treasury.

"Since that searing experience with Watergate," Gergen concluded, "I have always favored transparency."

> I have frequently disagreed with those I worked for, because the Watergate lessons were so vivid in my mind. They remind you that you have to stay true to your values. Nixon did not have a moral compass, and everything went off track.

Gergen's Watergate experience was formative in his development as an authentic leader. He recognized the glamour and prestige of a senior White House position had seduced him into abandoning his values. He strengthened his relationships with people who were there for him when his world was collapsing. Gergen's ability to process this early experience fortified his character, which in turn improved his ability to advise Presidents Ford, Reagan, and Clinton.

These days Gergen is teaching at Harvard Kennedy School and developing future leaders as director of the Center for Public Leadership. The center provides fellowships for talented leaders, with Gergen acting as their mentor and coach. As a CNN commentator, he shares his perspective on national affairs, bringing an important level of objectivity and wisdom to the public discourse.

Values, Leadership Principles, and Ethical Boundaries

Perhaps you have engaged in exercises in which you list your values and force-rank them in order of importance. It is relatively easy to be true to your values when things are going well. In defining your values, you must decide what is most important in your life. Is it maintaining your integrity? Helping other people? Devoting yourself to your family? There is no one right set of values. One person may value practicing kindness in all interactions. Another person may value championing excellence. Only you can decide what your most deeply held values are. When you do, you will be better positioned to align with people and organizations that share similar values.

Several of the leaders interviewed for this book referred to their values as being their moral compass. Former Johnson & Johnson chairman and CEO Jim Burke made the expensive but courageous decision to recall Tylenol products in the United States in 1982 after it was discovered that a terrorist had inserted cyanide into some Tylenol capsules. He observed, "Without a moral center, you will swim in chaos."

When you have a clear understanding of your values and their relative importance, you can establish the principles by which you intend to lead. *Leadership principles are values translated into practice.* They are like navigational instruments sailors use to get their bearings at sea, as they fix the direction of their travel. For example, a value, such as "concern for others," might translate into a leadership principle, such as "create a work environment where people are respected for their contributions, provided job security, and allowed to fulfill their potential."

All leaders operate with principles, even if they do so subconsciously. Take the basic question "What motivates people?" Some leaders believe people are motivated to do as little work as possible. They lead by principles that establish strict rules of conduct and behavior and enforce them rigidly to ensure people stay on task. Other leaders believe that people genuinely want to do a good job and find significance through their work. They operate with a principle of empowerment that gives people freedom to do their

---

Values: The relative importance of the things that matter in your life.

Leadership Principles: A set of standards used in leading others, derived from your values. Principles are values translated into action.

Ethical Boundaries: The limits placed on your actions, based on your standards of ethical behavior.

Figure 5.1 Defining Your Values, Principles, and Ethical Boundaries

work, encourages them to excel, and trusts them to monitor themselves.

After defining your leadership principles, you will need a clear understanding of your ethical boundaries. If values inform the positive principles you intend to live by, ethical boundaries set the absolute limits you place on your actions. You will encounter many gray areas in your life and work. Where do you draw the line between actions that are acceptable and those that are not? What lines will you refuse to cross?

Figure 5.1 demonstrates the relationship between values, ethical boundaries, and leadership principles. Those who develop a clear sense of their values, principles, and ethical boundaries *before* they get into crises are better prepared to keep their bearings and navigate through difficult decisions and dilemmas when the pressure mounts.

Narayana Murthy: Building a Company with Principles

Narayana Murthy is a successful entrepreneur who founded the global technology services company Infosys on a clear set of guiding principles from which he has never deviated. Murthy grew up lower middle class in southern India. His father was a civil servant who took pride in his high ethical standards. In his youth, Murthy was influenced by the teachings of Mahatma Gandhi and was involved with socialist youth organizations. He became a strong believer in redistributing wealth to alleviate India's massive poverty.

After Murthy's college graduation, his professor nominated him to go to Paris to install a logistics and baggage-handling system at Charles de Gaulle Airport. The intellectuals Murthy met at Parisian cafés in the late 1960s fascinated him. Describing his time there, he said, "As a 23-year-old Indian, I grew up on a heavy diet of Nehru's socialist philosophy. In Paris, I got the inspiration for compassionate capitalism. I learned how French people put the interest of community ahead of their own interests."

Returning to India, Murthy and a group of younger colleagues founded Infosys Technologies in 1982 and built it into India's leading information technology outsourcing company. Infosys gave Murthy the platform to translate his values into practice. "Our dream was to demonstrate that you could run a business in India without corruption and create wealth legally and ethically," he explained.

From the outset, Murthy and his colleagues wanted to create India's most respected company. Despite difficulties in starting the business, Murthy and his team adhered to a principled approach. Because Murthy refused to pay bribes, Infosys had to wait nearly a year for installation of a telephone line. "What drains your energy or enthusiasm is not the fiscal problem, but violating your value system," he said.

Leaders with principles are less likely to get bullied or pushed around because they can draw clear lines in the sand. We always believed that the softest pillow is a clear conscience. I feel fortunate we have never had a situation where we lost sleep because we did something wrong.

Eventually, the demands for bribes ceased. "If you refuse to buckle on the first couple of transactions," said Murthy, "they will go trouble someone else."

Compliance with the value system creates an environment that enables people to have high aspirations, self-esteem, confidence in the future, and the enthusiasm to take on difficult tasks. Leaders have to walk the talk and demonstrate their commitment to the value system. There is a direct correlation between the value system of our company and the success we have had over the last 24 years.

Murthy's experience living in France had a formative impact on his thinking about his principles and led to the growth and success of Infosys. I have rarely met a business leader who is as intentional about knowing his values and establishing his leadership principles as Murthy. He also had the courage to stick with these values even when they deviated from cultural norms.

More than 30 years after Murthy founded Infosys, it has achieved remarkable success. The company's market capitalization now exceeds $35 billion. When Murthy departed from the company at 68, he declined to become chairman emeritus, saying he believed corporate governance was best served if the current leadership assumed full responsibility.

Sam Palmisano: Leading by Values

As CEO of IBM from 2002 to 2012, Sam Palmisano shifted IBM's culture from management by objectives to leading by values. In doing so, he united IBM employees as a powerful global force in information systems. When he took over from Lou Gerstner, his iconic predecessor, Palmisano did not create new values or merely reiterate the values founder Thomas Watson established. Instead, he initiated a company-wide, online process in which all employees around the globe participated for three days in determining what IBM's values should be. In announcing IBM's 2003 Leading by Values initiative, Palmisano wrote:

Many people these days have grown cynical. They've lost faith in the idea that a business, a government or any other institution can run itself on the basis of enduring, commonly held beliefs. That's a shame. Maybe people wouldn't feel that way if more individuals in business—not just the leaders, but people at all levels—stood up, declared what they believe in, and then took meaningful steps to make it real, to put their values into practice.

How do you marshal the collective aspirations of 316,000 people serving customers in 165 countries? We could rely on traditional supervision, process and controls. But in the end, our clients simply wouldn't stand for that, because it would inhibit our ability to serve them responsively. And neither would all of you, because it would stifle your creative energies. We cannot apply Industrial Age management systems to address a post–Industrial Age need. And we can't just dust off the old mantras. These must be genuinely shared values. They can't, today, be imposed top-down.

Palmisano used the values that emerged from this process to align IBM's employees into a globally integrated network that could execute the company's strategy of delivering complete enterprise technology solutions. During the online "values jam," he posted frequently on the company intranet. He informally comments from that project was: "We have a unique opportunity for IBM to set the pace for *all* companies, not just the techs."

Working with Palmisano on the ExxonMobil board, I witnessed as he put his principle of trusting and empowering employees into action. "The old model of the heroic superman is increasingly archaic," he said. "Never confuse charisma with leadership. The most successful leaders today see themselves as part of the global community. The key is to build a sustainable culture." For Palmisano, values are the mechanism for building that culture.

Testing Values under Pressure

It is relatively easy to practice your values when things are going well. To understand your values, look at past situations when you were tested under pressure. What behaviors felt authentic? What behaviors do you regret? It is likely that your values shaped your behaviors. When you are forced to make trade-offs between your values under difficult circumstances, you learn what is most important in your life.

By reflecting on your behavior, you can understand the underlying values that shaped it. Did you uphold the value of honesty, even when it came at great personal cost? Or did you dissemble or stretch the truth and now feel shame or guilt? With reflection, you can assess whether your stated values match your own internal sense of right and wrong. With resolve, you can commit to overcoming vulnerabilities that may cause you to stray from your values. You will have many opportunities to realign your values with your compass and improve the way you are living out those values.

That's the test that Jon Huntsman faced.

Jon Huntsman: Testing Values under Pressure

In preparing for a day when your values conflict with those of your organization and with each other, you need to decide what you want to stand for in your life. How will your obituary read? What do you want people to say at your funeral?

The life of Jon Huntsman Sr., founder and chairman of Huntsman Corporation, the $13 billion chemical company, illustrates the way one person answered these questions. To the outside observer, Huntsman seems to lead an idyllic life, one marked by integrity, clarity of values, a large and successful family, and material success. Yet Huntsman has been tested at least three major times in the most severe ways. Each time he was forced to look deep inside himself to determine what he stood for.

Huntsman has strong views about his values and the importance of values in the lives of others.

> Each of us possesses a moral GPS—a compass or conscience programmed by parents, teachers, coaches, grandparents, clergy, friends, and peers. The compass is an integral part of our being. It continues to differentiate between proper and improper behavior until the day we die.

Born in a humble family in rural Idaho, Huntsman said his values and leadership style are inextricably linked to his family roots. Although he was close to his mother, he never developed a close relationship with his father, who was a stern disciplinarian. "My mother was a sweet, loving person who never said a negative word about anyone. Because of her, my heart has always been soft."

He observed, "I was taught to play by the rules: Be tough, be competitive, but do it fairly."

> *The principles we learned as children were simple and fair. With moral compasses programmed in the sandboxes of long ago, we can navigate career courses with values that guarantee successful lives, a path that is good for one's mental and moral well-being, and the opportunity for long-term material success.*

When Huntsman was just out of college, his mother developed breast cancer and died in her fifties. "She suffered so much that it broke my heart," he said. Nor was her suffering the family's only brush with cancer. His father died of prostate cancer, and his stepmother died from ovarian cancer. Huntsman himself has twice overcome cancer, the dark cloud hanging over the family.

Similar to David Gergen, Huntsman faced a test of his moral compass when working in the Nixon administration, shortly before the Watergate incident. After founding his own company, he was hired by Elliot Richardson, secretary of Health, Education, and Welfare (HEW), as associate administrator of social services. Huntsman's success in installing a management-by-objectives program that saved $100 million in six months brought him to the White House's attention, where Bob Haldeman hired him. Huntsman found the experience of taking marching orders from Haldeman "very mixed."

> *I had been CEO of a company and then was running a big division at HEW. I wasn't geared to take orders, irrespective of whether they were ethically or morally right. We had a few clashes, as plenty of things that Haldeman wanted to do were questionable. An amoral atmosphere permeated the White House.*

One day, Haldeman asked Huntsman to help him entrap a California congressman who had been opposing a White House initiative. The congressman partially owned a plant that reportedly employed undocumented workers, and Haldeman wanted to gather information that could be used to embarrass him. Huntsman said, "I was under the gun from Haldeman to call my plant manager and place some Latino employees from his facility on an undercover operation."

There are times when we react too quickly and fail to realize immediately what is right and wrong. This was one of those times when I didn't think it through. I knew instinctively it was wrong, but it took a few minutes for the notion to percolate. After 15 minutes, my inner moral compass enabled me to recognize this wasn't the right thing to do. Values that had accompanied me since childhood kicked in. Halfway through my conversation with our plant manager, I said to him, "Let's not do this. I don't want to play this game. Forget that I called."

I informed Haldeman I would not have my employees spy. Here I was saying no to the second most powerful person in the country. He viewed responses like mine as signs of disloyalty. I might as well have been saying farewell. I left within six months.

After resigning from the White House staff, Huntsman and his wife, Karen, faced a different type of values test when their youngest son, Mark, was born with severe cognitive disabilities. Mark's doctor told the Huntsmans their son would not be able to read, write, or go to school, because his mental capacity would never go beyond that of a 4-year-old. The doctor recommended Mark be institutionalized, which represented an impossible values conflict for the Huntsmans. Family was everything, and Mark was just as much a part of the family as the other children. Jon and Karen decided that whatever it took, Mark would live at home.

When Penny and I visited the Huntsmans to tour their cancer institute in 2002, Jon proudly introduced us to Mark, who greeted us with a friendly smile and a big hug. "Mark doesn't know what people do for a living, and can't tell a custodian from a CEO," Huntsman told us.

He judges people only by the goodness of their heart. He sizes up individuals quickly and spots phonies immediately. If their heart is good, he gives them a big hug. Every day, I learn from watching him. He has been the role model and anvil of our family.

In 2001, Huntsman faced the biggest challenge of his career. Because of a deep recession in the chemicals and packaging market, his company was on the verge of bankruptcy. Prices and profit margins were falling rapidly, just as energy costs and raw material prices were spiraling out of control. As a consequence, Huntsman's bonds were trading at 25 cents on the dollar.

On a somber day, financial experts, lawyers, representatives of his 87 lenders, and bankruptcy experts from New York City and Los Angeles gathered in Salt Lake City and presented Huntsman with their unanimous opinion. He had but one choice: Seek a court-supervised Chapter 11 bankruptcy or sit helplessly by as creditors shut the company down altogether by refusing to ship vital raw materials.

Listening patiently to their analyses and entreaties, he thought to himself, "I will not let this company be seized by corporate lawyers, bankers, and highly paid consultants. Not one of them can comprehend my notions of character and integrity." Huntsman answered in a single word: "No." To him, bankruptcy was not an option. His name was on the door—and on the debt. He believed his integrity was at stake.

> *There are times when consultants, lawyers, and outside advisers would like to tell us how to run our lives. Are we people of character, integrity, kindness, and charity, or are we going to be motivated by what somebody else says? At the end of our life, we have to determine what we want said at our funeral.*

Huntsman called his team together in this dark hour and told them:

> *We are going to make it. Our name is on the door. We will go to every one of our 87 bankers, and carve out deals that we can live with. We will bring in our bonds and redeem them for equity.*

The company went through three years of turmoil, while Hunts-man refused to give in. His wife's support proved essential.

> You have to have someone next to you who is tremendously sympathetic. My bankers and close associates abandoned me, so for years Karen was the only one there for me. She knew me best and understood how critical it was to me to maintain my integrity. If one person lost one penny anywhere along the line, I would have lost my character as a man.

During the process Huntsman had a heart attack and contracted Addison's disease—perhaps because of his run-down immune sys-tem. However, he said with pride:

> I repaid every single debt. As of today, the bondholders have been paid 100 cents on the dollar. Huntsman's creditors have been paid in full and have extended us more credit. Huntsman stock is doing well, and our earnings are the highest in history.

Reflecting on his financial crisis, Huntsman commented, "Build-ing goodwill, being honest and kind, and paying your bills along life's pathway will serve you when you're down and out."

> There are times in our lives when we have to ask ourselves, Are we going to let this erosion of our life happen, or are we going to step up and change it? Your life speaks for itself. If I had tried to cheat somebody during my lifetime or did not play by rules, they would have exercised their natural rights when I got in trouble.

Do you know how you will respond in similar situations? What do you stand for in your life? Once you know that, it is essential to be true to what you believe. The only way to prepare for crises like these is to understand your values and then apply them in practice. For living by his principles, his outstanding business success, and his generous philanthropic contributions, Huntsman was awarded the prestigious Bower Award for 2015 by the Franklin Institute, given annually to America's top businessperson.

Sallie Krawcheck: Putting Clients First

Sallie Krawcheck has often been called Wall Street's most powerful woman. She served as Citigroup's CFO and president of the Global Wealth & Investment Management division of Bank of America, the world's largest investment management business that includes Merrill Lynch and U.S. Trust. Krawcheck's values are driven by placing clients' interests first. She said:

> In the wealth management business, you have the ability to sit down with families, put together plans, and help them figure out how to live the life they want to live. This matters enormously to people. There's a mission to this, and it's a noble calling.

She has few kind words for Wall Street culture, though, saying that short-term financial pressures have destroyed the financial industry's focus on its mission. As CFO, she watched analysts roll their eyes if the CEO wasn't talking about how he would beat the quarter. Hedge funds and mutual funds were rapidly trading in and out of stocks with short-term focus.

> The financial services industry had the opportunity to make an enormous difference, but it got caught up in a game where this is the most important quarter in the history of the universe; we need the stock to go up. That's what they're focused on, not the ultimate mission.

As the head of Citigroup's Smith Barney wealth management business during the financial crisis, Krawcheck advocated returning client funds on certain products. She bluntly asserted that Citi had broken clients' trust by pushing low-risk alternative investments that were actually high risk. Vikram Pandit, Citi's CEO, vehemently disagreed. Krawcheck took her argument to the board of directors, saying:

> This is going to hurt the quarter, but we are going to have a more valuable company in the long run. If we don't do it, clients are going to be angry and they

should be. They're going to leave us and they should. We can do well and make money but not every quarter. We must have a long-term perspective.

Krawcheck asserted that refunding a portion of clients' losses was the right thing to do because it demonstrated the bank placed their interests first. The board sided with her, but Pandit fired her months later. Krawcheck said she knew taking this stand would get her fired. Asked if she ever regretted taking such controversial positions, she laughed and said, "My ability to see things differently is also why I was able to succeed."

Krawcheck's resume positions her as the consummate insider, but she has an outsider's mentality. She thoughtfully assesses each situation against her values. She had the courage to put her job on the line to be true to her values. She paid a high price, as her dismissal from Citi illustrates, but she sleeps well every night.

Keith Krach: When Values Conflict

You may not know for certain what your values are until you find yourself under the pressure of having your values in conflict or you find the values of the people with whom you work differ from your own.

The latter was the situation DocuSign CEO Keith Krach faced in his early thirties following a successful experience at General Motors (GM), where he was the youngest vice president ever. Krach left GM to become COO of a Silicon Valley startup named Qronos Technology with the promise of becoming CEO within a year. "It was like running the hundred-yard dash and getting smacked in the face with a two-by-four," he said.

> *The company didn't have the same values I had. The CEO used to say, "Let's hide this from the board." After a few months, it was crystal clear that I had made a mistake. With its values, the company was never going to survive. Although I had never resigned from anything in my life, I realized that if I stayed there much longer, I wouldn't be able to look myself in the mirror.*

Krach prided himself on being loyal and having integrity. Internally, he wrestled with the conflict between these values and his desire to conduct business transparently. His best friend told him, "You don't look good. If you have your attitude and enthusiasm, you're an A-plus performer. But you've lost it. You're like a D-minus. There is no in-between for you. You should quit."

The moment of reckoning came when Krach's wife was giving birth to their first child. Krach was at her side during labor, yet the CEO kept calling, demanding that he come to work. "We have a big partner meeting with IBM," the CEO told him. Krach responded, "That's anatomically impossible. I'm going to see my son born." After a few minutes, Krach reached clarity in his mind. He called his boss back and said simply, "I quit."

That was a big moment in my life. I immediately felt a sense of relief. I learned more at Qronos about what's important in terms of values, trust, and integrity. It was like a process of tempering steel that made me much more resolved about my values.

Now CEO of DocuSign, the rapidly growing online document signing service, Krach is able to employ the values he has held his entire life.

Setting Ethical Boundaries

Your ethical boundaries set clear limits on what you will do when you are tempted or under pressure or when you start rationalizing marginal decisions. If you establish clear boundaries early in life, your moral compass will kick in when you reach your limits and tell you it is time to pull back, even if the personal sacrifices may be significant. That's what Enron leaders Ken Lay and Jeff Skilling lacked as they lurched from deal making into dishonesty. Ultimately, they made a series of aggressive accounting decisions to inflate short-term profits. A rising stock price rewarded them for making these marginal decisions. Because they lacked clear ethical principles, nothing counterbalanced their growing greed.

One way leaders can stress test whether their actions exceed their ethical boundaries is to use the *New York Times* test. Before proceeding with any action, ask yourself, "How would I feel if this entire situation, including transcripts of our discussions, were printed on the front page of the *New York Times?*" If your answers are negative, then it is time to rethink your actions. If they are positive, you should feel comfortable proceeding, even if others criticize your actions later. When you operate with integrity, you will be comfortable having the media, your family, or other people you value examining your words and actions.

Judy Haberkorn: Transparency Is the Right Thing to Do

Verizon's Judy Haberkorn operated with a clear principle in dealing with customers: "Always be open and transparent." That principle was tested when one of her people made a significant mistake, one for which Haberkorn thought she herself might be fired. Attempting to save money, an employee sent consumers their telephone personal identification numbers (PINs) in unsealed envelopes. The envelopes wound up in building lobbies below the mailboxes, where anyone could steal the customer's name, phone number, and PIN.

When she took the issue and her concerns to her boss, Haberkorn was told not to worry. "It will die down," he said. Frustrated, she responded, "This is a test of how to handle a disaster, much like Johnson & Johnson [handled] Tylenol."

If you don't want to do this the Tylenol way, then fire me right now and put somebody else in this job. As long as I'm in charge, we're going the Tylenol route. I am sending a telegram to every one of our customers explaining what happened. We will pay for any calls made inappropriately as a result of this disaster, and immediately give customers a new calling card number and PIN. I will be on the local news shows tonight to explain what happened and what Verizon will do.

As a result, the issue went away. Reflecting on her experience, Haberkorn noted:

> It cost us some money, but there was no doubt in anybody's mind that we did the right thing. A mistake happened, and it was costly. To have our customers feeling we didn't care about their security and were careless with their privacy would have been a far greater disaster.

It isn't easy to take on your boss. For Haberkorn, her principles of how to treat customers were worth challenging her boss and taking the corrective action anyway. Her actions took a lot of courage, the mark of an authentic leader.

Values Challenges at Medtronic

Medtronic founder Earl Bakken first exposed me to Medtronic's values before I joined the company in 1989. For the next 13 years, we used the company's values to unify employees around a common purpose and philosophy of doing business.

At first, we had some employees in the international division who did not take us seriously and continued to do business according to local practices. Internal audit reports turned up repeated violations of company standards in these countries. I decided we had no choice but to make significant management changes. Rather than focusing on lower-level employees, we started by replacing the heads of international, Europe, Asia, and Latin America with leaders who were committed to leading by values.

When violations were uncovered, we made public statements about what had happened and what actions the company was taking. The new international leaders gave us the confidence that we could expand the business rapidly without constantly worrying about ethical violations. When the company went through a rapid growth phase in the 1990s, the leading-by-values philosophy was an invaluable tool for introducing new employees to the company's culture.

These days, Medtronic is expanding rapidly in international markets under the leadership of CEO Omar Ishrak, who was born in Bangladesh. Ishrak is using the company's solid system of values as its basis for expansion in China, India, and Latin America.

As we search for our True North, it is important to acknowledge just how easy it is to get pulled off course. The pressures to perform, our ingrained fear of failure, and the rewards for success can cause us to deviate from our values. By knowing our ethical boundaries and testing our values under pressure, we are able to stay on track.

Exercise: Practicing Your Values and Principles

1. List the values that are important to your life and your leadership. After you have done so, go back and rank them in order of their importance to you.

2. Recall a personal situation in which your values conflicted with each other. How did you resolve this conflict? How pleased were you with the outcome?

3. Recall a situation in which your values were tested under pressure.

    a. To what extent did you deviate from your values under that pressure?

    b. What resources did you call upon under this pressure?

    c. What would you do differently if you had to do it all over again?

4. List the leadership principles you use in leading others. Then go back and rank them depending on which are most important to you.

5. Recall a situation in which you deviated from your True North and your values to achieve your goals.

    a. How will you handle this situation if you face it in the future?

    b. How can you sense "the slippery slope" of minor deviations leading to major ones later on?

    c. When you find yourself being pulled away from your True North, how do you get back on track?

6. List the ethical boundaries that you will not cross.

6

SWEET SPOT

I get to do what I like to do every single day of the year. I tap-dance to work, and when I get there, I think I'm supposed to lie on my back and paint the ceiling. It's tremendous fun.

—*Warren Buffett, CEO, Berkshire Hathaway*

In this chapter, we will explore how to find your *sweet spot*, the intersection of your motivations and your greatest strengths. When you are operating in your sweet spot, you feel inspired to do great things and confident that you can accomplish them because you are using your strengths. Having an awareness of what motivates you and understanding your strengths and weaknesses enables you to discover your sweet spot. When you do, you create a powerful flywheel that enables you to be both successful and fulfilled. Operating in your sweet spot, you are aligned with your True North and have the greatest opportunities to make a difference in the world.

Warren Buffett Finds His Sweet Spot

No leader is clearer about his sweet spot than Warren Buffett is, and no businessperson in the past century has been more successful. Through his stewardship of Berkshire Hathaway, he has created hundreds of billions in value for his shareholders since 1965.

Despite delivering the most spectacular performance of any investor in modern history, Buffett has retained his modesty and humility. In person, he is remarkably open, without a touch of arrogance. At age 85, Buffett is still in his sweet spot: motivated by investing, not for the money per se, but for the thrill of using his strengths to build great companies.

In 2006, Buffett shocked the world when he announced he would contribute the vast majority of his fortune to philanthropic causes, outsourcing the management of more than $30 billion to his friend Bill Gates. The gift doubled the Gates Foundation's philanthropy in health care and education. Explaining the gift, Buffett said his skill lies in making money, not giving it away. Characteristic of Buffett, he sought someone he trusted to manage this benevolence, insisting that a minimum of $1.5 billion be given away each year.

In spite of his power and the demands on his time, Buffett is a relaxed and kind person. My MBA student Vitaliy Pereverzev told me about his experience with Buffett when he traveled to Berkshire Hathaway, Buffett's company in Omaha, Nebraska, at Buffet's invitation with 80 members of his investment club. After lunch at Buffett's favorite restaurant, Pereverzev realized he had left his camera back at the Berkshire Hathaway offices. Rather than sending a staff person back to get it, Buffett offered Pereverzev a ride in his Lincoln Town Car.

Buffett immediately offered the young Kazakhstani some advice. "Vitaliy, you have to do what you love. I do not want to live like a king. I just love to invest," Buffett said. "Money aside, there is very little difference between you and me in terms of lifestyle. I eat simple meals. I drive a regular car. I make decisions and, yes, I too make mistakes." Buffett went on to describe his childhood and what it was like working in his grandfather's grocery store.

Shortly before reaching the Berkshire headquarters, Buffett offered the young student concluding advice: "Be a nice person, Vitaliy. Look around at the people you like. If you like traits of other people, doesn't it follow that other people would like you if you have those same traits?" This sage counsel is typical Buffett. His lessons are simple, though rarely easy. Given his remarkable success over the past 60 years, it is surprising how few people follow his admonitions and his investing strategies.

Buffett also generously shares his advice with new CEOs. Anne Mulcahy told me about her interaction with him shortly after becoming COO of Xerox in 2000. Facing a liquidity crisis as $18 billion in debt matured, Mulcahy faced overwhelming pressure from bankers, lawyers, and financial advisers to declare bankruptcy. Determined to save the company she loved, she made a cold call to Buffett, who invited her to visit him in Omaha.

Mulcahy later said her ulterior motive was to get Buffett to put money into Xerox, in spite of his well-known aversion to investing in technology companies. The advice she received from Buffett proved even more valuable. After two hours of conversation, Buffett said:

> You're thinking the investors, bankers, and regulators are the people you need to survive. Put them aside and give priority to talking to your employees and your customers about what is wrong and what you have to do to fix it.

For the next six months, Mulcahy did just that as she toured the country, rallying support for the changes required to restore the company. Meanwhile, Xerox stock continued to decline, but she was unfazed. Buffett's advice proved valid. Mulcahy warded off bankruptcy, paid down $10 billion in debt, and continued to invest in research and development.

Finding His Sweet Spot

Born in Omaha, Buffett made his first stock market investment at age 11. As a teenager, he read Benjamin Graham's seminal book on value investing, *The Intelligent Investor*. Graham's thesis was to value stocks based on the company's business fundamentals. When the stock market traded away from the company's fundamental value, opportunity existed. After graduating from the University of Nebraska, Buffett went to Columbia University to study economics under Graham.

Although Buffett loves investing, his first full-time job as a stockbroker tortured him because brokers were rewarded for networking and selling, neither of which was his strength. He felt conflicted because he could generate commissions only by pushing clients to trade actively, even when it was against their interest. Instead of trying to turn himself into a master broker, he spent extraordinary amounts of time on fundamental analysis of stocks.

When Graham offered him a job at his firm, Buffett jumped at the opportunity, without even asking about the salary. He served as Graham's apprentice for several years before Graham decided to wind the firm down. Rather than work for someone else, Buffett moved back to Omaha and opened his own investing firm at age 26—an act of high self-confidence in that postwar era. This bold move positioned Buffett at the intersection of his motivations and his greatest strengths—his sweet spot.

Buffett has exceeded his mentor in many ways. His investment philosophy has evolved from focusing on cheap stocks to identifying companies with a sustainable competitive advantage and high-quality leadership. Buffett does only friendly acquisitions and brings a partnership spirit to working with executives of the companies he has acquired. A master evaluator of people, Buffett asks his partners, "Do you love the business, or do you love the money?" He only wants those who love the business.

Buffett versus Wall Street

Across seven decades, Buffett has consistently built his initial capital base from thousands of dollars into a personal fortune worth more than $60 billion. He operates from a basic set of principles, which any long-term investor can emulate. His remarkable success lies in the unique manner in which he has aligned his personal and professional abilities with his company's focus.

In sharp contrast with Wall Street, where hedge funds charge 2 percent annually for managing money and take 20 percent of the gains, Buffett charges no fees to his investors. As the funds churn their investments ever faster, Buffett says his preferred holding period is forever. He has proved the wisdom of his philosophy with long-term gains in companies such as American Express, Wells Fargo, and Coca-Cola.

Whereas activist investors pressure boards to fire CEOs who don't produce short-term results, Buffett has a nearly perfect record of retaining the leaders of his companies. His philosophy promotes full transparency, in contrast with hedge funds that fight to keep their investors and investments confidential. Buffett's famous shareholder letters contain the bad news along with the good, as he painstakingly points out his mistakes, often with a bit of self-directed humor.

During the 1990s boom in technology stocks, Buffett patiently outlasted his critics by avoiding the Internet stampede and continued to invest in value companies run by competent executives. At the 1999 Microsoft CEO Summit, I listened as he calmly explained to a leading Internet CEO that there was no amount of growth that could make his stock worth 100 times earnings. True to his prediction, the stock collapsed within the year and never regained its full value.

Wisely, Buffett also avoids his weaknesses. Often verbally attacked by his mother when he was a child, he has little interest in fighting with others. If he smells conflict in a deal, he avoids it. He also steers clear of hands-on management. Company leaders are welcome to call him for advice, but he places responsibility for decisions squarely on their shoulders. Because of Buffett's philosophy, Berkshire Hathaway's returns have more than doubled the Standard & Poor's 500 Index for the past 40 years. To put that success in context, Buffett has created twice the shareholder value of Goldman Sachs and Morgan Stanley *combined* with 24 people in a 5,000-square-foot office in Omaha.

Each March, more than 30,000 people make the three-day trek to Omaha for Berkshire Hathaway's annual meeting, known as "Woodstock for Capitalists." They hear Buffett and Vice Chair Charlie Munger take questions for four hours. Buffett said, "Berkshire is my painting, so it should look the way I want it to when it's done." His fondest hope is that Berkshire's success and adherence to his principles continue long after he passes from the scene. He noted,

"I'd view it as a tragedy if someone whose achievement was issuing the most junk bonds or having the silliest stock price took over the company, and all we've built evaporated."

Buffett is as remarkable for his humility as he is for his wisdom. He stays grounded in his values and thus eschews the temptations of the hot-money crowd. Buffett still lives in the Omaha house he bought for $31,500 in 1956, eats burgers and steaks at Gorat's, and drives an older car. He does fly privately, but he humorously named his first plane *The Indefensible*. When I have been with him, I had the distinct feeling his modesty and staying true to his roots were at the core of his success.

Having served on more than 20 corporate boards, Buffett also understands the responsibilities of sound corporate governance. When Salomon Brothers was embroiled in a major scandal with the U.S. Treasury Department, Buffett stepped in on a Sunday and took over as interim CEO. He saved the firm by offering federal investigators full disclosure and waiving attorney-client privilege, thus enabling Salomon to avoid a crippling criminal indictment. He told employees, "You don't need to play outside the lines. You can make a lot of money hitting the ball down the middle."

I had dinner with Buffett shortly after he fired David Sokol, a close Berkshire Hathaway colleague rumored to be named as his successor, for insider trading of Lubrizol stock. When I asked him how he felt about Sokol's betrayal, he replied, "I believe in trusting people. Occasionally, someone will violate my trust, but on balance I am better off in continuing to trust others."

Intrinsic and Extrinsic Motivations

To deliver high performance, leaders need to sustain high levels of motivation, just as Buffett has done. There are two types of motivations—extrinsic and intrinsic (see Figure 6.1). *Extrinsic motivations*, such as getting good grades, winning athletic competitions, or making money, are measured by the external world. Nearly every leader has had a strong achievement orientation since

Extrinsic Motivations	Intrinsic Motivations
• Monetary compensation	• Personal growth
• Having power	• Satisfaction of doing a good job
• Having a title	• Helping others develop
• Public recognition	• Finding meaning from efforts
• Social status	• Being true to one's beliefs
• Winning over others	• Making a difference in the world

Figure 6.1   Extrinsic and Intrinsic Motivations

childhood. Many competed in athletics in their youth and excelled in school. After graduating, many young leaders want a job with a prestigious organization. Eventually, their extrinsic motivations take the form of wealth accumulation, power, titles, elevated social status, and prestige.

Although they are reluctant to admit it, achieving success as the outside world defines it motivates many leaders. They enjoy the feelings of recognition and status that come with promotions and financial rewards. This cycle starts at an early age. However, each success leads to a desire for more money, fame, or power. That's why many people with great wealth and power are always comparing themselves with those who have more. Being driven entirely by extrinsic motivations is a dangerous trap that can lead you astray from your True North, as it did for Rajat Gupta and Lance Armstrong.

Intrinsic motivations are derived from your deepest inner desires, not the world's adulation. They are the basis for your True North and are closely linked to your life story. Examples of intrinsic motivations may include personal growth, helping other people, taking on social causes, creating great products or services, and making a difference in the world through your efforts.

Because modern society has placed unprecedented attention on visible achievements, extrinsic measures of success cause many leaders to seek the world's acclaim rather than pursue their inner motivations. The pressure starts early, when college graduates compare salaries. It evolves as they compare apartments or new home purchases. Alan Horn, chairman of the Walt Disney Studios, which includes Pixar, Lucasfilm, and Marvel, described how he consciously avoided these traps:

> Early in your career, the incremental dollar can change the incremental quality of life because it enables you to buy a better car or better house. At some point, the incremental dollar does not change the quality of life at all. In fact, incremental purchases just increase the complexity of life, not its enjoyment. I don't want more things because they simply wouldn't make me happier.

Debra Dunn, who has lived in Silicon Valley for decades as a Hewlett-Packard executive, advised emerging leaders to beware of getting caught up in social, peer, or parental expectations:

> The path of accumulating material possessions is clearly laid out. You know how to measure it. If you don't pursue that path, people wonder what is wrong with you. The only way to avoid getting caught up in materialism is to understand where you find happiness and fulfillment.

Finding Your Sweet Spot

The term *sweet spot* describes your motivated capabilities when your motivations and your strengths align (see Figure 6.2). Claremont professor Mihaly Csikszentmihalyi, a pioneer in positive psychology, provided us the following advice about motivation: "Find out what you are good at and what you like to do." In these two simple dimensions, Csikszentmihalyi cut through the jargon and summed up what our interviewees learned through hundreds of years of experience.

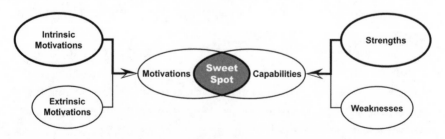

Figure 6.2   Finding Your Sweet Spot

You will be most effective as a leader when you find opportunities that highly motivate you and use your greatest capabilities. One without the other is insufficient. To find these opportunities, you must understand your deepest motivations and be honest with yourself about your capabilities. You won't be successful as a leader by pursuing something you're not good at or by pursuing leadership roles that don't motivate you. When you find a role that meshes your motivations with your capabilities, you will discover the sweet spot that maximizes your effectiveness as a leader.

Exploring Warren Buffett's Motivations

Applying this framework to Buffett, we clearly see extrinsic and intrinsic motivators at work in his life. Extrinsically, Buffett loves public recognition and being valued. Moreover, he has used his media savvy to raise his profile and gain unique access to deals. However, he is not motivated by accumulating possessions. Intrinsically, he is motivated by learning and teaching, sharing his knowledge through frequent media interviews, lengthy annual letters, and discussions at Berkshire's annual meetings.

The combination of these motivations has served Buffett well during challenging times, and has enabled him to become known as America's most trusted investor. During the financial crisis, leading firms, such as Goldman Sachs and General Electric (GE), turned to Buffett for investments and his stamp of approval. He has designed his life to take advantage of his strengths and focus on his motivations. No wonder he tap-dances to work each day!

Tracy Britt: Heeding Your Call

Often leaders who pursue their intrinsic motivations end up achieving the most. Tracy Britt, who worked for Warren Buffett as his financial assistant, illustrates this paradox of motivation. Britt grew up working long hours on her family farm in Kansas and became one of Harvard Business School's youngest graduates. Friends describe her as kind and honest. In my classroom, she had a grounded approach to looking at issues, recognizing the human dimension of business problems.

While still in school, she formed an unlikely friendship with Buffett. Britt dreamed of finding an investor with a long-term focus who would mentor her. They first met when she brought a group of students to Omaha, and thereafter she continued to correspond with Buffett. She also volunteered to help him on projects, such as reading the Lehman bankruptcy filings. Although she took a job at Fidelity upon her graduation, they continued to correspond.

Britt voraciously read everything she could about Buffett and relished opportunities to learn from him. As he got to know her, he sensed her talent and integrity. Eventually he asked her whether she'd be interested in moving to Omaha to join Berkshire. Britt didn't hesitate, saying yes without asking for details on her title or compensation. Five years later, Britt oversees investments worth billions, sits on the board of Heinz, and is chair of four Berkshire portfolio companies. Recently, Buffett asked her to be CEO of a Berkshire subsidiary, Pampered Chef. Only 30 years old, she has been profiled in *Fortune* and the *Wall Street Journal*, but it hasn't gone to her head. Her greatest joy comes in learning from the master.

Kevin Sharer: Discovering His Sweet Spot

Kevin Sharer is a talented leader who lost his way when he let his extrinsic ambitions to be CEO at a young age take him away from his sweet spot. Yet he learned from his experiences and found his sweet spot at Amgen, where he had two spectacular decades of leadership. His experiences with the navy and McKinsey prepared Sharer for the bare-knuckle intensity of the GE environment. His success at GE led to his first general management opportunity while he was still in his midthirties.

In 1989, Sharer encountered the most difficult situation of his life. Having succeeded at everything he had done, he was facing failure for the first time. A rising star at GE, he was eager—too eager—to get to the top. By age 40, Sharer ran GE's satellite business, was elected a corporate officer, and was promoted to the jet engine business. This would be heady stuff for anyone but especially for someone as ambitious as Sharer. When the headhunters came looking for a new head of sales and marketing for MCI, he seized the opportunity to leapfrog his career.

"The CEO race is wide open," MCI's vice chairman assured him. Sharer took the bait. This time, however, things did not go his way. Upon joining the company, Sharer learned the COO was in line for the top spot and didn't welcome competition, especially from the ambitious, young GE hotshot.

Sharer wasted no time in developing his strategy to transform MCI and position himself for promotion. Within six weeks, he concluded that the company's geographic marketing organization was improperly structured. "I was at the zenith of my arrogance at that time," Sharer said. "I marched into the chairman's office and proposed restructuring MCI's sales organization." His proposal was threatening to senior executives who had spent their careers building MCI. Lacking telecommunications experience, Sharer found he had little credibility within the organization. Having succeeded at everything he had done, he was facing failure for the first time.

"MCI was a crucible for me," Sharer observed later. "I learned that whether you are right or not, there is a price to be paid for arrogance." He also found out his style did not suit MCI's hyper-competitive culture. "People were personally competitive in a way that was inconsistent with my values," he explained.

> The internal competition was mean-spirited and at your throat. It was eating me up as I was becoming less effective and less committed to the company. If your values are not consistent with the people you're working with, you should not be there.

Desperate to escape from MCI, Sharer telephoned CEO Jack Welch and asked to return to GE. Welch wasn't happy with the way Sharer had bailed out after Welch had created so many opportunities for him. "Hey, Kevin, forget you ever worked here," Welch replied and hung up the phone. "At that moment," Sharer recalled, "I knew I had been cast adrift in a lifeboat."

> *I realized I had to make a go of this big operating job. I couldn't just bail out. It was a gut-wrenching two years for me, the most challenging and unhappy time of my professional life. I'm not a good knife fighter, and I was getting outmaneuvered. At first I went into denial. Then I became defeatist and cynical.*
>
> *It was grinding me down, and I began to retreat emotionally. My wife could not understand what I was going through because she had no corporate experience. She feared I would be fired, which only added to my feeling of isolation. Without question, it was the toughest time of my life.*

Sharer's story of abandoning his sweet spot parallels the difficulties that many leaders face. Their egos tempt them into situations that don't play to their strengths and don't inspire them. If they have self-awareness and insight, they readjust their compass to get back on the track of their True North and find opportunities where they can operate in their sweet spot.

Sharer's crucible at MCI proved invaluable. It humbled him, forcing him to control his ego and recognize there is more to life than just grabbing the next promotion. Caught up in the glamour of being a rising star, Sharer was brought down to reality. Two years after joining MCI, he received a letter asking whether he knew anyone who could be president of Amgen. Never having heard of the company, he went to the public library to learn about it. He decided to nominate himself for the job and was offered the position, under the tutelage of CEO Gordon Binder.

Having learned a painful lesson at MCI about being perceived as a know-it-all, he recognized he knew nothing about the biotechnology business. "If I hadn't had that chastening experience at MCI, I could easily have blown up at Amgen," he said.

> *My last brush with health care had been ninth-grade biology, so I asked one of our scientists to teach me biology. By being patient, I became an insider before I started making changes. I learned the business from the ground up, made calls with sales representatives, and showed my desire to learn.*

In contrast with his earlier experiences, Sharer patiently under-studied Binder for seven years. This time around, he avoided the seduction of the headhunters, telling them being number two at a rapidly growing company like Amgen was "better than anything else that was on the plate." A year before Binder's retirement, the board told Sharer, "Look, Kevin, you've got the job. For the next year spend your time learning R&D." Sharer studied the Amgen research process from the ground up, working in its labs, being tutored by scientists, and visiting competitors' research facilities.

When the board announced Sharer would become CEO, he met individually with the top 150 people in the company. Their feedback gave Sharer a thorough picture of what the company's top leaders wanted.

These interviews were the single most important thing I did upon becoming CEO. They gave me the mandate to create a shared reality for the company. That enabled people to align around the new vision and strategy for building Amgen for the next 10 years.

Kevin Sharer's searing experience at MCI enabled him to understand his strengths and motivations. By learning from the MCI debacle, he recognized changes he needed to make when he went to Amgen. He learned the business before taking charge, listened to the wisdom and experience of his colleagues, and was patient in reaching his goal. As a result, he led Amgen for a decade with spectacular success, transforming the company from a two-drug firm to a highly innovative organization that continues to produce breakthrough drugs from its labs.

Looking back at his MCI experience, Sharer reflected, "We are the mosaic of all of our experiences."

In retrospect, the MCI experience wasn't all bad. I discovered what a truly competitive company can do, and learned about entrepreneurship and innovation. A tough experience like that gives you genuine empathy for other people. It is vitally important that you love what you do because if you don't, you won't do your best. When I was at MCI, I never had an emotional connection with low-priced long distance. If somebody walks up to you and says, "Your product saved my life," the power of that connection is enormous.

Avoiding the Trap of Extrinsic Motivations

Moving away from the external validation of personal achievement isn't easy. Achievement-oriented leaders grow so accustomed to successive accomplishments in their early years that it takes courage to pursue their intrinsic motivations. But at some point, most leaders recognize they need to do what they love rather than achieving external acclaim.

Many leaders we interviewed turned down higher-paying jobs in early career decisions to pursue roles they were passionate about. In the end, they came out ahead—in both satisfaction and compensation—because they were successful in doing what they loved. Time Inc. CEO Ann Moore had a dozen job offers after business school and took the lowest-paying one—with *Time* magazine. "I had student loans hanging over my head, but I took the job because I loved magazines. At the time nobody in my class understood why I made that choice, but at our twenty-fifth reunion they understood completely."

Ann Fudge also took the lowest-paying offer she received out of business school. She explained, "You can't make career decisions just based on money. I hoped the money would come, and it did. If I had made my career decision based on the money, I would have been on a totally different career path." Jean-Pierre Rosso recalled, "I always focused on being happy in what I was doing. If I was motivated and did my job well, I knew the money would follow."

When Dave Cox was CEO of Cowles Media, a Stanford Business School student told him, "Maybe I have to get my satisfaction someplace else and just do the business part to make money." Amazed by the comment, Cox raised his eyebrows quizzically and asked:

> *Why would you want to spend your time doing work you don't enjoy? These should be the best years of your life. There is so much energy that results from feeling valued and connecting with your passions. That's when you add the greatest value.*

Balancing Your Motivations

Positive validation by the outside world is a natural consequence for leaders with high achievement orientation, because they cherish the recognition that comes with their accomplishments. It is natural to seek the esteem of peers, promotions in title, and the financial rewards that come with success. The danger comes when leaders become so enamored with these external symbols that they can never get enough. At this point, they are at the greatest risk of losing touch with their intrinsic motivations and abandoning things that give them a deeper sense of fulfillment.

As CEO of Medco, Per Lofberg challenged young business leaders to think carefully about the lifestyles they choose for themselves: "It is dangerous to get overcommitted to a high-flying lifestyle at a young age." Many young leaders are tempted to take high-salaried jobs to pay off loans or build their savings, even if they have no long-term interest in the work. They believe that after 10 years they can move on to do the work they love.

Yet many become so dependent on maintaining expensive lifestyles that they become trapped in jobs where they are demotivated and unhappy. Locked into the high-income and high-expense life, they cannot afford to do work they love. That holds a lot of people back from pursuing what brings them satisfaction and realizing their greatest potential.

Many leaders have learned the hard way that external recognition can be a fickle lover. When things do not go their way, external sources of gratification disappear very quickly. So do their superficial friends and acquaintances who are more interested in associating with their success than in supporting them when things go poorly. The key to developing as an authentic leader is not eschewing your extrinsic motivations but balancing them with intrinsic motivations that provide fulfillment in your work.

Build on Your Strengths

Truly great accomplishments come only from exploiting your strengths. Many of the most extraordinary people in history were tremendously flawed individuals. Margaret Thatcher, Mahatma Gandhi, and

Napoleon Bonaparte all had striking weaknesses, yet they used their gifts to achieve amazing things through their leadership.

Through intense reflection, Donna Dubinsky came to the realization in her midthirties that she wasn't playing to her strengths in her work. She was burned out after 10 years of 80-hour weeks at Apple and Claris, so she decided to take a yearlong sabbatical to live in Paris. There she found an apartment, learned to paint, studied French, and thought about what she would do next.

> I reflected on what I am good at, what I'm not good at, and what value I could bring. I'm not an innovative thinker and never will have the product savvy of Steve Jobs. In my 10 years in the technology industry, I had never thought of one big new idea.

As she thought further about her capabilities, she acknowledged her ability to recognize other people's good ideas, build strong teams, and design key business processes. "When I returned to Silicon Valley, I knew I needed a great product person to team with me," she said. Eventually she found Jeff Hawkins, creator of the PalmPilot, and she became Palm's CEO in 1992. The two have such complementary skills that they are considered inseparable business partners around Silicon Valley and are working on their third venture, Numenta.

When leaders step out of their comfort zones to take on new challenges, they often discover capabilities they did not know they had. When we first interviewed Cesar Conde, he was vice president of Univision, the largest Spanish-language television network in the United States. After the Castro revolution, his grandparents helped his mother flee Cuba because they wanted her to have better chances. At Univision, which employed many first- and second-generation Hispanic Americans, Conde created similar opportunities for his coworkers. One day, his boss took him to the company parking lot and told him, "Fifteen years ago, the parking lot was full of rickety old cars owned by our employees. With the company's success, the cars are new and employees can afford to send their kids to good schools."

Conde said, "I can identify with his pride. It is motivating to realize I have the opportunity to do something great for other people." Conde has since been promoted to executive vice president of NBC Universal. His internal passions propel his success.

Chuck Schwab's Journey to His Sweet Spot

Charles "Chuck" Schwab went through some very low moments in his midthirties. Recently divorced, he experienced a period of deep uncertainty about what to do professionally. He enrolled in law school at night in an attempt to follow in the footsteps of his father and grandfather. After just three weeks, he realized he lacked the required reading and writing skills and dropped out.

Schwab had struggled with reading all his life, but not until his early forties did he learn he was dyslexic. Although dyslexia caused him difficulty in school, he always knew he was good at math. So he began working part-time for an investment firm and discovered his interest in investments and his knack for investment research.

Like many leaders, Schwab needed time and experience to determine what motivated him. Eventually, he turned his passion for investments into building a company that would democratize the entire brokerage industry. Schwab's motivations and capabilities finally came together when at age 37 he founded Charles Schwab & Company.

Schwab traces his motivations to his upbringing in the post-Depression era. Times were tough in the small farming community of Woodland, California, where he grew up during the 1940s. During World War II, his family used ration stamps to buy food. Schwab's parents struggled their entire lives to be financially independent. "We were still suffering from the hangover of the Depression years," he recalled. "My father taught me the importance of being independent. I was motivated to be financially successful because I didn't want to have my life limited by resources."

When the Securities and Exchange Commission (SEC) deregulated brokerage services in the early 1970s, Schwab saw his opportunity to start a company. Before that time, stock market transactions went through large brokerage firms that charged fixed fees. Without competitive rates, many Americans could not afford to participate in the stock market. In 1974, Charles Schwab & Company entered the market, reducing brokerage commissions by 75 percent. Before long, individual accounts such as 401(k)s and individual retirement accounts (IRAs) were commonplace. "If you knew what you wanted to buy or sell, we could do it very efficiently. We'd complete the trade for a small commission without the interference of some hotshot broker."

The unfairness of brokerage industry practices that existed before deregulation touched a nerve deep inside him. In his interview, Schwab's face reddened and his hands gestured forcefully when he began talking about how Wall Street brokers took advantage of average American investors. "I always put the customer on top of a stool whose four corners are value, customer service, technology, and best price," he explained. "Wall Street flips the stool over, sitting on top of the stool with the client underneath." Leaning forward in his chair, he exclaimed, "Let me tell you, it was a den of thieves. Whatever the dealers wanted, they got."

> In a capitalist society, financial independence is fundamental. We are blessed in America with economic freedom and freedom of choice. I wanted to make Schwab a fully democratic place where people could come to us, disclose what they wanted, and get the best package available at the lowest cost, without the conflicts of interest so prevalent in the brokerage industry. Wall Street should be like your doctor, focusing on your interest, not its interests.

Schwab's strengths, talents, and motivations came together when he founded Charles Schwab & Company. He combined his investment research skills with the persistence and resilience learned from years of suffering with dyslexia. Building a company with a cause in which he passionately believed, he has helped millions become more independent while achieving financial independence himself. His company is an American icon, with 14,000 employees and a market capitalization of $36 billion.

Schwab's passion for helping Americans achieve financial independence is an intrinsic motivation that in the end made him wealthy. His life exemplifies the importance of discovering your sweet spot. You need to know what motivates you and have a realistic understanding of your strengths and weaknesses so that you can put your strongest capabilities to work. When you do so, you will discover the *sweet spot* of your motivated capabilities.

Exercise: Your Sweet Spot

The following exercise provides you the opportunity to find your sweet spot—that zone where you are able to use your abilities to the fullest and where you are highly motivated.

1. What are your extrinsic motivations? Which of them might become too dominant for you?

2. What are your intrinsic motivations? How do you ensure you are giving them priority?

3. Recall and then list one or more instances in which your extrinsic motivations conflicted with your intrinsic motivations. What did you do?

4. What are your greatest capabilities? How does your work and life use them?

5. List your motivated capabilities, areas where you are both highly motivated and very capable.

6. Envision future situations where you can apply your motivated capabilities in your sweet spot.

7

SUPPORT TEAM

> If you want to go fast, go alone.
> If you want to go far, go together.
> —*African Proverb*

If you were facing a major crisis in your life—such as losing your job, life-threatening illness, difficulties in your marriage, or death of a loved one—to whom would you turn? In challenging times, you need a solid network of trusted relationships with people who are available to counsel and care for you. Your support team is built upon long-term relationships and may include your spouse or partner, family members, best friends, mentors, and a small personal group.

Your support team has faith in you and understands your True North. Supporters don't care about your external successes or failures, but they do care about you as a person. Having people around you who support you gives you the confidence to listen to your inner voice, even when outsiders are attacking or criticizing you. Your closest confidants give you the resilience to get through hard times and enable you to recognize what is truly important in life.

Tad Piper's Support Team in His Crisis

Facing a crisis in his work, Piper Jaffray CEO Tad Piper learned just how essential his support team was in navigating difficult challenges. Even Piper is surprised to now find himself a member of three groups that support each other through life's difficulties.

Afforded early opportunities for business leadership, Piper was appointed chief executive of his family's growing financial services firm at age 36. A sophisticated leader, he felt he had little time for intimate groups because of his hectic life. He noted, "If you told me 20 years ago I would be part of three groups that meet regularly and talk about things like feelings and God, I would have said, 'Thank you, but I don't do groups.'"

Many of us find excuses—I'm too busy . . . The payoff isn't clear . . . I'll do it next year—to avoid building the types of relationships these groups engender. For Piper, the realization that he needed greater support came after he underwent treatment for drug dependency. "In treatment, my family had the opportunity to tell me about how my chemical use was affecting them," he explained. "It was horrible."

Afterward, he joined Alcoholics Anonymous (AA). He noted about his fellow AA participants, "These are not other CEOs." Yet in his AA group he found something far more valuable:

> These are nice, hardworking people who are trying to stay sober, lead good lives, and work with each other about being open, honest, and vulnerable. We reinforce each other's behavior by talking about our chemical dependency in a disciplined way as we go through the 12 steps. I feel blessed to be surrounded by people who are thinking about these kinds of issues and actually doing something, not just talking about them.

With the help of AA, as well as his couples group and Bible study group, Piper rebounded. Although the initial impetus for joining AA was dealing with his substance abuse, Piper credited all three groups with transforming his relationships and his life. "Most of us don't find the balance we so desperately seek," he said. "It is incredibly valuable to be reinforced by others who are wrestling with similar issues and actually doing something about them." In his groups, he learned to open up about the challenges he faced in his life, in sharp contrast with the many surface-level conversations he had previously with friends. These days his discussions are far deeper and more meaningful.

Founded by Piper's grandfather over a century ago, Piper Jaffray faced a financial and legal crisis of monumental proportions in 1994. As a Piper bond fund increased 90 percent in five years, its star manager began taking increased risks to sustain returns, using complex derivative instruments to leverage the portfolio. When interest rates decreased in 1994, the fund declined 25 percent.

Investors cried foul, and their lawyers went on the attack. Suit after suit was filed, charging Piper Jaffray with failing to inform clients of the fund's risks and with falsely designating the fund as conservative. Piper tried working with the clients to resolve the issues, but doing so became increasingly difficult. He found that even some of his closest friends were turning against the firm. "When you get into problems," he pointed out, "you find out quickly how strong your relationships are, which people are real and which aren't, and who will abandon your relationship for money."

The uproar over the bond fund's decline placed the firm's reputation and financial structure at risk. "We had a 99-year history of serving clients well and being known for trust and integrity," he said. "The mutual funds we positioned as relatively safe, conservative investments turned out not to be." When a *Wall Street Journal* article estimated potential liabilities from lawsuits was three to four times the firm's capital, Piper recognized the company's future was in jeopardy. He felt incredible pressure to preserve the firm and his family's legacy:

> I remember working unbelievably hard for long hours trying to sort through the possible resolutions. I was feeling helpless and powerless as the problems were just overwhelming. I was going to let down tens of thousands of clients. I worried about our 3,500 employees and their families, and all the ramifications. I kept thinking, "Oh, my God, I can't do this."

Fortunately, Piper's past experience with chemical dependency taught him how to handle challenging situations. He began by sharing all his emotions in a long, tearful conversation with his wife, and then shared the pressures with his closest friends. "Our friendships weren't based on whether I succeeded or failed on this problem," he said. Acknowledging to these close confidants that the situation was out of his control brought Piper a sense of relief. With their support, he faced his fears and finally accepted his situation.

Piper's faith and his relationships brought him a sense of clarity and peace, instead of making him feel isolated. This inner assurance proved of paramount importance, because he needed to maintain the confidence of the company's employees and clients. As problems in his asset management division escalated, Piper needed high performance from his remaining businesses. Because he had support from meaningful relationships, Piper was willing to be vulnerable with his senior team, and even with front-line employees.

Piper said one experience in particular taught him the power of being vulnerable, something he had never experienced before. "We brought together our leaders and their spouses from branch offices around the country," he explained.

> My wife and I decided to be completely honest with them and totally vulnerable. We showed them we were real people, feeling just like they were. We stood in front of them and told them we were scared. I also talked about my chemical dependency and about my faith. That was the most powerful thing we have ever done. People never forgot that day because we showed our vulnerability. All of a sudden everybody on our team trusted us, even the skeptics.

"Most leaders are afraid to be vulnerable," he said. "They think, 'I'm supposed to be strong and have all the answers.'" Paradoxically, his vulnerability, honesty, and clarity inspired others to stay the course. Piper eventually settled the lawsuits and began building the business once again. Shares rebounded more than threefold from the 1994 nadir. After the repeal of the Glass-Steagall Act in 1999 permitted commercial banks to acquire investment banks, U.S. Bancorp acquired Piper Jaffray, providing the latter a broader capital base.

Building Support Teams

If you were facing a highly challenging problem like Piper was, whom would you turn to for support? Many leaders try to hunker down and fix problems themselves without reaching out for help. Without confidants to provide perspective in crisis, it is very easy to lose your way, as Lehman's Richard Fuld did. That's a risky course of action, because during a crisis is when you most need to depend upon people with whom you have built trusting relationships over a long period.

Leaders do not succeed on their own. The loneliness of leadership has been well documented, but the remedies have not. Everyone has insecurities; some people are just more open about them than others. Even the most outwardly assured executives need support and appreciation. Authentic leaders build close relationships with people who will counsel them in times of uncertainty, be there in times of difficulty, and celebrate with them in times of success.

Essentially, leaders facing personal or professional turmoil face two choices: Wear a mask or reveal their innermost thoughts and feelings to those closest to them. Many leaders choose to wear a mask even with their spouses, advisers, leadership teams, and friends. If you do not reveal your vulnerabilities to these trusted people, giving voice to your uncertainties and acknowledging your fears as Tad Piper did, leadership becomes a very lonely place.

Having people in your life with whom you share confidentially ensures that you will have support when you need it most. Your support team can provide affirmation, advice, perspective, suggestions for course corrections, and, above all, love. During their most difficult times, leaders find comfort in being with people on whom they can rely so that they can be open and vulnerable. During the low points, they cherish the friends who appreciate them for *who* they are, not *what* they are.

Leaders need a multifaceted support structure that includes their spouse or significant other, family members, mentors, close friends, and personal and professional support groups. Their support team helps them stay on track, especially when outside forces pressure them to deviate. Many leaders have built their support networks over time, as the experiences, shared histories, and willingness to be vulnerable create the trust and confidence they need in times of uncertainty. Leaders must give as much to their relationships as they receive so that mutually beneficial bonds can develop.

The Power of Sharing Openly

One of the greatest gifts you can give yourself and another person is to build a relationship where you can be completely vulnerable and open, warts and all, and still be accepted unconditionally. When someone knows and accepts your weaknesses, your inner fears, and your struggles, he or she becomes a true partner. Most leaders have their closest relationships with their spouses or partners. When leaders feel unconditionally loved by another person, they are more likely to accept themselves for who they are. This enables them to become less dependent on external reinforcement.

Paula Rosput Reynolds, CEO of Safeco, found such a person in her second husband.

> When you go home at the end of the day and your employees think you're a jerk, or something has gone so wrong it seems hopeless, you've got to have somebody who says, "I love you unconditionally." I know I can always go home and my husband will love me.

Your partner is someone who will also hold up a mirror to tell you the truth in a compassionate way when you have strayed from your True North. In your partner's eyes, positions and accomplishments mean little, but the essence of who you are means everything. Because most leaders face frequent criticism, they may develop protective armor to combat it. Only those with whom they have genuinely loving relationships can penetrate the armor protecting their core.

Big Brothers Big Sisters' Judy Vredenburgh and her husband each have a deep appreciation for the values, character, and humanity of the other. She said, "I married someone who is not threatened by my power or position."

He made it clear that my position would not give me negotiating strength in our relationship. He doesn't care about the things that impress the external world, but he deeply values my humanity as well as my achievement orientation, my sense of responsibility, and my values.

There may be times, however, when your marriage is strained, and things are not going well at work. In these situations, you need someone else with whom you can share everything. It could be your best friend, mentor, another family member, or therapist. The important thing is not to go it alone in these difficult times. Those who do find it very difficult to maintain their perspective and objectivity.

Most leaders find comfort in being with their families. Younger leaders maintain close connections with their families of origin, seeking out opportunities to share high-quality time with siblings, parents, and grandparents. In knowing their parents at a deeper level and learning more about their parents' pasts, they wind up understanding themselves better.

As working hours have increased, some leaders have sharply limited their social lives in order to make time for family. John Donahoe, eBay president, and his wife imposed a moratorium on social events so that they could spend quality time with their four children. When George Shultz was U.S. secretary of state, he and his wife skipped all Washington social events unless the president or vice president insisted they attend. Jamie Dimon, J.P. Morgan's CEO, said he sacrificed superficial types of social events, such as attending football games and playing golf, to prioritize time with his three daughters.

Mentoring: A Two-Way Street

Many authentic leaders have mentors who changed their lives by helping them develop the skills to become better leaders and the confidence to lead authentically. What some people fail to recognize, especially aspiring leaders, is the importance of the two-way relationship with their mentors. *Lasting relationships must flow both ways.*

The best mentoring interactions spark mutual learning, exploration of similar values, and shared enjoyment. If people are looking only for help from their mentors, instead of being interested in their mentors' lives as well, the relationship won't last for long. Mentoring is a two-way street in which both people learn a great deal from each other, and the bilateral connection sustains it.

By mentoring many leaders from the next generation, I have been able to walk in their shoes, appreciate what's important to them, understand their work lives, and see how they are struggling to live integrated lives. In my relationship with Dean Nitin Nohria, I have a mentor who is much younger than I am, yet his wisdom has been invaluable in my 12 years on the Harvard Business School (HBS) faculty.

As a young entrepreneur building a fledgling company, Howard Schultz realized he needed someone with whom he could share his fears and vulnerabilities. When Starbucks had only 11 stores, Schultz heard Warren Bennis lecture on leadership and said to himself, "Here is someone I can learn from."

> *Who do you talk to when you're afraid to demonstrate vulnerability and insecurity to others? You can talk to your wife or close friends, but you also need advice from someone who has been there before. I asked Warren for his help, calling him once or twice a month. He taught me that vulnerability is a strength and a characteristic people value. Demonstrating your values, emotions, and sensitivities empowers others, as no one is impervious to having doubts.*

Many people are afraid to approach potential mentors because they do not want to impose on others. They fail to realize how much they can offer to their mentors. Warren Bennis tells young leaders they have to recruit great mentors. He likens this process to a dance where the two engage in mutual learning. Reflecting on how he developed close relationships with his own mentors, he recalled, "They appreciated my openness, energy, follow-up, and discipline."

When I was in business school, Dean Leslie Rollins took me under his wing and helped me develop as a leader with heart and soul, guiding me to understand the deeper purposes of leading in business and society. He coached me, goaded me, challenged me, and offered me countless opportunities to develop my deeper qualities. He made me furious at times, but it was his penetrating challenges that had long-lasting impact.

Mentors are not necessarily people who make you feel good about yourself or tell you that you can do anything. Sometimes the best mentors provide tough love by being critical as a means of teaching. Kroger's David Dillon told the story of the mentor he had early in his career. At age 29, he was named merchandising vice president (VP) for the Fry's supermarket division of the Dillon Company. One day, Dillon got a call from Chuck Fry, the entrepreneur whose family business Dillon's company had bought, inviting him to walk through a Fry's store together. As they stopped in front of a soft drink display, Fry spent a long time questioning Dillon about what he saw. Dillon failed the interrogation, because Fry's questions showed him he wasn't observing what was happening in the store. Fry explained, "The display had not been built with the customer in mind, but was based on maximizing the vendor's profits."

Years later, Dillon learned that the real purpose of Fry's visit was to decide whether he was willing to learn from Fry as a teacher and mentor. If he wasn't, Fry planned to have him pulled out of his job. For the next year, Dillon and Fry spent an hour of every day together, in person or on the phone.

Looking back, I realize I was failing terribly as merchandising VP, but didn't even recognize it. It was a very valuable lesson. You can't put leaders into a totally foreign job and expect them to perform; you have to teach them the leverage points of that job. Without Chuck, I would not have succeeded in the grocery business.

Dillon's story illustrates the importance of having mentors who challenge rather than just support you. Too many leaders prefer mentors who are always there for them but don't push them to change or improve. As a mentor, it is relatively easy to be a good listener and support other people's ideas but harder and riskier to point out their weaknesses and blind spots.

Yet it is also important for your team to know that you will be there to support it if necessary. Ecolab's Martha Goldberg Aronson shared the story of a boss who was willing to bet on her in stretch roles while supporting her. When she took a new position, her boss told her:

> On certain days you will feel that you're way out on this limb. The wind is going to start to blow, and you're going to feel like the limb is going up and down. You're going to hear it crack, and you're going to come crashing down. That's when I'll be there to catch you.

It wasn't long before Aronson encountered a quality problem with her new line of catheters. She noted, "The branch cracked a few times, and my boss was really there." Just knowing you have support from your leaders if things go wrong is very empowering. It enables you to recognize that you will not be hung out to dry, so you can take on significant challenges and stretch goals without fear of someone sawing off the limb behind you.

Mark Zuckerberg's Mentors Accelerated His Growth

Mark Zuckerberg, founder and CEO of Facebook, is one of very few people who have turned their idea into more than $100 billion of market value. Zuckerberg has been supported on his journey by several mentors, particularly Don Graham, CEO of the Washington Post Company. Early in 2005, Zuckerberg met Graham, whose family had controlled the *Post* for 50 years. Graham's own mentor, Warren Buffett, had advised him and helped shape the *Post*'s focus on long-term value creation.

From their first meeting, Graham and Zuckerberg felt an immediate connection. Zuckerberg recalled wanting to emulate Graham. In turn, Graham was so attracted to the Facebook founder that he offered to invest in the company on the spot. Zuckerberg verbally accepted a $6 million investment from the *Post*, only to later renege when Accel Partners offered to invest at a significantly higher valuation. That trying experience actually brought Zuckerberg and Graham closer together, because Graham was impressed by the way Zuckerberg balanced his duty to Facebook shareholders and his desire to do right by Graham.

Later that year, Zuckerberg spent several days shadowing Graham to learn how CEOs spend their time. Graham counseled him on key decisions, such as recruiting Sheryl Sandberg as COO. Graham also encouraged Sandberg to accept the position reporting to the much-younger Zuckerberg. As their relationship deepened, Graham sought Zuckerberg's advice for online initiatives to engage the *Post*'s readers.

Zuckerberg's roster of mentors has evolved as the company has grown. Early on, he relied on Sean Parker to help him understand how to attract equity capital while retaining control over his company. These days, he seeks counsel from Bill Gates and Silicon Valley venture capitalist Marc Andreessen, but his relationship with Graham has been constant. Today, Graham is lead director of Facebook's board.

Coach Campbell: Silicon Valley's Leading Mentor

Intuit chairman Bill Campbell is the dean of mentoring in Silicon Valley. Many venture capitalists and board members in Northern California will not hire a new CEO without first checking with him. Although he keeps a low public profile, "Coach Campbell" is one of Silicon Valley's most respected executives.

Campbell has mentored dozens of entrepreneurs and business leaders, including three leaders we interviewed: Randy Komisar, Donna Dubinsky, and Bruce Chizen. His selfless spirit, cultivated on the football fields of his youth, has enabled him to develop a loyal network of mentees, supporters, and friends. People are drawn to him because he unleashes the leadership potential of those whom he touches.

Campbell played offensive guard at Columbia University with an intensity that still emanates from his eyes. On first impression, his broad shoulders, tight jaw, and tough talk make it seem like he is going to tackle you. Despite all the muscle, he genuinely cares about people. "When you're with Bill," said Komisar, "you never have the sense he's worrying about himself."

While an Apple executive, Campbell led the 1987 spin-off of Claris and recruited a talented team to join him, including Komisar, Dubinsky, and Chizen, all of whom eventually became CEOs. Each of them speaks with great nostalgia about the Claris years and their strong affection for Campbell. They still call him regularly for wisdom, advice on difficult decisions, friendship, and laughter. They are like a tight-knit family.

Relationships between Campbell and his mentees have been highly interdependent. Dubinsky, Komisar, and Chizen recognized Campbell could help them enhance their skills while they helped him build Claris. Dubinsky said, "Bill taught us how to build a team, operate the company, and communicate with employees."

Campbell helped them discover authentic leadership by modeling it for them. Dubinsky recalled the respect he showed for others. "Bill would walk in and spend a few minutes every day talking to the receptionist. He knew her problems in life and could relate to what her kids were doing." Campbell also knew how to give tough love. He challenged his team to think beyond their own narrow interests to focus on the entire company. Dubinsky noted, "He pushed me a lot. He saw me as a champion for my people, but insisted that I look out for the company's best interests as well."

Most important, Campbell empowered all three of these leaders by regularly asking for advice and revealing his own vulnerabilities. Komisar recalled, "Bill exposed himself to us as a human being."

He would give a speech to the whole company, imploring us, "We're going to do this!" Then we would go in his office, shut the door, and he would say, "I'm worried. Do you think the team can do this?" I saw a vulnerable human being and was able to support him when he was down.

By being vulnerable and making subordinates his advisers, Campbell gave Komisar, Dubinsky, and Chizen the confidence and license to be authentic. Komisar said he learned to be comfortable with himself from being mentored by Campbell:

Bill brings tremendous knowledge and experience to the table. He does not give you a fish, but teaches you how to fish. You sense from Bill an overwhelming belief in you and deep caring for what happens to you. That is the highest expression of love.

The best mentors put the interests of their mentees first. As a result, their relationships grow into personal friendships, as mine did with Warren Bennis. The cycle continues when those who benefited from strong mentoring offer to mentor others.

Building True Friendships

Close friendships are built over years of shared experiences, with each person having a genuine appreciation for the other. Most people have no more than a handful of close friends, but they stay in regular contact with them. Close friends provide reinforcement when leaders feel discouraged and need a boost. It is often by sharing vulnerabilities that their friendships deepen, because openness is the sine qua non for cultivating relationships. Like mentoring, friendship is a two-way street where both parties benefit from the relationship. If it devolves into a situation where one person is doing all the giving and the other all the receiving, the friendship will not last for long.

DaVita CEO Kent Thiry uses redwood trees as a metaphor for the way to develop close relationships. "Redwood trees are the tallest, strongest, longest-living tree in the forest. How do you get a tall, strong, long-lived redwood tree? It takes time." After college, Thiry worked hard to maintain close contact with a handful of friends, traveling to see them and organizing reunions throughout the year. He also let them know how much their friendship meant to him. "You can start to grow another tree, but it's going to take 10 years or more. Wouldn't it be a crime to cut a tree down just because you were tired of it?"

With friends of many years, you develop special bonds of shared life histories. However, relationships need to be nurtured and cannot be taken for granted. Traditions help create lasting friendships. Chris O'Connell, executive vice president of Medtronic, has a group of seven classmates from business school who are among his closest friends. "Once a year, we get together for a four-day retreat. In 12 years, not one person has missed a single year."

When people grow together through the phases of life, they develop a deeper understanding of each other. Having been through it all together, close friends notice the little things, such as when you need a kick, even when no one else can see that. They can sense when you are getting off track and they aren't afraid to tell you.

True North Groups

One way of cultivating deep and authentic friendships is through True North Groups, a term I coined with my friend Doug Baker Sr. to label peer groups that meet regularly to talk about important issues in their lives. True North Groups provide a safe environment in which to open up, share your vulnerabilities and challenges, and engage in intimate discussions. A carefully conceived structure causes members of the group to probe their beliefs and relationships and to describe the challenges they face. In 2011, Baker and I wrote the book *True North Groups* as a guide for people who want to form their own group.

In preparing for the unexpected in life, Warren Bennis tells leaders, "Have some group that will tell you the truth and to whom you can tell the truth."

If you have people like that around you, what else matters? You're never going to be prepared for 9/11, nor can you figure out what's going to happen. All you can do is make sure there's some way of understanding reality beyond what you know yourself.

In 1974, Baker and I formed a men's group after a weekend retreat; 40 years later, we're still meeting weekly at a nearby Minneapolis church. Having a group with whom you can share your deepest feelings is a true blessing. We discuss our spiritual and religious beliefs and doubts, career difficulties, marriage and family problems, and the process of personal development.

Each week, one group member initiates discussion about an area of faith or his developmental journey. Typically, discussions are drawn from readings, poems, or editorials that challenge us to share more deeply. In a recent meeting one group member asked to suspend the program so that he could seek our advice about a deeply personal challenge he was facing. The discussions are intense but never judgmental. Our faith journeys have led members of the group in different directions, but we come together with mutual caring and respect.

Over the years we have developed a sense of shared history—from having a member who died from Alzheimer's disease to coping with chemical dependency, divorce, challenging sons, death of a child, loss of one's job, and personal health issues. One issue we never stop talking about is our relationship with our fathers, because most of us had complex relationships that we are still trying to understand. Being a part of this group has been a great boon to me over the years, enabling me to share more of myself—my weaknesses and my vulnerabilities—with my colleagues at work and to behave more authentically.

We all consider the group to have been one of the most important aspects of our lives, enabling us to clarify our beliefs, values, and understanding of vital issues, as well as providing a source of honest feedback when we need it most. The key to its success is what we call "honest conversations," saying what you really believe without fear of judgment, criticism, or reprisal.

There are multiple forms of support groups. For example, Penny and I formed a couples group with three other pairs of friends 20 years ago. We have rich discussions at our monthly meeting about our faith, our lives, our families, and personal growth. We also travel together regularly.

In my HBS course, Authentic Leadership Development (ALD), we create six- to eight-person Leadership Development Groups as an integral part of the classroom experience. Since its inauguration in 2005, ALD has become one of the most popular electives for both MBA students and executive education participants. In the past decade, 6,000 people have participated in these groups. Remarkable conversations have emerged, and more important, strong bonds have developed between group members, even in a one-week executive program. At the end of each course, we ask participants to evaluate what has been most meaningful to them in the course; without exception, small groups sessions rank higher than any other form of learning.

Your journey to leadership is likely to take many unexpected turns. Life is full of challenging situations, including ethical dilemmas, midcourse career changes or burnout, seemingly intractable interpersonal challenges, marriage and family issues, failures, and loneliness. At times, you may feel you are losing your way or have gotten off course from your True North.

Getting back on track alone is very difficult, perhaps even impossible. During these moments, you need your support team. It is important to build these relationships long before there is a crisis in your life. In fact, developing these relationships now may be one of the most important ways to prevent crises from occurring and help you stay on the course of your True North.

Exercise: Building Your Support Team

The following exercise will allow you to determine the kind of support team you want to build.

1. Make a list of the most important relationships in your life, right now and in the past.

    a. What is your most important relationship?

    b. Why is this person important to you?

    c. In what ways do you look to this person for support?

2. What role has your family of origin played in your development as a leader?

3. Who has mentored you as a leader? Have you had a particular teacher, coach, or adviser who has been influential in your interest in leadership and your development as a leader? How have you helped your mentor and built a two-way relationship?

4. Which friends could you count on if things did not go well for you? Do you have friends with whom you can share the challenges you face openly? Can you give each other honest feedback?

5. Do you have a personal support group? If so, what is its value and meaning to you and your leadership?

8

INTEGRATED LIFE

The world will shape you if you let it. To live the life you
desire, you must make conscious choices.

—*John Donahoe, CEO, eBay*

Successful leaders live complex and demanding lives. As the frequency of communication has intensified, the pace of business has
increased. Yet many of us have not learned how to deal with this new
reality. There is never enough time to do everything you want to do,
because the world around you makes ever greater demands on your
time. Nor will you be able to achieve a perfect balance between all
aspects of your life—your career, family, friends and community, and
personal life. Inevitably, you will have to make trade-offs. How you
do so will determine how fulfilling your life will be.

Authentic leaders are constantly aware of the importance of
staying grounded. In doing so, they avoid getting too cocky during
high points and forgetting who they are during low points. Spending
time with their families and close friends, getting physical exercise,
having spiritual practices, doing community service, and returning
to places where they grew up are all ways they stay grounded. This
grounding is essential to their effectiveness as leaders because it
enables them to preserve their authenticity.

To avoid letting endless professional commitments dominate their
time, authentic leaders must give priority to their families and take
care of themselves personally, in terms of their health, recreation,
spirituality, and introspection. There is no silver-bullet solution to this
issue, but neglecting to integrate the facets of life can derail you.

To lead an *integrated life*, you need to bring together the major
elements of your personal life and professional life, including work,

family, community, and friends, so that you can be the same person in each environment. For authentic leaders, being true to themselves by being the same person at work that they are at home is a constant test, yet personal fulfillment is their ultimate reward. Doing so will make you a more effective leader in all aspects of your life.

John Donahoe: Choosing to Live Fully

On a tranquil Boston evening in the fall of 1983, eBay's John Donahoe, then an energetic 23-year-old, enjoyed a relaxing dinner with his fiancée, Eileen. Just a year out of college, Donahoe had already earned an excellent reputation as a consultant at Bain & Company. His eyes lit up as he talked about his career prospects.

As dinner continued, Eileen voiced concern about the toll John's career could take on his life. She worried that the long hours, constant travel, and stress might limit his ability to have close relationships. Then she asked him pointedly, "Is that really what you want in life?" John answered adamantly, "No!" He reached into his wallet to find a piece of paper and wrote on the back of a Shawmut Bank receipt, "I will not live the life of a management consultant," and signed his name. John recalled, "Her challenge to me was, 'Be who you are.'"

As Donahoe rose through the ranks to become Bain's worldwide managing director, he worked hard at leading an authentic life. "My ultimate goal is to have an impact and be an authentic businessperson, as well as the kind of father, husband, friend, and human being I want to be. The human side is the highest goal and the ultimate challenge."

According to Donahoe, "Leading a satisfying life is a quest worth taking." He believes integrating his life has enabled him to become a more effective leader. "There is no nirvana," he said.

The struggle is constant, as the trade-offs and choices don't get any easier as you get older. My personal and professional lives are not a zero-sum trade-off. I have no doubt today that my children have made me a far more effective leader in the workplace. Having a strong personal life has made the difference.

Integrating their lives is one of the greatest challenges leaders face. Donahoe stressed that being authentic takes continuous effort.

The challenges of maintaining authenticity, sense of self, learning, and growing are the same no matter where you are. The world can shape you if you let it. To have a sense of yourself as you live, you must make conscious choices. Sometimes the choices are really hard, and you make a lot of mistakes.

One of his first big decisions came during his first year at business school. The final term was the most intense academic experience of his life. On the eve of finals, Eileen went into labor with their first child. When Donahoe asked himself what was more important, the birth of his child or his grades, the answer became obvious. Having achieved in every academic environment, he had to let go of his desire to get top grades. "In a strange way, I had an excuse for not doing well. I had to accept the fact that I was not going to get straight As." As finals approached, Donahoe spent more time with Eileen. As his colleagues became increasingly stressed, he felt oddly relaxed.

Much to his surprise, Donahoe earned the highest grades possible that quarter. "It was only because I had a bit of perspective. I certainly was not the smartest person in the room," he said. "I remember watching the inefficiency that kicked in when people stressed out." That experience showed him a strong personal life could be an ally in achieving professional success.

A few years later, Donahoe faced another choice that confirmed his belief that he could integrate his life in an authentic way. After graduating from law school, Eileen received an offer to clerk for a federal judge, but the job required her to be at work by 7:30 AM. Donahoe had no alternative but to take their two kids to school every day. Because his job required him to travel extensively, he went to Tom Tierney, then managing director of Bain's San Francisco office, and told him that he had no choice except to quit. Tierney just laughed and said, "John, we can find a way to work around this." He reassigned Donahoe to a local client, enabling him to take his kids to school before heading to the client site.

Donahoe was amazed that his clients appreciated the choices he was making. He honestly shared his situation with the client: "It is important to me to be doing this. I'm committed to working hard, but I can't be there before 10 AM."

> The client responded positively as he appreciated my commitment and contributions even more. I didn't have the courage to think about it that way before. There's an inclination in business to put on a tough exterior to give the impression that you have everything under control.

Donahoe learned that the more he integrated his life and embraced his humanity, the more effective he became as a leader. "That was my best year of client work. Our client understood, and I became more relaxed," he recalled. By showing his team and clients his vulner-abilities, he discovered his teams performed better and his client relationships strengthened.

The following year, Donahoe was named head of Bain's San Francisco office. After six years in that role, he felt burned out by the fast-paced life and wanted to spend more time with his two oldest sons before they became teenagers. So he handed off his work to his colleagues and took a three-month sabbatical. "It was an opportunity to bring our family closer together," he explained.

First the family went to Europe, and then Donahoe took separate weeklong trips with his wife and each of his four children. He returned to Bain reenergized. A year later, he was named worldwide managing director, succeeding Tierney. The announcement came just as the economy was plummeting in the first decade of the 2000s and the health of one of his children tested him as never before. "The health issue emerged soon after I became managing director, just as the consulting industry faced its biggest downturn in 30 years."

> This was the hardest thing I've ever had to work through in my life. My family, friends, coaches, and colleagues were unbelievably helpful. Real life forced me to bring a sense of authenticity and vulnerability to the workplace, because life humbles you.

Sharing his personal situation helped him connect with his partners, so they could rally during the downturn. By accepting his vulnerabilities, Donahoe was able to maintain an even keel. "I had faith in our people. We could talk about where we were going and how we were going to make it happen," he said. He believes he was effective precisely because he was able to integrate his personal and professional lives during stressful circumstances.

Because so much emotional energy was going to my family, I didn't take the downturn personally. As a result, I was more effective as a leader. My legacy to my Bain partners will be the way I led us through the downturn.

After concluding his leadership of Bain, Donahoe became CEO of eBay, succeeding Meg Whitman and transforming the company into a vibrant competitor in the high-tech world of Silicon Valley. Donahoe retired from eBay in 2015 after completing the spin-off of highly successful PayPal.

Although 30 years have passed since their conversation that night in Boston, Eileen Donahoe has not forgotten the signed Shawmut Bank slip. "I still keep it inside my purse," she said. "I've brought it out many times over the years." The Donahoes have successfully weathered challenging stages of their lives and continue to strive for an authentic life together. Their partnership serves as an excellent example not only of how to be intentional in building a meaningful life but also of how rewarding it can be.

Blending Careers with Family Life

These days, developing leaders wonder, "Can I have a great career *and* a great family life?" This is the number one question I am asked by my MBA students and those I mentor. Psychologist Ellen Langer challenges the notion of work/life balance. "The idea I think to replace work/life balance, which treats these categories as independent, is work/life integration. You're treating yourself whether you're at work or at play in basically the same way."

Increasing pressures and time demands on the job and the complexities of two-career marriages have made this integration more challenging than ever before. Younger leaders have seen many in their parents' generation sacrifice their families for their careers and have lived through the pain of broken marriages and estranged relationships. They are committed to doing it differently, but often they don't know how.

Integrating your work and home life is one of the most difficult issues leaders face. There are no clear answers, and you must make continual trade-offs. Most of us want to have a successful career *and* a rewarding marriage and family life. That is certainly admirable. The problem comes when you get into the habit of sacrificing yourself and your family for the company. Years later, you may find yourself in a career trap that you can't withdraw from because your living expenses are so high that you can't afford to quit. Yet you may not realize the trap in the early stages of your career. My advice is to establish clear ground rules for your work/life integration and stick to them, rather than getting into the habit of doing whatever it takes to get ahead.

When I was at Litton, my boss was one of the top five people in the company. He owned an expensive home in Beverly Hills and belonged to exclusive country clubs, yet he called regularly to tell me how much he hated his job. One day I said to him, "If it's that bad, why don't you quit?" Instantly he replied, "With all my expenses, I can't afford to." A few years later, he died of lung cancer from smoking to relieve his stress.

To find that delicate balance, it is essential to set clear boundaries between work and home life. If you do so, you will be pleasantly surprised about where life will lead you. After all, the alternative is to earn a lot of money and not have the time to share it with your family or to become estranged from your spouse and children because you neglected them.

Managing Dual Careers

From the time I was a teenager, I was committed to leading a great organization *and* having a great family life. I had friends whose fathers sacrificed their families to excel in their careers, and I worried about this happening in my life. When Penny and I were dating, we talked about how we could support both our careers and still have plenty of time for our family. Before our children were born, finding a balance was pretty easy. With both of us working, we were able to adapt our schedules and spend our nonworking hours together.

When our sons, Jeff and Jon, were born, everything changed. Penny was working as a consulting psychologist after obtaining her master's degree in psychology. She took time off from her job after each boy was born and then went back to work part-time. Meanwhile, the intensity of my work was heating up. I traveled regularly to Japan and Europe, sometimes on trips spanning 10 days. My absences put a lot of pressure on Penny to raise the boys *and* get her work done.

I tried to do my full share of the child rearing, the chores, and the boys' transportation to day care or to sports, as well as carry my share of the emotional load. I cannot say I succeeded. As hard as I tried, Penny wound up with a much greater share of the burden, especially when I was traveling. These days, I am a lot more realistic about the challenges involved for our sons and their families.

Hitting the Wall at Home

Marriage is *not* a static state. To have a successful long-term marriage, you and your spouse have to work at it continuously, talking openly about your differences, your fears, and your vulnerabilities. Penny has been the barometer in our relationship, forcing us to talk through the issues when we seem to be drifting apart or too caught up in our own worlds. This has been an enormous help to me in opening up more.

Not surprisingly, the high level of stress at Honeywell I experienced in the late 1980s also carried over into my home life. During those years, I was traveling almost constantly, which was hard on both Penny and me. I found myself less happy with my work and began turning to activities outside the company for a sense of fulfillment. Meanwhile, I was in denial about how the stress was affecting my family and me. It was a good thing Penny confronted me about my behavior and the toll it was taking on her and the boys. Our marriage survived that period, but it wasn't easy. Moving to Medtronic not only was more satisfying to me personally, but it also made life better for our family.

When you feel a great deal of pressure, it is hard to recognize its impact on those closest to you. In retrospect, it took pain at work *and* at home for me to face up to the reality that I needed to change directions in my career and focus on what is truly important in life.

An Integrated Life Makes You a Better Leader

Let's confront directly the notion of who are the better leaders: the 80-hours-per-week executives who live for work and subordinate everything to the company's perceived needs or the leaders who work equally hard during 50 to 60 hours but balance their work with the needs of their families? Integrated leaders develop healthier organizations. By appropriately delegating their work, they make more thoughtful decisions and lead more effectively. Their employees make higher levels of commitment to the organization. In the end, they achieve better results on the bottom line.

My leadership flourished when I found congruence among my work, my personal life, and the company's mission. Today's emerging leaders know from experiences in their families that integration is imperative for leading a fulfilling life. They are committed to excelling in their work but know that there is much more to life. They certainly do not lack the passion to lead. Quite the contrary: They will be better leaders *because* they are living integrated lives.

If we sell our souls to the company, at the end of the day, we may find we have little to show for our efforts. If we seek organizations that nourish our souls, permit us to grow into fully functioning human beings, and enable us to integrate our lives, we can find fulfillment.

Making Choices and Trade-Offs

Ellen Langer wasn't alone; Warren Bennis also never liked the word *balance*.

> Balance *is an engineering term that means you put the little weights on each side, and if you're really a good person, you'll come out equal. We have to be aware that we swing back and forth. It is choices all the time, not balance.*

We make dozens of choices every day, many of them subconscious or intuitive, and try to learn from those that turn out to be mistakes. *Ultimately, our lives are an expression of the choices we make.* When leaders talked about their crucibles, they said those experiences forced them to ask, "What is most important in my life?" Asking that question allows leaders to make conscious choices.

Xerox's Anne Mulcahy said:

> *I like to work hard and have a serious career, but the most important thing in my life is my family. I love Xerox and I'd kill for it, but it is not even on the same scale as my family.*

She and her husband, a 36-year Xerox veteran who traveled a great deal himself, decided that one of them would be at home with their kids every night. They also decided they would not move. Instead, they commuted, even when their jobs required them to travel great distances. "To be CEO of Xerox never having moved is quite extraordinary, but it's doable. At Xerox, we expect people to put their families first. Unacceptable trade-offs should not be part of the work environment."

Martha Goldberg Aronson: Taking on Added Responsibility

Emerging leaders are often identified as having the talent to lead across a much wider business spectrum, and their companies test them in more challenging settings. In her early years at Medtronic, Martha Goldberg Aronson developed a reputation as a high-potential leader. She joined the company's acquisitions group and was selected two years later to attend business school as a Medtronic Fellow. Rejoining Medtronic as product manager, she was soon promoted to run a start-up venture and eventually became general manager of the business. As her business grew, Aronson's career prospects brightened.

One day, she was home alone with her two children when the phone rang. Medtronic's head of human resources asked her, "What would you think about an international assignment?" Aronson recalled, "I hemmed and hawed and told her this wasn't the best day to talk about a move." Aronson was skeptical about whether an international move was right for her career or her personal life. Being far from the support of her parents and siblings with a baby and a toddler was not part of her game plan. She also balked at walking away from her current job before it was done and worried about the impact on her husband's career.

When she discussed the European opportunity with her husband, Dan, his immediate reaction was, "Let's go," although it meant a break in his career. So she accepted the job, realizing it was a unique opportunity to live and work overseas. Aronson flourished in the European environment. She grew professionally and personally from the daily exposure to the wide range of cultures in her region as her multicountry team produced significant results. She took the risk when an opportunity came, and was willing to learn more about leading in a complex geographic environment without knowing the next step in her career.

After three years in Europe, she was pregnant with her third child and felt she needed to be closer to her family in Minnesota to continue her career and support her family. Her husband was also eager to resume his career. She called Medtronic CEO Art Collins to explain her dilemma. Collins immediately offered her the position as head of investor relations. Just a year later, she was promoted to the company's executive committee as head of human resources.

Eager to return to line management, Aronson left Medtronic three years later and became national sales manager for a Chicago-based health care company. Recognizing that constant travel was keeping her away from her family, Aronson reconsidered her latest move, and accepted a position at Minnesota-based Ecolab to build its fledgling medical business. At last report, she is thriving both at work and at home.

Aronson's story offers some important lessons. All leaders have to face difficult questions about work/life integration. Aronson's European role proved to be a formative experience for her career and her family. However, too many sacrifices for your career may be a signal that you're out of balance. Although there is no perfect balance between career and family, you have to put boundaries around your work decisions, or you may find that work takes over your life—and then you will not be effective in either domain.

The Buckets of Your Life

Many leaders think about integration in terms of bringing the major parts of their lives together: family, work, friends and community, and personal time. Philip McCrea, CEO of ClearPoint, said, "I have four buckets representing the important areas of my life." (See Figure 8.1.)

One is my career. The second is my family. The third is my community and personal friendships, and fourth is the personal activities I enjoy. The third and the fourth are very removed for me right now. This is not frustrating because I'm tremendously fulfilled by the first two today. By age 40, I'd like to be in a position where I have a better ability to fill buckets three and four—community, friendships, and personal activities. Long term, I will not continue the career I'm in if it leaves a void.

McCrea and his Swedish-born wife, Annika, who has a promising career herself as a consultant, made the difficult decision to

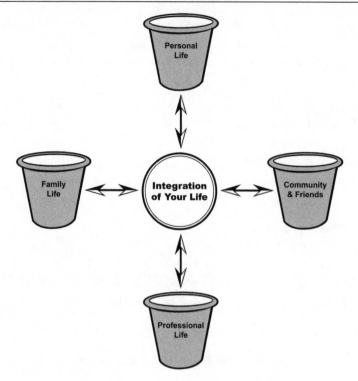

Figure 8.1   Integrating Your Life

plunge in and start a company just as they were starting their family. Living in San Francisco, McCrea found he was traveling coast-to-coast virtually every week because his customers—primarily large pharmaceutical companies—were on the East Coast.

Eventually, he was faced with a stark choice: Give up his family life or move his family to New Jersey to be close to his customers. He and Annika chose the latter route, as she was able to convince her company to transfer her to its U.S. headquarters in Connecticut. Recently, McCrea and his family moved to Stockholm for three years so that his teenage children could learn about their Swedish culture and language and Annika could work at the headquarters of her Swedish company.

Leadership can require significant sacrifices, especially during intense periods of work, when certain buckets get less time. Gail McGovern, CEO of the American Red Cross, framed it concisely:

> A lot of people ask if it is possible to have a rich personal life and a great work life. I say unequivocally, it is entirely possible. You just have to recognize you can't give 110 percent to everything. There are many mundane things in your life you have to let go of and not feel guilty about.

To ease the pressures, McGovern hires people to help with child care and does not worry if her house isn't perfectly clean. "If you accept you can't be super housewife, super career person, super mom, and super wife, there is absolutely no reason why you cannot have it all," she concluded. Now that her children are grown, McGovern is at the peak of her career as CEO of the American Red Cross, where she is transforming one of America's greatest treasures into a well-governed, vibrant organization.

Staying Grounded by Integrating Your Life

To integrate your life, you must remain grounded in your authentic self, especially when the outside world is chaotic. Well-grounded leaders have a steady and confident presence. They do not show up as one person one day and another person the next. Integration takes discipline, particularly during stressful times, when it is easy to become reactive and slip into bad habits.

Leading is high-stress work. There is no way to avoid stress when you are responsible for people, organizations, outcomes, and the constant uncertainties of the environment. For global leaders, long overseas trips intensify the stress. The higher you go, the greater your freedom to control your destiny but also the higher the level of stress. The question is not whether you can avoid stress but how you can manage and relieve it to maintain your own sense of equilibrium.

When Medtronic's Chris O'Connell gets stressed, he said:

I feel myself slipping into a negative frame of mind. When I'm at my best, I'm very positive and feel I can accomplish anything, both at work and home. When I become negative, I lose effectiveness as a leader and become even less effective at home. Both positive and negative emotions carry over between work and home.

Prioritizing Your Family

Facebook COO Sheryl Sandberg integrates the buckets of her life through a fundamental belief that success lies in the identification of real priorities at work and at home and an acceptance that no one can possibly do it all. In her book, *Lean In*, Sandberg defines success as "making the best choices we can and accepting them." She encourages leaders, particularly women trying to integrate work and family, to "learn from Icarus to aim for the sky, but keep in mind we all have real limits."

Each week, Sandberg and her husband, David Goldberg, CEO of SurveyMonkey, sit down to plan who will take their two children to school and discuss upcoming travel commitments to ensure at least one parent can be at home. Sandberg and Goldberg both put high priority on leaving the office in time for dinner. They dedicate their weekends to spending time with their children, although Sandberg admits to sneaking in e-mails from the local soccer field while watching their kids' games. Even with careful planning, Sandberg acknowledges her family life and professional life are not perfectly in sync. "I still struggle each day with trade-offs between work and home," she said. "Every woman I know does."

Focusing on What Matters

When Sandberg worked as a McKinsey management consultant, her manager implored her to take more control over her career, telling her, "McKinsey will never stop making demands on our time, so it is our responsibility to draw the line . . . We need to determine how many hours we are willing to work and how many nights we travel." After the birth of her son, Sandberg adjusted her in-office hours at Google to 9 AM to 5:30 PM, enabling her to nurse her son. To compensate, Sandberg got up in the early morning hours to check e-mails and worked at home after her son went to bed. She learned that by focusing her time, she did not need to spend 12 hours a day in the office.

> I focused on what really mattered and became more efficient, only attending meetings that were truly necessary. I was determined to maximize my output while away from home. I also paid more attention to the working hours of those around me; cutting unnecessary meetings saved time for them as well.

Sandberg also lets family life and professional life blend together. In Facebook's early days, CEO Mark Zuckerberg hosted strategy sessions at his home on Monday evenings. Instead of missing dinner with her family, Sandberg brought her children into the office instead, fondly recalling her time with them. She observed:

> Facebook is incredibly family friendly, so my children were in heaven, entranced by pizza, endless candy, and the huge pile of LEGOs the engineers share with young visitors. It made me happy my kids got to know my colleagues and vice versa.

Many leaders are reluctant to combine their work and family lives, but bringing the two together can lead to more productive and fulfilling lives, both personally and professionally.

Staying True to Your Roots

Returning to where you came from is another important way to stay grounded. Just as Howard Schultz goes back to Brooklyn from time to time, Bill Campbell stays in regular contact with his old friends in Homestead, Pennsylvania, which helps him keep perspective on life in Silicon Valley. Akshata Murthy, who grew up in Bangalore as the daughter of Infosys founder Narayana Murthy, returns to India regularly to see her old friends and extended family. She is committed to making an impact there someday.

To restore themselves and keep their sense of perspective, leaders may have a special place they can go with their families on weekends and vacations. Many renowned leaders found they can think more clearly away when they escape: Thomas Jefferson had Poplar Forest and Winston Churchill had Chartwell. For decades, former secretary of state George Shultz and his wife went to an old family farm they own in Massachusetts. "I once told the president, 'This is my Camp David.' When I go there, I put on an old pair of pants and old shoes. I am so relaxed, I don't worry about anything."

I experience that same sense of relaxation when Penny and I retreat to our second home in Colorado. I have written most of my books there, inspired by the beauty of the mountains. Although owning a second home may be out of reach financially, you can always escape to a nearby park or a local Starbucks where you can read and think uninterrupted, like my son Jon does.

Finding Time for Yourself

To manage the stress of our leadership roles, we need personal time to reflect. As Chapter 4 described, some people practice meditation or yoga to center themselves and relieve anxiety. Others find solace in prayer. Some people find they can release tension by jogging at the end of a long workday. Still others find relief through laughing with friends, listening to music, reading, or going to movies.

It's not important what you do, as long as you establish routines to relieve your stress and think clearly about life, work, and personal issues. It is critical not to abandon these routines when you're facing an especially busy period, because that is when you need your stress reduction techniques most of all.

Spiritual and Religious Practices

Understanding our role in the world by asking questions, such as "What is the meaning and purpose of my life?" or "Why am I here?" is the most personal and profound area of our leadership development. Many leaders have an active religious or spiritual practice to engage these issues, either privately or with like-minded people. Some seek the answers through a process of introspection. Others explore them through discussions with people closest to them.

Authentic leaders who are religious talked in our interviews about the power of prayer, being a part of church groups, and finding solace at church. Venture capitalist Denise O'Leary, who sits on several prestigious corporate boards, listens to Gregorian chants at a local church, while her husband, DaVita CEO Kent Thiry, reads Buddhist texts to center himself. She explained, "Church is the place where I find real solace. I remember loving this style of music as a child. It is my meditation as it allows me to be introspective."

Community

Being in direct contact with those who are less fortunate also provides leaders invaluable perspectives about what is happening in the world around them. Lisa Dawe, regional operations director with DaVita, emphasized that human interactions in an AIDS hospice helped her stay in touch with reality. "It is crucial to connect with people one-on-one, not just to create a fundraising plan for a nonprofit board."

> Being in touch with AIDS victims enabled me to feel human. I sat by the bedsides and watched, one by one, as people died. That helped me understand what I'm going to do when I get to that point and provided perspective on how fortunate I am. It helped me get to the core of what it means to be human.

Measuring Your Success

Have you clearly defined how you measure your success in life? If not, you are at risk of defaulting to metrics such as money, fame, and power, or letting other people measure success for you. Clay Christensen's book *How Will You Measure Your Life?* acknowledges an uncomfortable truth: It is significantly easier to measure the return on investment of an incremental hour at work than of spending that same hour with your young children. As a result, we unintentionally sacrifice investments in our families—not because we don't care about our families, but because the benefit is harder to see. Once the cost of these decisions becomes apparent, it's too late to recapture that precious time. Christensen challenges his students to set goals for their whole lives and then define priorities to achieve them. Only when you define what is most important in your life can you set the right priorities and become an integrated leader.

Integrating All Aspects of Your Life

Being authentic is not just something you are at work. It must be reflected in all aspects of your life. Unfortunately, the pressures of society and work often cause us to behave differently in the various aspects of life—work, family, social, and spiritual. As a result, we wind up compartmentalizing our lives.

Can you imagine yourself trying to be a strong, mature leader at work, impervious to all the pressures? A rising leader in your community? A laid-back person at home? And practicing a private spiritual life? That's what I was doing in my early thirties. To cope with all these different roles, I created internal compartments for each of them and behaved according to the expectations I encountered in each environment. Anyone who knew me well saw I was anything but authentic in all these roles.

In 1974, Penny and I went on a spiritual retreat weekend that was a life-changing experience for us. Throughout the weekend, the sharing of love we experienced deeply moved us, but I also saw clearly for the first time how I was compartmentalizing my life. I did not have the courage to share all of myself and who I really was with people in these different environments, especially my superiors at work. I was so afraid to tell my boss at Litton where I was going that I set up a special arrangement with my secretary to contact me if he called during the retreat. I was more focused on managing my boss's image of me than on being myself. I perceived it was acceptable to tell him I was golfing but not to tell him I was growing spiritually.

Emerging from the weekend, I decided to knock down these artificial walls and decompartmentalize my life. I committed to be the same person at home, at work, in the community, and in church. During this time, Penny was a great reality check, challenging me when she observed me behaving differently in social settings. This wasn't easy, and it took many years before I felt fully comfortable letting people in each aspect of my life see who I really was.

What does it mean to live your life with integrity? Real integrity results from merging all aspects of your life so that you are true to yourself in all settings. Think of your life like a house, with a bedroom for your personal life, a study for your professional life, a family room for your family, and a living room to share with your friends. Can you knock down the walls between these rooms and be the same person in each of them? When you can act the same in each setting, you are well on your way to living your life with genuine integrity. Living that way, you can be an authentic leader leading a fulfilling life.

Leading an authentic life requires openness to all that life has to offer and a willingness to go with the flow of life. It is important to seek this richness early in life, when you are still in a formative stage and open to the breadth of your experiences. You will be surprised at the way early experiences open up new avenues of exploration, lead you to interesting people, and shape your thinking about your professional life as well as your personal life. At the end of the day, you will be able to tell your grandchildren that you had the courage to dive into life, experience its joys and sorrows, and leave the world a better place.

Exercise: The Integrated Leader

1. What is most important to you in your personal life? In what ways do you nurture your inner life?

2. What do you do to ensure that you stay grounded professionally? In what ways do your family life, personal life, friendships, and community life add to or detract from your professional life?

3. How do you cope with the seductions and pressures of professional life and still stay focused on your True North?

4. What is the most difficult choice or trade-off between various aspects of your life that you have made in the past? What would you do differently in the future? What is the most difficult trade-off or choice that you are facing right now?

5. How do you measure success in your life? What is your personal scorecard? What long-term achievements would you like to realize? What will bring you the greatest amount of happiness?

Part Three

Your True North Meets the World

Parts I and II were inward-looking as you explored your leadership journey and your development as an authentic leader. In Part III, the focus shifts to the world around you. Having discovered your True North, you can now learn how to be more effective as a leader within your organization.

Leaders don't operate in a vacuum: You have to apply your leadership in real-world settings with significant challenges. The real measure of your effectiveness as a leader is your ability to use your True North to lead and empower people to have sustainable impact in solving challenging problems. This is where you realize your full potential as a leader.

By shifting your focus from yourself to serving others, you make the transformation from *I* to *We*. Then you will be prepared to discern your purpose in leading others and how it aligns with your organization's purpose. Having this clarity enables you to empower your teammates to lead around a common purpose and shared values. Finally, we examine the additional qualities you need to be an authentic global leader in today's global world.

9

I TO *WE*

In the middle of the road of my life, I awoke in a dark
wood, where the true way was wholly lost.
—*Dante Alighieri*, The Divine Comedy

Having focused on essential areas of your development as a leader, we are ready to tackle the greatest challenge of your journey: the transformation from *I* to *We*. In your early years, you are measured primarily for your individual contributions. Thus, it is difficult for emerging leaders to recognize that leadership is not about them and their ability to attract followers but is about serving others to bring out the best in them. *We* leaders are servant leaders.

I first encountered the notion of servant leadership in 1965, when I invited Robert Greenleaf to present his emergent ideas on this subject to the Musser Seminar on Business and Christian Ethics. Greenleaf described his views on the leader in his 1970 essay, "The Servant as Leader":

> *The servant-leader is servant first. One wants to serve first; then one aspires to lead. This is sharply different from one who is leader first, perhaps because of the need to assuage an unusual power drive or to acquire material possessions. A servant-leader focuses primarily on the growth and well-being of people and the communities to which they belong. The servant-leader shares power, puts the needs of others first, and helps people develop and perform as highly as possible.*

Jaime Irick, a rising star at General Electric and West Point graduate, explained this transformation in practical terms. "You have to realize that it's not about you," he explained.

To get into West Point or General Electric, you have to be the best. That is defined by what you can do on your own—your ability to do well on a standardized test or be a phenomenal analyst or consultant. When you become a leader, your challenge is to inspire others, develop them, and create change through them. If you want to be a leader, you've got to flip that switch and understand that it's about serving the folks on your team. This is a very simple concept, but one many people overlook. The sooner people realize it, the faster they will become leaders.

Nelson Mandela: Seeking Reconciliation, Not Retribution

Nelson Mandela's transformation from *I* to *We* is one of the most powerful ever experienced. He endured all forms of pain: hard labor, racist taunts, extreme illness in minimal conditions, and 27 years in prison for a political crime he didn't commit. Because of his efforts, he saved South Africa from civil war and became a role model for leaders all over the world.

On February 11, 1990, Mandela walked out of his prison cell at Robben Island, a free man for the first time since 1963. He described the scene:

As I walked toward the prison gate and was among the crowd, I raised my right fist and there was a roar. I had not been able to do that for 27 years. It gave me a surge of strength and joy.

That evening, Mandela spoke to a large crowd at the Grand Parade in Cape Town. His brief but carefully chosen remarks set forth his plan for the future of South Africa:

I stand here before you not as a prophet but as a humble servant of you, the people. Your tireless and heroic sacrifices have made it possible for me to be here today. I therefore place the remaining years of my life in your hands.

In those few words, Mandela declared that his purpose was to be a servant leader for *all* South Africans. Note that there is no bitterness in his words. Mandela wanted democracy for all, not just black South Africans. In his book, *Long Walk to Freedom*, Mandela elaborated, "I knew people expected me to harbor anger toward whites. But I had none."

> *I wanted South Africa to see that I loved even my enemies while I hated the system that turned us against one another. We did not want to destroy the country before we freed it, and to drive the whites away would devastate the nation. Whites are fellow South Africans. We must do everything we can to persuade our white compatriots that a new, nonracial South Africa will be a better place for all.*

Mandela Emerges as a Leader

When the Afrikaners took power in South Africa in 1948 and created apartheid, Mandela became a founding member of the Youth League of the African National Congress (ANC), aligning with young leaders that included Walter Sisulu, Oliver Tambo, and, years later, Thabo Mbeki. Eventually, the Youth League took over the ANC.

In the 1950s, Mandela was an angry young man who was repeatedly arrested for sedition. Later, he joined the South African Communist Party and founded a militant group to sabotage the Afrikaners' apartheid government. Mandela frequently organized boycotts and demonstrations against apartheid that erupted in violence.

In 1956, the Afrikaner government arrested him for high treason in causing violence. He endured the four-year Treason Trial and was eventually declared not guilty. That didn't satisfy the Afrikaner government, which arrested Mandela for political crimes in 1962. During the ensuing Rivonia Trial, Mandela gave his most important speech, defending the ANC's actions and laying the groundwork for South African democracy three decades later. He concluded his three-hour oration with these words:

> *I have dedicated my life to this struggle of the African people. I have fought against white domination, and I have fought against black domination. I have*

cherished the ideal of a democratic and free society in which all persons will live together in harmony and with equal opportunities. It is an ideal for which I hope to live and to see realized, but it is an ideal for which I am prepared to die.

It was to no avail. On June 12, 1964, Nelson Mandela was sentenced to life imprisonment.

During his long years in prison, Mandela went from being an angry man to a transformative leader who realized his greater purpose was to serve his nation by saving it from civil war and reuniting *all* the people of his country. He reframed his leadership purpose from the *I* of leading black South Africans to become servant leader of all South Africans, someone who could reconcile blacks and whites to create the new South Africa, centered on social justice and opportunity for all.

As a servant leader, Mandela rose above discrimination, injustice, and hatred. If ever a person had a right to be bitter toward his captors and the injustice done to him, it was Mandela. How then could he honor the prison guards who looked after him and forgive the judge who sentenced him? How was he able to negotiate with the leader of a minority government that repeatedly ordered his people beaten and killed to stay in power? When Mandela was elected president, how was he able to cast aside calls for revenge and offer reconciliation to his oppressors?

To know the answers to these questions, one would have to walk in Mandela's shoes or look into his soul.

When I met with him privately in 2004, he was passionate and calm—no longer the angry activist of his thirties. He was focused on his mission of reconciliation from racial injustice. His vision deeply moved me. Mandela's leadership transformation inspires us to serve and lead others in greater callings.

From Hero's Journey to Leader's Journey

As we enter the world of work, most of us envision ourselves in the image of a hero who can change the world for the better. This is a perfectly natural embarkation point for leaders. After all, so much of our early success in life depends upon our individual efforts, from the grades we earn in school to our performance in individual sports to our initial work assignments. Admissions offices and employers closely examine those achievements and use them to make comparisons.

As we are promoted from individual roles to leadership, we believe we are being recognized for our ability to get others to follow us. If we think leadership is just about getting others to follow us and do *our* bidding as we climb the organization ladder, we risk derailment. You may reach the point in your journey when your way forward is blocked or your worldview is turned upside down by events. This may trigger a rethinking of the purpose of your life and your leadership.

To become authentic leaders, we must discard the myth that leadership means having legions of supporters following us as we ascend to the pinnacles of power. Only then can we realize that authentic leadership is serving people by aligning them around a common mission and values and empowering them on their leadership journeys. This transformation from *I* to *We* is the most important process leaders go through in becoming authentic. How else can they unleash the power of their organizations unless they motivate people to reach their full potential? If supporters merely follow the leader, they are limited by the leader's vision.

Only when leaders stop focusing on their personal needs and see themselves as serving others are they able to develop other leaders. They feel less competitive with talented peers and subordinates and are more open to other points of view, enabling them to make better decisions. As they overcome their need to control everything, they learn that people are more interested in working with them. A light bulb turns on as they recognize the unlimited potential of empowered leaders working together toward a shared purpose.

Figure 9.1 captures some distinct differences between *I* leaders and *We* leaders.

I Leaders	*We* Leaders
• Leaders attain power and position	• Leaders serve others
• Self-interest drives decision making	• Purpose drives decision making
• "I can do it on my own"	• "It takes a team with complementary strengths"
• Pace setter: "I'll be out front; follow me"	• Empower: "Work together to fulfill mission"
• Ask for compliance with rules	• Seek alignment through values
• Arrogant	• Humble
• Leaders direct others	• Leaders coach and mentor others
• Focus on near-term results	• Focus on serving customers and employees
• Fire in their eye–extreme conviction	• Inspire and uplift
• Develop loyal followers	• Empower people to lead
• Leaders get credit	• Team gets the credit

Figure 9.1   *I* versus *We* Leaders

Challenges in Making the Transformation

Making the transformation from *I* to *We* is not an easy task. It not only requires a mental rethinking of your leadership, but it also necessitates changes in behavior to focus on others rather than yourself. Let's look at several leaders who struggled with this transition and emerged as exceptional leaders.

Gail McGovern: "It's Not Fair"

As CEO of the American Red Cross, Gail McGovern has never forgotten struggling with leadership upon her first promotion as a telecommunications manager. "Within one month, I went from being the best programmer to the worst supervisor in Pennsylvania Bell," she said.

> It's unbelievable how bad I was. I didn't know how to delegate. When somebody had a question about their work, I'd pick it up and do it. My group was not accomplishing anything because I was on the critical path of everything. My boss saw we were imploding, so he did an amazing thing: He gave me every new project that came in. It was unreal. At 4:30 PM, my team would leave, and I'd be working day and night trying to dig through this stuff.

Finally, I couldn't take it any longer. I went to his office, stamped my foot like a 5-year-old, and said, "It's not fair. I have the work of 10 people." He said calmly, "Look out there. You have 10 people. Put them to work." It was such a startling revelation. I said sheepishly, "I get it."

Doug Baker Jr.: A Call to the Heart

One of the hardest things for leaders is to see themselves as others see them. When they receive critical feedback, their initial response is often defensive, challenging the validity of the criticism or the critics themselves. If leaders can process the criticism objectively, however, constructive feedback can trigger a fundamental reappraisal of their leadership and propel them on the journey from *I* to *We*.

That's what Doug Baker Jr. learned when he was rising through the ranks of Minnesota-based Ecolab. After working in marketing in Germany for three years, Baker moved to North Carolina as deputy head of a newly acquired company. To integrate his team, Baker hired a coach to conduct 360-degree assessments and facilitate group sessions. "I elected to be first to go through the high-impact leadership program."

At 34, Baker saw himself as a fast-rising star, moving rapidly from one leadership role to the next. "I had become arrogant and was pushing my own agenda," he said. Then he got the results from the assessment, in which his colleagues told him all this and more. "I got a major dose of criticism I didn't expect."

As part of this process, I went away for five days with a dozen strangers from different companies and shared my feedback with them. Since I had been so understanding in this session, I expected people to say, "How could your team possibly say you were ego-driven?" Instead, I got the same critical assessment from this new group.

It was as if someone flashed a mirror in front of me at my absolute worst. What I saw was horrifying, but also a great lesson. After that, I did a lot of soul-searching about what kind of leader I was going to be. I talked to everyone on my Ecolab team about what I had learned, telling them, "Let's have a conversation. I need your help."

Meanwhile, Baker's division was challenged by a larger competitor that threatened to take away its business with McDonald's, which accounted for the bulk of its revenues. When he forecast a significant shortfall from his financial plan, the corporate CEO traveled to North Carolina to find out what was going on. Asked by the CEO to commit to saving the McDonald's business in the face of intense new competition, Baker refused. This raised the CEO's ire, but Baker held his ground, unwilling to be pressured into commitments he wasn't sure he could fulfill. Reflecting on confronting his powerful boss, Baker commented, "I'd rather have a bad meeting than a bad life."

> *If we had lost McDonald's, it would have been embarrassing for me, but it was all these folks in the plant who were really going to be hurt. There was unemployment all over North Carolina as many factories were shutting down. If they don't have a job here, they don't have a job, period. Suddenly, you find the cause is a call to the heart. Saving the McDonald's account created a lot of energy. Fortunately, we retained the business. It was a traumatic time, but ultimately a great learning experience for me.*

Doug Baker Jr. received critical feedback about being an *I* leader just in time. On the verge of becoming overly self-confident and thinking leadership was about his success, the criticism brought him back to earth. It enabled him to realize his role as a leader was to unite the people in his organization around a common purpose. Saving the McDonald's account provided a rallying point for that unity.

Under pressure from the CEO to deliver short-term numbers, Baker kept his organization focused on the long-term objective of building the business. This experience paved the way for him to become Ecolab's next CEO. After 10 years at the helm, Baker has a record that speaks to his leadership: Ecolab's stock tripled as he made timely acquisitions in the energy field. He has also assumed important leadership roles in the business community as chair of the Minnesota Business Partnership and Greater MSP.

Zach Clayton: It's Not about Your Resume

Like many achievement-oriented leaders, Zach Clayton grew up defining his identity by his accomplishments. "At age 13, I visualized creating the perfect college application," he admitted, "and worked painstakingly to build it." In high school, he was elected class president, was named valedictorian, wrote a book on post-9/11 youth politics, and was elected co-chairperson of the National Association of Student Councils.

Clayton ultimately decided to attend the University of North Carolina at Chapel Hill on the Morehead-Cain scholarship. There he wrote another book on politics and started a software business. At 22, he became one of the youngest students admitted to his class at Harvard Business School and graduated as a Baker Scholar, at the top of his class.

> When I graduated, I ended up declining an offer from McKinsey in order to launch Three Ships, a digital marketing company. It was the height of the 2009 recession and I was nervous about giving up a prestigious position. I remember thinking, "One day we will build the company to 20 employees and several million in revenue. Then it will be worth it."
>
> When that day came, I was ready to raise the goal to $20 million, and then it hit me. My God, I am on a treadmill promising myself I will be satisfied when my next big accomplishment comes. This is the fifth time I've gone through this cycle, and I'm about to do it again.

During this period, I talked frequently with Clayton as he came to the realization he would be unfulfilled if he measured his life by his resume.

> I hit a wall in 2013 that made me realize I had to claim my identity apart from Three Ships in order to be happy. If I am only aiming for accomplishments, I can never get enough. I was neglecting the idealistic thread in my life that has always been drawn to service.

Following these realizations, Clayton resolved to connect his idealism with his business aspirations. He involved his entire team at Three Ships in creating a written purpose and set of values for the business. One of the aims is to empower people to fulfill their full potential. In 2015, his team launched Three Ships University, providing professional and personal development training for employees and clients.

"Every day I am trying to make the transition to a *We* leader," Clayton said, "but getting past my personal desire for outward success hasn't happened overnight—as my 360 feedback showed."

> *Looking back at the transition of the past year, I feel more energized, motivated, and happier. My team is more engaged and feels trusted. As I've shifted my focus to developing others, we have strengthened our value proposition for customers and employees—and the business is more successful.*

Have you ever become so caught up in success that you think it's all about your leadership? Did you have truth tellers around you? Hard as it is to take in, feedback provides the opportunity to make the transformation from focusing on yourself to understanding how you can be an effective leader of other people, just as McGovern, Baker, and Clayton did. This requires letting go and trusting others.

Crucibles Help Make the Transformation

Often, having a crucible can force you to reflect on your life and propel your transformation from *I* to *We*. That's what Steve Jobs and John Mackey learned through their painful experiences.

Steve Jobs: Learning in the Wilderness

Steve Jobs once asked plaintively, "How can you get fired from the company you started?" That's precisely what happened when Jobs lost a power struggle with Apple CEO John Scully. The Apple board concluded he was so disruptive in pursuing his own projects that he intentionally undermined everyone else. Decades later, Jobs reflected on the experience in his 2005 Stanford University commencement address:

> *Getting fired from Apple was the best thing that could have ever happened to me. The heaviness of being successful was replaced by the lightness of being a beginner again, less sure about everything. It freed me to enter one of the most creative periods of my life.*
>
> *During the next five years, I started a company named NeXT, another company named Pixar, and fell in love with an amazing woman who would become my wife. Pixar created the world's first computer animated feature film,* Toy Story, *and is now the most successful animation studio in the world.*

When Apple bought NeXT, Jobs returned to Apple. During his wilderness experience, Jobs realized he didn't have to do everything himself and that his greatest gift was inspiring innovative people to create great products. At Pixar, he worked with two of the world's most creative leaders, Ed Catmull and John Lasseter, and recognized the benefits of nurturing great teams. Watching them, Jobs learned to moderate his competitiveness. As Jobs said, "None of this would have happened if I hadn't been fired from Apple. It was awful tasting medicine, but I guess the patient needed it."

Jobs was a wiser, more mature leader when he returned to Apple in 1996 after an 11-year absence. He had learned how to nurture great teams and recognize their contributions. As one of his direct reports told me, "Steve still acted like a jerk on many occasions, but when he returned, he surrounded himself with high EQ (emotional intelligence) leaders like Tim Cook, Jonny Ive, and Ron Johnson, who moderated his impact on others."

Jobs had a practice of looking in the mirror each morning and asking himself, "If today were the last day of my life, would I want to do what I am about to do today?" Whenever the answer was no for too many days in a row, he knew he needed to change. He said, "Your time is limited, so don't waste it living someone else's life. . . . Have the courage to follow your heart and intuition."

Steve Jobs wisely followed his own advice, living every day to the fullest before cancer cut his life short. He left Apple in the strongest position of any company in the world and passed the baton to his successor, Tim Cook. Cook has the self-esteem not to emulate Jobs but to march to the beat of his own drummer.

John Mackey: Learning to Share Power

Whole Foods Market cofounder John Mackey dropped out of college in 1978 and borrowed $45,000 from family and friends to found his first health food store, SaferWay. He lived above the store as he got the business going. When he acquired another natural foods store, he renamed the business Whole Foods Market. Through a series of acquisitions, Whole Foods morphed from a health food store into a supermarket selling healthy foods. Although he has created $17 billion in value for his shareholders, Mackey takes no salary or bonus and owns only 0.2 percent of the company's stock.

When you meet John Mackey, you know you're talking to an authentic leader: a committed capitalist who is exceptionally passionate about healthy foods and transforming unhealthy eating patterns. He is devoted to his customers and his employees and outspoken in his views. He asked, "If Whole Foods doesn't take a leadership role in educating people about healthy diets, who the heck is going to do it?"

I first encountered Mackey's philosophy through his remarkable debate with Nobel Prize–winning economist Milton Friedman about whether the purpose of the corporation was to serve its customers and fulfill its mission *or* maximize returns to its shareholders. As he said, "We don't sell healthy foods to earn a profit. We earn a profit to sell healthy foods." I was pleased when Mackey asked me to write the foreword to his signature book, *Conscious Capitalism*. In it, he wrote, "We should commit ourselves to following our heart and doing what we most love and what is most meaningful to us."

Mackey had to overcome many obstacles to get on the path to sustained success. In 2008–2009, he faced the greatest challenge of his career. It started with Michael Pollan's criticisms of Whole Foods in his popular book *The Omnivore's Dilemma*. Then Whole Foods' acquisition of Wild Oats was challenged by the Federal Trade Commission (FTC) for monopolizing the natural foods market. In the midst of the FTC investigation, the Securities and Exchange Commission discovered that Mackey had been posting criticisms of Wild Oats for eight years on Yahoo Finance's message boards, using the pseudonym Rahobed.

Meanwhile, Whole Foods' spectacular same-store sales growth began to slow. In the face of this pressure, its stock price collapsed, declining 88 percent from $38.70 to $4.72 by December 2008. The drop caused hedge fund raider Ron Burkle to buy 7 percent of Whole Foods and agitate for changes in its leadership. As a consequence, the Whole Foods board stepped in to determine what was required to preserve the company.

Mackey, who had a reputation for being a lone ranger and very outspoken, realized he needed to change. He eventually welcomed the board's constructive inputs, recognizing that he had to transform his leadership from operating so independently to become more of a *We* leader. Ultimately, the board settled the FTC suit, agreeing to sell 32 Wild Oats stores in overlapping markets. It stripped Mackey of his chairman title, appointing longtime board member John Elstrott in his place, and ordered Mackey not to make public statements. The following year, Whole Foods veteran Walter Robb became co-CEO alongside Mackey.

Since these changes, the business has done exceptionally well. Whole Foods expanded from 284 stores to 400, revenues grew from $8 billion to $15 billion by 2014, and the company's stock soared 10 times from its 2008 low to $48. Whole Foods' co-CEO leadership structure has worked well, because Mackey and Robb created a formidable partnership based on mutual respect. Although Mackey's outspokenness occasionally gets him in trouble, he has proved himself to be much more than a passionate entrepreneur. Today, he is a great *We* leader of the Whole Foods team, something I witnessed in person when I spent two days at Whole Foods in 2012.

My Defining Leadership Experience

In the middle of our careers, it is common to find ourselves in situations from which we think we cannot escape. Often our blind spots cause us to miss what is happening to us. As Dante wrote in the beginning of *The Divine Comedy*, "In the middle of the road of my life, I awoke in a dark wood, where the true way was wholly lost." Have you ever felt this way? I know I have. Like me, you may be in a midcareer crucible and not even recognize you need to make the *I* to *We* transition.

The most agonizing time in my career came when I least expected it.

In the mid-1980s I was on my way to the top of Honeywell. What began as a huge promotion turned into a decision to reassess my career and to move in a new direction. By 1988, I had been promoted several times, taking over more responsibility for Honeywell's most challenging businesses. At the time, I was responsible for three groups, nine divisions, 18,000 employees—and a raft of problems.

I had developed a reputation as "Mr. Fixit," the guy who could turn around Honeywell's troubled businesses. I knew *how* to turn businesses around, but I never had time to reap the fruits of my labor before moving on to the next set of troubled operations.

In my last assignment, I uncovered losses exceeding $500 million that had not been recognized or accounted for properly. This caused a great deal of consternation for the Honeywell board and its shareholders. We could do nothing except get all the problems on the table and correct them. As I was fond of saying, "I didn't create the problems. I'm just the guy who's trying to fix them."

During this period, I started questioning whether Honeywell was really the place for me. I had always seen myself as a growth-oriented leader, not a turnaround specialist. When presented with problems, I was quite willing to get them resolved, but I yearned to build sustainable-growth businesses.

On a beautiful fall afternoon while driving around the lake near my home, I looked in the rearview mirror and saw a miserable person—me. On the surface, I appeared to be energized and confident, but inside I was deeply unhappy. I wasn't passionate about Honeywell's businesses and realized I was out of sync with Honeywell's slow-moving, change-resistant culture. Worse yet, I was becoming more concerned with appearances and attire than with being the values-centered leader I had always tried to be. One visible signal that I was playing someone else's game was that I had started to wear cuff links. Reluctantly, I faced up to the reality that Honeywell was changing me more than I was changing it—and I didn't like the changes I saw in myself.

I drove home and told Penny just what I was feeling. She said compassionately, "Bill, I've been trying to tell you this for a year but you refused to listen." That evening, we had a long talk about our lives and our careers. We recognized my lack of job fulfillment was having a negative impact on our marriage, our sons, and our friendships.

Penny helped me realize that, like Dante, I was "in a dark wood." I was too fixated on being CEO of a very large corporation rather than following my heart and working toward a worthwhile purpose. Reluctantly, I acknowledged I was letting my ego get in the way of my values. If indeed I was in a trap, it was a trap of my own making. I was focusing too much on external measures of success and losing my passion to help others let their light shine.

In this position it is difficult to see things clearly, and we may miss the opportunity that is staring us in the face. Over the years, I had three opportunities to join Medtronic, dating back to 1978. I turned them all down, mostly because I didn't feel Medtronic was a large enough company for me; it was only one-third the size of my Honeywell sector. Yet the opportunity kept nagging at me. Had I done the right thing? It finally dawned on me that I was so caught up in my drive to run a major corporation that I was in danger of losing my soul. In the process, I realized I had sold Medtronic short and maybe myself as well.

The next morning, I talked with my men's group and asked them for candid feedback. They had seen what was happening and were pleased I was recognizing I had lost sight of the purpose of my leadership. I kept thinking about the vision I had in my teenage years: leading a mission-driven, values-centered company where I was passionate about the company's products and the opportunity to serve others.

At this point, I had not fully made the transition from *I* to *We*. What better place to do that than Medtronic? I called Medtronic CEO Win Wallin and reopened the door. Several months later, after conversations with Wallin, founder Earl Bakken, and several board members, I became Medtronic's president and COO.

I finally found the place—or it had found me—that offered everything I wanted: values, passion, and the opportunity to help people suffering from chronic disease. The Medtronic mission to restore people to full health inspired me from the moment Bakken described it. In midcareer, I had the good fortune to find congruence between Medtronic's needs and my personal desires.

My 13 years there was the best professional experience of my life. I fully embraced the Medtronic mission of restoring people to full health and discovered the purpose of my leadership in serving patients and empowering 26,000 employees. Had it not been for my midcareer crucible, I might never have seen the light. Only in going my own way did I become fully alive as I finally made the transition from *I* to *We*.

Taking the *I* to *We* Journey

Making the transformation from *I* to *We* requires introspection and cognitive reframing. To get started, ask yourself these basic questions:

- Does my life matter? To whom?
- What's the purpose of my life and my leadership?
- Will I leave a legacy behind?

I suspect your introspection will not lead you to the conclusion that your life's purpose is to accumulate possessions, material wealth, fame, or power over others. After all, at the end of the day, you cannot take your possessions with you. Material wealth is a currency with no intrinsic value, and it contains the extrinsic risk of pulling you off the course of your True North. Fame is fleeting. Like mercury, it can build up for many years and slip right through your fingers. Seeking power over others is the ultimate corrupter of the human character.

My friend Peb Jackson told me about a wealthy man in his late forties who had accumulated more than $100 million in personal wealth. The man told Jackson his life lacked fulfillment and satisfaction, and he had a hollow feeling inside. Then the man asked, "Is this all there is?" Jackson gave him a compassionate, but honest, answer: "If all you're chasing is money, then that's all there is."

So what does that leave? Just this: Life is about serving something or someone greater than ourselves—a worthy cause, an organization important to you, your family, or a friend in need. In my experience, that's the best way to know that your life matters. Becoming a servant leader propels you on the *I* to *We* journey.

Your True North shows the way to finding and fulfilling your life purpose—the way in which you use the unique gifts you bring to the world. Ask yourself, "How can I leave a lasting mark on the world?" Your answer to that question will be a clear expression of your life's purpose and the way you will use your leadership gifts.

Exercise: Your Transformation from *I* to *We*

After reading Chapter 9, think back over your life, and recall the experiences that enabled you to go from hero's journey to leader's journey.

1. Do you ever see yourself as the hero of your own journey?
2. Have you made the transformation from *I* to *We*? If so, what experience or experiences triggered this transformation for you?
3. If you have not yet made this transformation, what would have to happen in your life and leadership for a transformation like this to occur?

10

PURPOSE

> There is a thread that you follow. It goes among
> things that change. But it doesn't change . . .
> While you hold it you can't get lost . . .
> You don't ever let go of the thread.
> —*William Stafford, "The Way It Is"*

Having focused on the transformation from *I* to *We*, you are ready to discern the purpose of your leadership. Understanding your life story, your crucibles, and the transformation from *I* to *We* all help you discover your purpose. As an authentic leader, you must choose your purpose carefully, because your passion for that purpose is what draws people to you as a leader. If you aren't clear about your purpose, why would others want to follow you?

For you as a leader, your purpose is the way you translate your True North into making a difference in the world. For your organization, purpose is the motivating force that binds people together to drive the organization toward common goals. For society, it is the way leaders and organizations contribute to better lives for all people.

Ken Frazier: Medicine for the People

Ken Frazier has led his life with a clear sense of his True North. Now CEO of one of the world's leading pharmaceutical companies, he has found great alignment between his True North and his organization's mission. He said,

Merck founder George W. Merck declared, "Medicine is for the people. It is not for the profits." On the organization chart, it looks like I'm in charge, but every employee knows that George Merck quote by heart, and they look constantly to see whether my actions are consistent with it. It's aligned with my personal sense of who I want to be and what I hope to contribute to the world.

Frazier has traveled a long road since he was born in inner-city Philadelphia, overcoming many difficulties along the way. His grandfather was born into slavery in South Carolina. His father was sent north at age 13 to escape from indentured servitude but never had the opportunity for formal education. "My father was by far the most influential human being I have ever known," said Frazier. "He was self-taught, read two newspapers daily, and spoke immaculate English."

Frazier's parents were deeply committed Christians with a faith that carried them through the most difficult of times, just as it did for him. His mother died unexpectedly when he was 13. He explained:

Our life was turned upside down, and we had to become more independent. The day she was buried, my father told my siblings and me, "This is a good day because your mother won't suffer anymore." That is what I call faith in action.

Since his father worked as a janitor, Frazier and his siblings had to fend for themselves after school, avoiding the gangs that inhabited the streets outside his house. "I learned very early from my father that one has to be one's own person and not go along with the crowd."

He taught me the most important lesson of my life: "Kenny, what are you to do as the grandson of the man who started this narrative of being free and being your own person? You better do what you know is right, and not be fixated on what other people think of you." I didn't have to be popular, or feel like I had to join a gang. I have experienced discrimination and know that life is not fair, but feeling victimized gives one a sense of false power. You don't want bitterness to control you. That is the opposite of taking responsibility for one's own life.

At 15, Frazier was appointed to West Point but denied admission because he was too young to be inducted into the U.S. Army. Instead, he attended Penn State on a scholarship. While there, he decided he wanted "to become a great lawyer like Thurgood Marshall, effecting social change." At Harvard Law School, he was acutely aware he wasn't from the same social class as his classmates. He wryly noted, "Lloyd Blankfein [CEO of Goldman Sachs] and I were among the few students who 'were not of the manor born.'"

Defending Merck Science

Upon graduation, Frazier joined a law firm with an ethos of public service, making partner at age 30. Once again, he found himself crossing social barriers, observing, "I was an African American from the inner city in a firm of people from the upper crust of Philadelphia." Within his law firm, Frazier did lots of pro bono work, including teaching at a law school to black lawyers in South Africa in the midst of apartheid. He said, "My proudest moment came from winning freedom for an innocent prisoner who was on Alabama's death row for 20 years."

> I was a stranger in a strange land. My first day in the courtroom, the bailiff told me, "Down here we don't wear blue suits," which were reminiscent of the Union Army. Next time I wore a gray suit. My client was one of the greatest people I have ever met. He is such a hero to me because he has no recrimination for having spent 20 years on death row. In that situation, you either become consumed by bitterness, or rise to a different state of awareness.

When he joined Merck in 1992 as general counsel of its joint venture with Astra, Frazier's purpose shifted to using his legal skills to help a company whose purpose is to create medicines that save lives. After only a year, Merck CEO Roy Vagelos proposed making him senior vice president of public affairs. Initially, he was not inclined to accept the promotion until Vagelos persuaded him that he could do much more for Merck than just be a lawyer. Six years later, Frazier was promoted to general counsel. There, he confronted 50,000 lawsuits filed by patients who used Vioxx after Merck voluntarily withdrew the drug.

Frazier made the courageous decision to try the cases, one by one. He noted:

> These cases went to the heart of who we are as a company. When plaintiffs alleged that Merck put profits ahead of safety, did low-quality science, and had questionable integrity and commitment to humanity, we knew we had to defend Merck science. We lost our first case in rural Texas, as the jury returned breathtaking damages of $253 million for a single patient. The next day, the New York Times read, Merck could find itself "bankrupt," and they can blame it all on the "ineptitude" of their lawyer. That was not a good day.
>
> We learned from that experience and started winning cases. After we won eight cases or so in a row, the judges told the parties to settle the remaining cases. We eventually did, not for anything close to the estimated $30 to $50 billion the plaintiffs were seeking, but for $4.85 billion. The New York Times called it a brilliant litigation strategy. It wasn't a litigation strategy at all, but a defense of our science, our people, and Merck's mission.

After Frazier spent a brief stint as Merck's head of Global Human Health, the board elected him CEO of Merck on January 1, 2011. He immediately reaffirmed Merck's mission: "To discover, develop and provide innovative products and services that save and improve lives around the world."

His strategy to fulfill the mission was to develop transformational medicines and vaccines that focused on unmet medical needs. He committed to spend a minimum of $8 billion per year on research and development (R&D), just as archrival Pfizer and others were paring back R&D staffs. Resisting shareholder pressure to cut research, he invested in a new generation of drugs coming to market, such as Januvia for diabetes, human papillomavirus vaccine Gardasil, and Keytruda for melanoma. To concentrate on Merck's mission, Frazier sold the company's consumer products business for $14 billion and acquired antibiotic maker Cubist Pharmaceuticals for $8 billion.

He concluded, "At Merck, you have the opportunity to make tangible contributions to humanity."

> *There's a yearning in all of us to leave something meaningful behind, because we know we have a short time on earth. Merck gives me the chance to leave something to people 20, 50, or even 100 years from now because we did the right things today. My purpose as CEO of Merck is to create an environment where world-class scientists want to focus on the most important issues facing mankind, such as our late-stage program for treating Alzheimer's. The quality of science in our industry is what separates the winners from the losers.*

Frazier never forgot the influence of his father, "Looking back at the days sitting at my father's table, [I remember] he told me, 'Believe in yourself, and get up in the morning to help somebody.' If he were alive today, he would say, 'The boy did what he was supposed to do.'"

Ken Frazier is proud of his roots, and he found his True North in them: a call to serve. Frazier has focused on his leadership purpose in multiple roles and used this purpose to invigorate a major global pharmaceutical company. His contributions are genuinely a gift to humanity, and his story is an inspiring one from which we can all take hope and learn.

A Mentor's Story

Frazier's mentor at Merck, former CEO Roy Vagelos, carried out founder George Merck's passion for discovering lifesaving drugs for two decades. He had been a medical researcher for 19 years when he was asked to become dean of two prestigious medical schools, the Universities of Chicago and Pennsylvania. Vagelos turned down the opportunities because he believed being a dean was a dead end. "I was horrified about becoming a dean, because you don't teach or do research; you just shuffle papers and push people around," he explained. Then he got an offer to lead Merck's research.

> *I thought if I could use my knowledge of biochemistry to discover new drugs, I could impact human health far beyond what I could do as a practicing doctor, and I could possibly change the technology of drug discovery. I never thought of*

*myself as being a leader, but asked myself instead if I was contributing
something to what's going on in the world.*

I first met Vagelos when he was selected for the U.S. Business
Hall of Fame for his leadership in eliminating the African disease
known as river blindness. Merck discovered a cure, the drug
Mectizan, but market projections indicated Africans could not afford
it. Vagelos took the courageous course of completing the drug's
development and distributing it for free throughout Africa—until all
river blindness was eradicated. He explained, "Here's a drug that can
prevent blindness in 18 million people. That single decision put
Merck in a position where we could recruit anybody we wanted for
the next decade."

During the 1980s and early 1990s, Merck had the most productive record in producing lifesaving new drugs of any pharmaceutical
company, in large part because of the inspiration Merck's researchers
drew from Vagelos's passion and sense of purpose. Not surprisingly,
Merck's shareholder value increased 10 times in 10 years. Now in his
mideighties Vagelos is still going strong. As chair of biotechnology
firm Regeneron for the past decade, he has guided the creation of
numerous breakthrough drugs using monoclonal antibodies—and
created $42 billion in shareholder value, a 6,700 percent increase.

"Given a choice of working just to make a living, or benefitting
the people of the world, the majority of people will choose the
latter," Vagelos concluded.

What's the Purpose of Your Leadership?

Most leaders find the purpose of their leadership emanates from their
life story. By understanding the meaning of key events in your life and
reframing them, you can determine your leadership purpose. Understanding your purpose is not as easy as it sounds. You cannot do so in
the abstract; discerning it takes a combination of introspection and
real-world experiences before you can determine where you want to
devote your energies.

For some leaders, a transformative event in their lives inspires them and lights the way to their purpose. Others, like me, require many leadership experiences before discovering their purpose and alignment with an organization where they can pursue it in an authentic way. When you gain clarity about your purpose and find or create an organization aligned with it, you are ready to make important differences in the world through your leadership.

Often young leaders are too eager to get ahead and go for promotions and titles rather than patiently wait to find their purpose. When Avon's executive vice president Andrea Jung was passed over for CEO at age 39, her board member Ann Moore, then CEO of Time Inc., gave her invaluable advice to "Follow your compass and not your clock." Jung decided to stay, and two years later she was named CEO, a position she held for a dozen years. By the time she became CEO, Jung's purpose was clear: the empowerment of women. She commented, "There is purpose in my work: enabling women to be self-empowered, learn to run their own businesses, and achieve economic means to provide education. At the end of the day, that trumps all things."

Dedicating Your Life to Public Service

Everyone who knew Seth Moulton while he was an undergraduate at Harvard College recognized his commitment to public service. He delivered his class's commencement speech, challenging his peers to commit to service. But he didn't just goad his classmates. After graduating, he joined the U.S. Marine Corps, and served four tours of duty in the Iraq War as an infantry officer.

Moulton's choice surprised—maybe even infuriated—his liberal parents, who had been opposed to the Vietnam War. They were shocked that one of their children would want to join the military, let alone fight on the front lines in Afghanistan or Iraq. Moulton recalled his mentor, Reverend Peter Gomes, telling him, "Believing in the right thing is not good enough. You have to go do it."

I first became aware of Moulton when he appeared in the documentary *No End in Sight*, which criticized the handling of the Iraq War up to 2007. I was struck by how he could be so loyal to the military yet entirely honest in his criticisms of civilian leaders in their execution of the war. Later, I got to know Moulton much better when he was a George Leadership Fellow in the three-year, joint-degree program between Harvard Business School and Harvard Kennedy School. By then he had completed five years of military service, working in later years directly under General David Petraeus, who commanded all U.S. forces in Iraq. Moulton was intense, thoughtful, and committed to serving his country.

After completing graduate school, he became project manager for a high-speed rail venture in Texas. Moulton said that he had "hoped to find the same sense of public mission in the private sector" that he had experienced during his military service. However, the project was constantly delayed by overseas investors, and after one year on the job he resigned to pursue other opportunities.

Yearning to apply himself to a cause he could invest in fully, he decided to run for Congress. "I want to serve in order to make a difference," he said. Just six months before the 2012 elections, he began considering a long-shot campaign against an entrenched Democratic incumbent in his home district on Massachusetts's North Shore, a race that many party elders advised him to avoid. "I was disappointed that so many people discouraged me from participating in the democratic process," he said. "That democracy was what we were fighting for every day in Iraq."

Recognizing the futility of such a short campaign, he declined to run, but was intrigued enough by the idea to consider running in 2014. Moulton officially announced his candidacy in July 2013, and worked tirelessly for the next 12 months, getting to know his constituents, staking out policy positions in speeches, and raising money locally and nationally. In spite of his efforts, he still trailed the incumbent in the primary by 30 points in the polls in late June. For the next two months, he worked even harder to deliver his message to the district's constituents. On September 9, Moulton won by an

11-point margin, taking an improbable victory after trailing by as many as 53 points earlier in 2014. His election was the only Democratic primary upset of the entire 2014 cycle.

In the general election, Moulton faced an experienced and well-financed Republican who was considered by the Republican Party to be one of their top prospects nationwide. Polling showed a close race, but on Election Day Moulton emerged with a 56 to 41 percent victory. In his victory speech, Moulton's passion and voice rose as he talked of Congress's misunderstanding of the military and its lack of support for veterans. "I am going to Washington to change that," he declared.

Although he is one of the youngest members of Congress, Moulton is focused on making an immediate difference, by getting the Veterans Administration back on track to help veterans returning from Afghanistan and Iraq. Americans will hear a lot more from Moulton in the years ahead. Congress needs more authentic leaders like him who bring clarity of purpose to the public sector.

Opening up Opportunities

When Baxter Healthcare's Michele Hooper was a child, she had a close friend who lived on her street. One day, she went to her friend's house but was met at the door by her father. "He told me my friend was no longer allowed to play with black children. That had a huge effect on me. It was horrible." The shock of that blatant discrimination stuck with Hooper and provided the impetus for her leadership. After that painful experience, she was driven to excel academically. "I planned to use my intellectual capacity as a stepping stone to get ahead," she said. Although she had no role models in the corporate world, she decided to become a corporate leader because she excelled at economics and business courses.

At Baxter, Hooper earned her first general management opportunity: to lead the turnaround of its Canadian operations. The work was so stressful that she broke out in hives and acne. Yet, she said,

"I could not quit because I was the first black female to run an organization like that and first in my family to move into these lofty executive ranks. I could not fail." As she advanced in Baxter's leadership, she found her purpose: to be a role model for people coming up and provide them opportunities. Hooper believes many talented people never get opportunities they deserve because no one recognizes their potential. "It goes back to my days when I was rejected by my friend's father," she said.

> *You have to accept people for who they are. There are so many good people out there. All they need is an opportunity and a platform. People gave me that in my career and allowed me to take stretch assignments to grow in ways that I would have never dared.*

These stories reflect both the struggle that leaders go through in discerning their purpose and the fulfillment they feel when they find it and can share it with others. Ann Fudge sees leadership as serving, not self-serving. She asked, "How can I use my talents to give back in some positive way?"

> *Anyone can figure out ways to drive a business for two years, make a boatload of money, and move on. That's not leadership; that's playing the game. Leadership is leaving something lasting, whether it is how you treat people or how you deal with problems.*

Turning Purpose into Action

Your leadership purpose does not become meaningful until you apply it to the challenges you encounter in the real world by bringing people together around a common purpose.

Jim Wallis: Taking Faith to the Streets

Shortly before our interview, Sojourners founder Jim Wallis returned from Ferguson, Missouri, where he had gone to meet with the young people who were leading the protests against their police department's racial bias and the faith leaders who were trying to support them, speak to public officials, and bring people together. Wallis, one of America's leading religious figures engaged in social justice, said his new book will be on race in America. He believes purpose has little meaning unless it is translated into action:

> My whole vocation is for faith to hit the streets in our work, our neighborhoods, our nation, and the world. If it's not a driving force in your life, it won't be sustained. Through Jesus, God hits the streets. That means religion has to have a street test. We can talk and talk about religion, but if it doesn't ever change things on the street, it has little impact. In my courses at Georgetown, I ask students, "How does your faith hit the streets?"

Wallis grew up in a white neighborhood of Detroit. As a teenager, he was troubled by the disparities he saw in black sections of Detroit just a few blocks away, concluding, "Something is terribly wrong with my city and my country. I went into the city to find answers."

> As a janitor at Detroit Edison, I became friends with young black guys, and that changed everything. One day, I came back to my home church, where a church elder told me, "Jim, you have to understand that Christianity has nothing to do with racism; that is political and our faith is personal." That's the night I left my church as a teenage kid. The issue of race was consuming me in my mind and heart. I knew something was wrong, yet nobody would talk about it. I said to myself, "If Christian faith has nothing to do with racism, then I want nothing to do with Christianity."

While studying at Michigan State University, Wallis got deeply involved in civil rights and antiwar movements, and has been arrested 20 times since in nonviolent civil disobedience for justice and peace. He said, "As a radical student activist, I could put 10,000 people on the streets in about two hours." In 1970, when tensions over the Vietnam War and the gunning down of three students at

Kent State University brought emotions to a boil, he led the student strike that temporarily shut down Michigan State. His alma mater awarded him an honorary degree 44 years later for his unwavering commitment to social justice.

During college years, Wallis had his conversion experience when he encountered Jesus's words in the Gospel of Matthew, "Inasmuch as you have done it to one of the least of these my people, you have done it to me." He explained:

Here is the Son of God saying, "I'll know how much you love me by how you treat them." Them is the marginal, the vulnerable, the poor, the oppressed. This is more radical than Karl Marx, Ho Chi Minh, and Che Guevara combined. How we treat the poorest and most vulnerable is the real test of our faith. The rest of my life has been trying to figure out the public meaning of faith.

At Trinity Evangelical Divinity School, Wallis continued to engage in social causes. He founded Sojourners in the early 1970s as a faith-based social organization, network, and movement with the mission of "Putting faith into action for social justice." For the past 40 years, he has vigorously pursued that mission, never wavering in his commitment to help the oppressed in society.

Wallis makes a sharp distinction between climbing the career ladder and pursuing a vocation. He said, "Career is putting your skills and assets on a resume, and trying to climb the rungs of the ladder of success. Vocation is discerning your gifts and your calling. Your vocation *is* your True North, what you're called to do. Otherwise, you're working at some job, trying to advance on the career ladder, and maybe engaging in your vocation in your extra time."

Your vocation, which comes from the Latin word vocari, is where the crying needs of the world intersect with your gifts. Rather than looking for opportunities to ascend, ask what are you called to be. If your vocation is just an extracurricular activity, you're in trouble. This difference between career and vocation is central to your leadership. Your leadership is what you're doing every day in your work and your relationships. When people ask how to find their True North and their vocation, I tell them, "Trust your questions and follow them wherever they take you."

True to his calling, Wallis has taken his work to the streets of South Africa, to the inmates at Sing Sing Correctional Facility, to the poorest residents of inner-city Washington, DC, and to President Barack Obama in the Oval Office, never ceasing in his efforts to help society's underprivileged people. He has demonstrated enormous courage in taking on powerful bodies, yet he refuses to be identified with any part of the political spectrum. At the World Economic Forum, he has advocated for a New Social Covenant. In part the Covenant calls for "transformational, values-based leadership in every field . . . We must engage the people . . . who will build and leave behind a more just, generous, and sustainable world."

Penny George: It's Never Too Late to Become a Leader

My wife, Penny, never thought of herself as a leader, nor did her parents encourage her to become one. Quite the contrary: They discouraged her from taking the risks that come with leading. She became a skilled organizational psychologist, valued by her clients for helping talented individuals realize their potential. However, Penny avoided organizational leadership roles, even on nonprofit boards.

Tragedy struck in 1996, shortly after she received her doctorate in psychology, just as she and a partner were launching their new consulting psychology firm. She recalled, "A day after a routine mammogram I returned home from work to find a message on my answering machine: 'Penny, it appears you have breast cancer. Please schedule an appointment with a surgeon.'"

Although her oncologist told her, "The goal is cure," Penny went on an emotional roller coaster, convinced she was going to die. She opted for a modified radical mastectomy, followed by seven months of chemotherapy and five years of hormonal therapy. Yet she had a constant fear that the cancer would return. Unwilling to be passive, she experimented with many complementary therapies. She embraced rigorous lifestyle changes, including a new diet, exercise, and stress reduction, tried herbal medications, and did psychotherapy to reframe the difficulties of her teenage years. She found taking responsibility for her return to wellness was profoundly healing and restored her sense of control.

Shortly after her surgery, our son Jon canceled his spring vacation plans to come home to be with his mother. That personal experience led to his decision to go to medical school. Today he is emerging as an exceptional head and neck cancer surgeon at the University of California, San Francisco, Medical Center, and is deeply committed to his patients. His older brother, Jeff, has also followed a path to a career in the medical field, and is currently global head of Alcon, the worldwide leader in eye care, which is owned by Novartis.

As part of her recovery, Penny went on an 11-day vision quest in the barren Four Corners region of Colorado, including a 4-day solo fast. After her return, she decided to concentrate her energies on advancing integrative medicine. Her vision for a new way of approaching medicine combined the best of traditional Western practices with complementary therapies to treat the whole person, just as she was doing for herself.

One day, as we were driving to Colorado, she told me with determination, "We are going to change the way medicine is taught and practiced." Penny proposed that she run the family foundation we had created in 1994. With the help of an exceptional foundation director, she directed half our giving to integrative medicine. Together they conceived an innovative idea to bring together medical leaders of integrative medicine with philanthropists who were funding in the area. This led to the formation of the Bravewell Collaborative, a group of 25 foundations pooling their funding to support the transformation of medicine.

Although her leadership of the collaborative was acclaimed by its members, she kept insisting, "I am not a leader." Why this dichotomy? Rather than be the powerful out-front leader, she was quietly leading from behind by encouraging individual members of this peer network to step up and lead. It was her passion and vision, coupled with the values of collaboration, that inspired the group's members. Her story illustrates how discovering your passion can empower you to step up to lead and find the purpose of your leadership.

Steve Rothschild: Finding His Calling

Sometimes in your career you will find that your work does not align with your leadership purpose. At this point, you have to make a choice: Either you find ways to bring your work into alignment with your purpose, or you shift direction to find the opportunity that enables you to fulfill your purpose through your work. That's the choice Steve Rothschild had to make.

Rothschild was a rising star at General Mills. He created the Yoplait yogurt business in the United States and put it on course to become a $1 billion business. Promoted to executive vice president while still in his thirties, he faced many new challenges, but after eight years in this role, he became restless. He felt like a person in the middle, missing the satisfaction of leading his own team. He also disagreed with the company's direction, judging it had to become more global.

His frustration came to a head when he was asked to present the company's international business strategy to its board of directors. "I concluded we ought to be doing more internationally, because we couldn't rely solely on domestic growth," he explained. While in Spain on business, he got a frantic phone call from the company president, who told him the CEO wanted to pull the recommendation to expand internationally. Rothschild replied, "I can't do that because I don't believe it." He explained, "The CEO wanted me to heel, but never talked to me directly."

Shortly after that incident, Rothschild faced the reality that he was marching to a different drummer and wasn't enjoying his work. After some reflection, he decided to leave General Mills. "I was stuck in a job I no longer enjoyed. I needed to feel alive again," he said.

Leaving General Mills was a godsend for me. It allowed me to explore things that were underneath my skin and in my soul and gave me the opportunity to refocus on my marriage and family. Since leaving, my relationships with my family have become much closer and deeper. Making this move has made me a more complete person, happier and fulfilled.

Having made the decision to get out of the frying pan at General Mills, Rothschild decided not to jump back into the fire. Instead, he gave himself the time and freedom to understand his passions and to recognize he wanted to work on issues that meant something to him. In the process, he shifted his priorities to helping underprivileged people get back on their feet.

When you're focused on something professionally for so long, you're afraid to let go. It's like standing inside a giant hoop. When you let go a little bit, you do so with one arm. You're afraid to let go with two arms and fall out of the hoop altogether, because you could fall flat on your face. In my case, I had to let go of the hoop altogether.

He realized his passion was in helping underprivileged people become financially self-sufficient and develop stronger families. Using his own money, he founded Twin Cities RISE! Its mission is to provide employers with trained workers by preparing unemployed adults for skilled jobs paying fair wages.

My decision to start Twin Cities RISE! evolved out of the recognition that I like solving meaningful problems. The challenges faced by underprivileged people of color, many of whom have been incarcerated, weren't being adequately addressed. The nature of the problem shifted from building a business to building lives.

Aligning Your Organization and Shared Purpose

Leaders don't operate in a vacuum. Their responsibility is to bring people together to pursue a shared purpose. Gaining alignment around a purpose is the greatest challenge leaders face. Authentic leaders, such as Ken Frazier, convey such a sense of passion for their purpose that the mission inspires people.

Cynics would say it is easy to create a sense of purpose when your company is saving lives like Merck does, but what about the grocery business? Kroger CEO Dave Dillon is a strong believer in creating a purpose shared throughout the organization. Kroger may not save lives, but it is a company where employees feel they are part of something important. Dillon gained alignment around the proposition that serving the public in a service-oriented grocery operation is a dignified, proud profession. "All human beings want to find meaning in their lives. Our objective is to give them that meaning," he said.

> We have opportunities to make customers' lives better by making them feel good about the world around them because someone was friendly to them. Little touches of human kindness can literally change their day. If I deliver that human kindness, I wind up feeling better about myself as well. At the end of our careers, we can look back and say, "I was part of something special."

PepsiCo Chair and CEO Indra Nooyi has a clear vision of what makes up a good company. She cited four characteristics: (1) returns value to shareholders, (2) nourishes people and societies, (3) minimizes its impact on the environment, and (4) cherishes its employees. Her multifaceted purpose expresses how organizations should add value to all of their stakeholders. She said, "Every company has a soul, made up of all the people who comprise the enterprise."

> Employees do not want to park their persona at the door. They want to work for a company where they can bring their whole selves to work—a company that cares about the world. Every good CEO has to remain focused on their True North.

Nooyi was born in Chennai, India, and attended Madras Christian College and the Indian Institute of Management Calcutta before immigrating to America in 1976 to attend the Yale School of Management, where she received her master's degree. After working in strategy at several leading organizations, she joined PepsiCo in 1994.

When she was elected CEO in 2006, Nooyi foresaw that the coming health crisis would lead people to shift to healthy foods and beverages. So she embarked on a strategy to broaden PepsiCo's product mix from primarily sugar-based drinks and high-fat foods to a much better balance of healthy products, such as Quaker Oats, Gatorade, Tropicana juices, and many newer health-oriented products.

She labeled her strategy "Performance with Purpose" to emphasize the importance of achieving near-term performance targets while the company was moving toward its long-term purpose. Nooyi took major steps in executing this strategy, including making acquisitions in emerging markets. In every meeting she had and every speech she gave, she rallied PepsiCo's 275,000 employees around this common purpose.

Meanwhile, archrival Coca-Cola, led by Turkish-born Muhtar Kent, focused primarily on Coke's traditional soft drink brands. In 2009, Coke gained the upper hand when it captured the top two spots in soft drink market share, leading to criticism of Nooyi for neglecting Pepsi's traditional strengths in soft drinks. Instead of backing down, she beefed up Pepsi's soft drink marketing while continuing with her 2006 diversification strategy and made several changes in her top management team. Her moves paid off in results between 2011 and 2014 as PepsiCo regained lost share and broadened its business. In those three years, PepsiCo handily outpaced Coke as its stock price increased more than double its major competitor.

Well after PepsiCo's turnaround and the success of Nooyi's strategy was clearly established, activist investor Nelson Peltz bought 0.7 percent of its shares and proposed that Nooyi abandon her strategy. Instead, he demanded that she purchase Mondelez, the spin-off of Kraft's international business; combine it with PepsiCo's food business; and spin off its beverage business. Nooyi was prepared for such an assault. PepsiCo's internal analysis attributed $1 billion in annual profits from the combination of snacks and beverages. Nooyi held her ground and continued to pursue her purpose-based strategy. In early 2015, Peltz agreed to drop his breakup campaign in exchange for PepsiCo adding the former CEO of H. J. Heinz to its board.

Nooyi's example demonstrates the importance of tenacity in pursuing a clear mission, and aligning everyone around it, which is essential to ensuring realization of the strategy. Naturally, there will be setbacks, such as PepsiCo's shortfall in 2009, and voices calling for alternative approaches, as Peltz did. These are the test of the depth of your belief as a leader in your purpose and in your organization.

Keeping Your True North and Purpose in Sync

Your leadership purpose is how you activate your True North to make a difference in the world. If you're starting an organization, its purpose should reflect your True North. On the other hand, if you work in an organization that already has a mission, you need to find congruence between your True North and the organization's mission. If you cannot, you won't find fulfillment from your work.

Looking back on Ken Frazier's story, we can see he has aligned his True North of serving others with Merck's mission of medicine "for the people." Similarly, when I walked into Medtronic I felt called by its mission of restoring people to full health. In both instances, we were joining an organization that already had a strong mission we believed in.

In other cases, the alignment is less strong. At PepsiCo, Indra Nooyi sensed this, and as CEO, she ultimately made hard decisions to change the mission and strategy of PepsiCo to emphasize the company's purpose in leading the shift to healthy foods and beverages. Earlier in my career, I struggled to relate to the mission of Honeywell and tried to use my executive role to improve the company. When I realized Honeywell was changing me more than I was changing it, I decided to move to Medtronic.

Occasionally, leaders find their work and the mission of their organizations are incompatible with their True North. For instance, Seth Moulton exited from the railroad company that had a paralyzed leadership structure and dysfunctional culture. Steve Rothschild left General Mills because he could not relate to the company's mission.

For many of us, how and where we apply our purpose evolves throughout our lifetime—the thread William Stafford writes about in the poem at the beginning of this chapter. Yet a constant source of our purpose—our True North—stays the same as we navigate life's changes and new opportunities present themselves. As long as you stay on the course of your True North, you are moving inexorably through life with commitment and passion.

Exercise: The Purpose of My Leadership

In this exercise, you will focus on the purpose of your leadership and how your purpose is derived from your life story, your passions, and your motivated capabilities.

1. Recall your early life story (addressed in the exercises for Chapter 1 and Chapter 3), and use it to identify sources of the passions that are close to your heart.

2. By reframing your life story, can you discern your passions more clearly?

3. In what ways do your passions lead you to the purpose of your leadership?

4. Write a letter to yourself describing the long-term purpose of your leadership. For the near term, what is your purpose in leading? In what ways does the purpose of your leadership relate to the rest of your life? Is it integral to it or separate from it?

11

EMPOWERMENT

Where is the spiritual value in rowing? The losing of self
entirely to the cooperative effort of the crew as a whole.
—*George Yeoman Pocock, boatbuilder,*
1936 Olympic gold medal winner

Leaders who make the transformation from *I* to *We* and know the purpose of their leadership are able to develop an emotional connection with their followers that gives them the credibility to lead. They need the skills to empower people throughout their organizations, especially first-line employees, around a common mission and set of values.

In the past, many leaders relied on their positional power over subordinates to drive performance. That hierarchical approach rarely works with today's employees, especially the younger generation of millennials, who are highly resistant to being directed by their bosses. Instead, they seek leaders who inspire them and give them the freedom to decide *how* they will achieve results.

Authentic leaders focus on building personal relationships with people and empowering them to lead, each in his or her own way. In the long run, empowerment is far more successful in developing leaders, building healthy cultures, and achieving sustainable results than the traditional hierarchical approach.

Anne Mulcahy: Empowering People in Crisis

Anne Mulcahy is an exceptional leader who was called upon to lead Xerox through the greatest crisis in its history. Thrust into a

position she never anticipated, Mulcahy demonstrated a remarkable ability to rally Xerox's 96,000 employees around a common
purpose. Her empowering approach not only averted bankruptcy
but also built the healthy culture that today her successor, Ursula
Burns, leads.

Back in 2000, becoming CEO of Xerox was the furthest thing
from Mulcahy's mind. One day, as Mulcahy was preparing for a
business trip to Japan, chairman Paul Allaire came to her office and
told her he planned to recommend that the Xerox board terminate
its current CEO and promote her to COO and eventually CEO. She
was so shocked that she asked for the evening to discuss it with her
family. The next day she accepted the job.

The board's decision surprised Mulcahy as well as everyone else.
In her 25 years at Xerox, she built a network of strong, trusting
relationships. She worked in field sales and on the corporate staff but
not in finance, research and development (R&D), or manufacturing.
At the time, she was enjoying her first general management assignment, running a relatively small business outside the Xerox
mainstream.

> *It was like going to war, knowing it was the right thing for the company and
> there was so much at stake. This was a job that would dramatically change my
> life, requiring every ounce of energy I had. I never expected to be CEO, nor
> was I groomed for it.*

What no one understood was that Xerox was facing a massive
liquidity crisis and was on the verge of bankruptcy. Its revenues were
declining, its sales force had been unraveling, and its new-product
pipeline was depleted. The company had $18 billion in debt and its
credit lines were exhausted. Morale inside the company had plum-
meted, and its share price was in free fall. Xerox had just one week of
cash on hand, so its external advisers were recommending that the
company consider bankruptcy. To make matters worse, Xerox's CFO
was preoccupied with a Securities and Exchange Commission
investigation into the company's revenue recognition practices.

As the situation moved from bad to worse, Mulcahy recognized how high the bankruptcy risks were.

> My greatest fear was that I was sitting on the deck of the Titanic and I'd get to drive it to the bottom of the ocean—not exactly a moment to be proud of. Nothing spooked me so much as waking up in the middle of the night and thinking about 96,000 employees and retirees and what would happen if things went south.

How did Mulcahy cope with this crisis when she had had no financial experience? She brought strong relationships and an impeccable understanding of the organization. She bled Xerox and everyone knew it. To ameliorate the gaps in her experience, she asked the treasurer's office to tutor her on finance and surrounded herself with a diverse set of leaders.

As she discovered the depth of the company's problems, Mulcahy's purpose became clear: to save Xerox from bankruptcy and restore it to its former greatness. Her challenge was to unite the disheartened organization and get leaders throughout the company to step up. "I get things done by identifying with the people in the company and trusting them," she said. "I care most about building a good team to lead the company."

Mulcahy met personally with the top 100 executives to ask whether they would stay with the company despite the challenges ahead. "I knew there were people who weren't supportive of me," she said.

> So I confronted a couple of them and said, "Hey, no games. Let's just talk. You can't be thrilled. If you choose to stay, either we're totally in sync or when you go, it won't be pleasant, because I have no appetite for managing right now. This is about the company."

The first two people she talked to, both of whom ran big operating units, decided to leave, but the remaining 98 committed to stay. They did so because they believed in Mulcahy. She also appealed to their character and to their desire to save the company they loved.

Ursula Burns, who succeeded Mulcahy in 2009, expressed her own loyalty to the company that had given her so much.

> *I have been to almost every country in the world. I have a wonderful life and great friends, more than I ever imagined. It all came from a partnership between me and this company. What do you say when times are tough? "Thank you very much, I'll see you later?" That's not what my mother taught me.*

After the initial conversations with Mulcahy, the team came together quickly and was heartened by the number of their colleagues who stayed on. "We had dinner in the conference room off the cafeteria," said Burns. "We all looked around, pleased at how many stayed, and said, 'Okay, fine, we're in this together. Let's go. What do we have to do to survive?'"

Instead of endless rounds of meetings at headquarters, Mulcahy visited customers' offices and rode with field salespeople to see whether she could help stem the tide of customer defections and field-sales resignations. She told the sales force, "I will go anywhere, anytime, to save a Xerox customer." Her customer engagement contrasted sharply with that of her predecessor, who rarely traveled outside headquarters. It sent an important signal that solidified the Xerox field organization and restored customer confidence.

Yet Mulcahy was both challenging and demanding, holding people publicly accountable for their results. Despite the tremendous pressures the company was under, she set realistic expectations. "You can't wish your way to good performance," she said. "If you set the bar someplace that buys you 90 days of stock market esteem, you will eventually get killed. Boy, is it ugly."

She encouraged senior managers to engage each other directly. "We talk about everything," said Burns. "Anne is really clear: 'Make sure you get it.'" Mulcahy did not take the lead in every discussion, playing instead what Burns described as an orchestrating role. "She's very good at reading people," Burns explained, "and getting us to work together."

The bankruptcy question came to a head in October 2000. Earlier in the month, Mulcahy candidly told the company's shareholders that Xerox's business model was unsustainable. The next day, the stock dropped 26 percent. She noted, "This was my baptism by fire."

Mulcahy had traditionally drawn support by interacting with her peers, but in her new role she had to provide her team confidence that the company could survive—in spite of personal doubts she had. "As a touchy-feely people person, the hardest thing was that my new role required some distance I wasn't prepared for." Yet Mulcahy was not immune from uncertainty and stress.

One day I came back to the office from Japan and found it had been a dismal day. Around 8:30 PM on my way home, I pulled over to the side of the Merritt Parkway and said to myself, "I don't know where to go. I don't want to go home. There's just no place to go."

Have you ever felt like that? In my experience, feelings of loneliness and despair are quite common for leaders, but most do not have the courage to admit it. In times like these, you need the support of your colleagues. Mulcahy explained, "I picked up my voice mail and listened to a message from chief strategist Jim Firestone: 'This may seem like the worst day, but we believe in you. This company will have a great future.'" That was all Mulcahy needed to drive home and come to work inspired the next day. "The team gave me incredible supportive strength. We fight, we debate, but at the end of the day, they've been extremely loyal and supportive."

When the company's external advisers argued that Xerox should prepare for a bankruptcy filing to relieve the $18 billion debt burden, Mulcahy exploded.

I told them, "You don't understand what it's like to be an employee in this company—to fight and win. Bankruptcy's never a win. I'm not going there until there's no other decision to be made. There are a lot more cards to play."

I was so angry because they could not comprehend the passion and drive that's required to succeed and the impact of bankruptcy on the company's employees. Our people believed we were in a war we could win.

Anne Mulcahy did win in the end. She staved off bankruptcy by cutting billions in operating expenses without touching R&D or field sales and by reducing debt by 60 percent. In launching 60 new products with new color and digital technology, she restored revenue and profit growth.

What distinguished Mulcahy's leadership was her ability to empower people to rise to the challenge and to keep them focused on the shared mission of saving and restoring Xerox. Authentic leaders, such as Mulcahy, recognize the collective power of an empowered team far exceeds that of any single individual, and they rally teams around a common cause.

The Engaged Leader

The capacity to develop close and enduring relationships is one mark of empowering leaders. Unfortunately, many leaders of major companies believe their job is to create the strategy, organizational structure, and organizational processes. Then they delegate the work to be done, remaining aloof from the people doing the work.

The detached style of leadership will not be successful in the twenty-first century. Today's employees demand more personal relationships with their leaders before they will give themselves fully to their jobs. They insist on having access to their leaders, knowing that it is in the openness and the depth of the relationship with the leader that trust and commitment are built. Bill Gates, Steve Jobs, and Jack Welch were so successful because they connected directly with their employees and realized from them a deeper commitment to their work and greater loyalty to the company. Welch, in particular, was an interesting case because he was so challenging and hard on people. Yet those very challenges let people know that he was interested in their success and concerned about their careers.

In *Eyewitness to Power*, David Gergen writes, "At the heart of leadership is the leader's relationship with followers. People will entrust their hopes and dreams to another person only if they think the other is a reliable vessel." Authentic leaders establish trusting relationships with people throughout their organizations. The rewards of these relationships, both tangible and intangible, are long lasting.

Woody Allen once remarked, "Eighty percent of success is showing up." Surprisingly, many leaders get so busy that they don't take the time to be there for people. They don't bother to attend award ceremonies, company picnics, or sales meetings. Nor do they walk around the offices, factories, labs, and field sales and service locations. Often they are too busy to come to important customer meetings or trade shows. As a result, their teammates never get to know them personally. Their only contact with their leaders is through impersonal media, such as speeches, voice mail, videotapes, and Web streaming of company events.

Target CEO Brian Cornell makes frequent visits to stores around the country, often going alone and unannounced, shaking hands and getting to know people, as well as using his astute powers of observation to see how effective Target team members are in connecting with their guests. These visits have given him a clear understanding of his new organization and what needs to be improved. It also led to what he termed "the most difficult decision of my career"—to close his predecessor's ill-fated foray into Canada. Not only did Cornell have multiple business analyses prepared to search for a way forward, but he also visited nearly empty stores the week before Christmas and realized that Target's efforts should focus entirely on the lucrative U.S. market.

Likewise, Howard Schultz told of visiting a Starbucks store one Saturday morning:

> I walked in, dressed so nobody would recognize me. When I sat down, the manager came up and said, "Howard, is that you?" I said, "Yes, it is." She told me about receiving Starbucks stock and what it did for her and her family. Then

she started crying and said, "I'm so moved that you're in my store." Later I got a voice mail from her, saying how powerful that moment was for her. I immediately called her back and thanked her for sharing with me.

Stories of basic human interactions like this one are very powerful. All Cornell and Schultz had to do was show up. Being at important events or engaging on the front lines at unexpected times means a great deal to people and enables them to take their leaders off their proverbial pedestals and see them as real people.

Mutual Respect: The Basis for Empowerment

To bring out the best from teammates, authentic leaders must develop trusting relationships based on mutual respect. There is no substitute. Like loyalty, respect provides a basis for empowerment, but leaders must earn it. Here are some of the things empowering leaders do to gain the respect of their colleagues:

- Treat others as equals
- Listen actively
- Learn from people
- Share life stories
- Align around the mission

Treat Others as Equals

We respect people who treat us as equals, especially when they are successful investors, such as Warren Buffett. He has the same sandwich and Cherry Coke combination with a group of wide-eyed students as he does with his close friend Bill Gates. Buffett does not rely upon his image to make people feel he is important or powerful. He genuinely respects others, and they respect him as much for those qualities as for his investment prowess. By being authentic in his interactions, Buffett empowers people to lead in their own authentic way.

Listen Actively

We are grateful when people genuinely *listen* to us. Active listening is one of the most important abilities of empowering leaders, because people sense such individuals are genuinely interested in them and not just trying to get something from them. Warren Bennis was an example of a world-class listener. He patiently listened as you explained your ideas and then thoughtfully contributed astute observations that came from a deep well of wisdom and experience.

Learn from People

We feel respected when others believe they can learn from us or ask for our advice. The best advice I ever got about teaching came from my Harvard Business School (HBS) colleague Paul Marshall, who was one of HBS's greatest teachers. He told me, "Bill, don't ever set foot in an HBS classroom unless you genuinely want to learn from the students." I have taken his advice into every class I have taught for the past 12 years, telling MBA students and executives, "I feel certain I will learn a lot more from you than you do from me." The students find that hard to believe at first, but they soon see how their feedback helps me understand how today's leaders and MBA students think.

Share Life Stories

When leaders are willing to be open and share their personal stories and vulnerabilities, people feel empowered to share their own stories and uncertainties in return. On Thanksgiving eve in 1996, I sent an e-mail to all Medtronic employees, expressing my gratitude for the support Penny and I received following her ordeal with breast cancer and chemotherapy. We were overwhelmed by the number of people who spontaneously shared their stories with us.

Align around the Mission

The most empowering condition of all is when the entire organization aligns with its mission, and people's passions and purpose
synchronize with each other. It is not easy to get to this position,
especially if the organization has a significant number of cynics or
disgruntled people. Nonetheless, it is worth whatever effort it takes
to create an aligned environment, including removal of those who
don't support the mission.

Individuals usually have their own passions that drive them. If
the organization's leaders can demonstrate how employees can fulfill
their purpose while achieving the organization's mission, then
alignment can occur. Authentic leaders empower others to use their
gifts and step up to leadership, regardless of their titles or roles in the
organization.

Several years ago, I visited Medtronic's heart valve factory in
Southern California, where employees reconfigure valves from pig
hearts to replace failed human heart valves. The process requires
extremely skilled workers because it is more art than science. On the
factory floor, I met the top producer, a Laotian immigrant who made
a thousand valves a year. When I asked her the key to her process,
she looked at me with passion in her eyes and said, "Mr. George, my
job is to make heart valves that save lives."

> Before I sign my name to a completed valve, I decide whether it is good enough
> to put in my mother or my son. Unless it meets that standard, it does not pass. If
> just one of the valves I make is defective, someone may die. To the company
> 99.9 percent quality may be acceptable, but I could not live with myself if I
> caused someone's death. But when I go home at night, I fall asleep thinking
> about the 5,000 people who are alive today because of heart valves I made.

Can there be any question that she is a leader among her peers?
She has a passion for her work that is tied directly to the company's
mission, she sets high standards for herself, and she sets an example
for everyone else to emulate. That's the kind of leader we need at
all levels.

Creating an Empowered Culture

How do leaders create a culture that infuses empowerment throughout the organization? It starts with how the leaders on top behave every day. They cannot preach empowerment and then behave in a hierarchical manner to get near-term results, or they lose credibility with their colleagues. Nor can they reward or even tolerate power-driven managers who behave like jerks to get results and often play political games in their organizations. These people need to be moved out of the organization for the culture to be internally consistent with empowerment. Then they need to reward leaders at all levels who empower their colleagues and subordinates and recognize them publicly.

Empowering leaders engage actively with their colleagues by counseling them, offering suggestions, or assisting them in making vital contacts. For example, as CEO of Merck, Roy Vagelos ate regularly in the company cafeteria, where he asked people about their work and the challenges they were facing. He took notes about the conversations and then thought about the specific problems for a few days before calling the employees back with his ideas.

Imagine how Merck researchers must have felt when they picked up the phone to hear Vagelos getting back to them. "I'd call them up and say, 'That's a tough problem, but here are a couple things you might try,'" Vagelos said. "People love to have involvement of the leader. They feel you want to help them and are part of the solution." These interactions reinforced the importance of the researchers' work and had a multiplier effect upon employees.

Marilyn Carlson Nelson: From Sweatshop to Empowerment

Carlson chair and CEO Marilyn Carlson Nelson dramatically transformed the company founded by her father, Curtis Carlson. Carlson was a consummate salesman and a tough, demanding boss. Seeing her leaving the office at 7:30 one night, Carlson asked his daughter whether she had lost her enthusiasm for the business. "Monday through Friday are about staying even with the competition," he often said. "Saturday is when you get ahead."

The elder Carlson taught his daughter about business but didn't encourage her to join the company until her children were grown, believing that the workplace was not meant for mothers. After giving birth to her first child, Nelson worked from her home as publisher of Carlson's employee newspaper and was promoted to department head. When she told her father, his response was blunt: "You're getting too involved in the business. You should be at home with your children." Added Nelson, "My father fired me on the spot. I left the building with tears running down my face."

While raising her family, Nelson got deeply involved in the Minneapolis community, chairing the Minnesota Orchestral Association, creating a "Scandinavia Today" celebration and bringing the 1992 (and later the 2018) Super Bowl to Minnesota on the coldest weekend of the year. She also became the first woman to serve on the boards of major local corporations and was coowner of a rural bank. As her business profile rose, her father repeatedly rebuffed her interest in the family company.

When her last child went off to college, Nelson finally rejoined Carlson at age 48. In her first month, she accompanied her father to a presentation by MBA students at Minnesota's Carlson School about their research into Carlson's corporate culture. Nelson recalled asking how the students saw Carlson. No one dared to answer. Finally, one student said, "Carlson is perceived as a sweatshop that doesn't care about people. Our professors don't recommend we work for Carlson." Nelson was stunned. "That meeting lit a fire under me," she said. She realized then she needed to shift the corporate culture away from her father's top-down, autocratic style.

When Nelson's brother-in-law abruptly departed as CEO two years later, her 80-year-old father returned to active management. Nelson took on more prominent operational roles but still was not designated as successor. Meanwhile, key executives left the company, frustrated by Carlson's command-and-control style. Eventually,

Nelson assumed responsibility for key Carlson divisions and began to reshape the company's leadership and strategy.

At the celebration for her father on the company's sixtieth anniversary, she was finally named CEO. Undaunted, Carlson cautioned his daughter against relying on others. "Be very careful," he told her, "You can't trust anyone besides yourself." Nelson had just the opposite point of view, feeling that trust would work in a caring environment. "If you create a supportive environment, you can attract people who are trustworthy, so long as you trust them and you are trustworthy yourself," she explained.

Nelson transformed a fear-driven culture into a more supportive culture by focusing on employees and customers. "In the command-and-control environment," she explained, "my dad robbed himself of the opportunity to hear contrarian views."

> The contrarian view forces you to either understand or change your position. I moved to a collaborative mode of management. Now we rely on everybody to bring their wisdom and experience to bear on decisions. I believe that collective wisdom has great value when it comes from solid thinking. Ultimately, the leader still has to make the final decision.

Nelson decided to reinvent Carlson as a company that cared for customers by creating the most caring environment for its employees. She shifted emphasis away from stewardship of financial capital toward acquiring and cultivating human capital. She looked for three characteristics in employees: character, competence, and caring. "The need for character as absolute trustworthiness, and competence in the form of global experience, expertise, and judgment, are not surprising," Nelson explained, "but the characteristic of caring was not self-evident."

> I looked for people who had "a servant's heart." Servant leadership is an important driver of the culture we want to create. Satisfied employees create satisfied customers. In the service business, customers understand very quickly whether you legitimately care about serving them.

Nelson recognized these values had to be embraced by Carlson locations worldwide if they were to become key behaviors for every Carlson employee. She traveled tirelessly to meet with company employees and customers around the world. "We can build relationships only if employees are affirmed and empowered, have clarity of direction, and understand the company's mission," she said. "We cannot just teach restaurant employees to put a meal on the table. They have to customize the experience depending on whether customers want privacy or an evening of fun."

Reflecting on the changes she led at the company, Nelson proudly said that no MBA student today could conclude that Carlson does not care about people. "You cannot change a culture in six months," she explained. "It takes time to build transparency and collaborative discussion into the culture." Having suffered from her daughter's death 20 years before, Nelson reaffirmed her personal mission "to use every tool at hand as an opportunity to give back or make life better for people." Her transformation of Carlson's corporate culture to a collaborative environment is a remarkable example of how leaders can inspire employees around a common vision and empower them to lead.

Kent Thiry: The Mayor of DaVita

To outsiders, the culture of DaVita, which runs kidney dialysis centers, appears highly unusual, perhaps even a bit weird. Company meetings are filled with sports-event-like cheers and skits, and CEO Kent Thiry runs around in a *Three Musketeers* costume, brandishing a sword. Even Thiry acknowledges, "People new to the village think these practices are cheesy, foolish, and superficial."

Every country has sports teams, military organizations, and religious groups with their own chants, cheers, songs, and slogans. It isn't the DaVita culture that is weird, but rather the companies that have emotionally sterile environments that don't inspire people in their work. Given the percent of people's lives spent at work, why shouldn't it be fun and fulfilling at the same time?

Thiry's approaches to creating an empowering culture emanated from his unfortunate experience of liquidating his previous company, Vivra Specialty Partners (VSP). Physically and emotionally drained, Thiry believed the failure of VSP marked the end of his private-sector career. He and his wife, Denise O'Leary, agreed to take time off from their careers to devote their energy to their family. When Thiry was offered the opportunity to lead DaVita a few weeks later, his wife was furious. "That is a disgustingly testosterone-driven idea!" she exclaimed. So he turned it down initially. When she saw how depressed he was, she told him, "You're a head case. Just go do the darn thing."

When Thiry became CEO of DaVita, he recognized the emotional challenges his employees faced working in dialysis centers where patients spent an average of 12 hours per week and 20 percent died each year, even with the best care available. Thus, he sought ways to create an upbeat, communal atmosphere in each center and a deep sense of caring between patients and DaVita employees.

Throughout DaVita, he wanted to create a differentiated organization that behaved like a community, where people supported each other and felt the same passion for their workplace as they did for their churches and local sports teams. Thiry wanted to replicate the community he found in the old-style, small Wisconsin town where he grew up. He gave himself the title of Mayor of DaVita and adopted themes from his favorite movie, *The Three Musketeers*.

Hearing Thiry speak often about his company's culture, I decided to experience it firsthand. I quickly saw the exceptionally high level of passion, enthusiasm, and commitment on the part of every DaVita employee I met. Rather than judging DaVita's culture as different, I found myself agreeing with Thiry's contention that it is the emotionally sterile culture of many companies that is weird.

Just as we created a strong sense of community built around patients at Medtronic, I asked myself, "Why shouldn't all companies do the same?" Multiple surveys by Gallup have shown that only 30 percent of employees are engaged with their work. That's a disaster and tragic loss of human potential. No wonder so many employees feel burned out and turnover is so high. Think what inspiring workplaces we could have if most companies created empowering working environments like Carlson and DaVita have.

Tony Hsieh's Radical Transparency

As CEO of Zappos, Tony Hsieh has a maniacal focus on culture. Zappos is the only shoe retailer in the world that has created tours of its call center because of the constant demand of business leaders who wanted to see the zany, exuberant, and customer-obsessed culture in action. Hsieh built the entire business on clear values and purpose. He communicates openly and often with everyone in the company, particularly front-line employees. In a company-wide e-mail he sent in November 2008 following a layoff, he wrote:

> Remember this is not my company, and this is not our investors' company. This company is all of ours, and it's up to all of us where we go from here. The power lies in each of us to move forward and come out as a team stronger than we've ever been in the history of the company.

In good times and bad times, Hsieh's communications are authentic, funny, and informal. He speaks directly and personally to his colleagues. His relentless focus is on the values that allow the company to create incredible customer service with few rules and little bureaucracy constraining Zappos employees. For instance, most call centers measure employee performance on average handle time to reduce call length and maximize productivity. Zappos eliminated this metric as well as call scripts and upsells to enable their employees to connect directly with customers and deliver better service.

Hsieh's empowerment of employees has unlocked incredible potential in the organization. He said if you get the culture right, everything else falls into place. As a result, Zappos grew rapidly for 10 years until its $1.2 billion acquisition by Amazon.com in 2009.

Leaders like Mulcahy, Nelson, Thiry, and Hsieh have discovered that empowering people throughout their organizations with passion and purpose delivers far superior results than what can be accomplished by forcing subordinates to be loyal followers. By giving others the latitude to lead within the organization's broad purpose, they are able to delegate more of their leadership responsibilities while expanding the impact of their leadership to more people.

Empowerment Is Accountability

The term *empowerment* is often misunderstood as "freedom to do your own thing." Actually, real empowerment must be accompanied by a high degree of accountability to deliver on your commitments. I encountered this misunderstanding when I first joined Medtronic and spoke frequently about creating a culture of empowerment. One day, I was confronted by a senior executive, saying it was not very empowering for me to challenge her results. Several weeks later, she came back and said, "Now we understand you better. When you talk about empowerment, you really mean 'empowerment with accountability,'" to which I responded, "Is there any other kind?" Successful leaders are closed-loop managers who follow up regularly with their team to ensure they are getting results and provide assistance as needed.

Alan Mulally: Empowerment with Closed-Loop Accountability

Alan Mulally is an empowering leader who brings his team together to gain agreement on goals and objectives yet is rigorous in following up to get candid reports on progress. Throughout my career, I have heard middle managers who don't respond well to careful monitoring classify Mulally's approach as "micromanagement." I disagree. Empowered leaders must be wholly accountable for their actions and transparent about their results, or the results are anarchy and politics, both of which lead to poor performance.

In 2006, Mulally arrived at Ford from Boeing as the new CEO, wearing a sport coat and slacks, attire quite distinct from Ford's buttoned-up executives. He noticed when he drove into the company parking garage that there were no Fords in the garage, strange for a company whose eponymous auto was also its largest seller. He was immediately escorted up to his enormous office, where a cadre of aides—a total of 30—greeted him, offering to take his coat and pour his coffee. Within a month, they were all gone, replaced by the assistant who came with him from Boeing.

Walking into the enormous office that Henry Ford II once occupied, Mulally gazed out the panoramic windows at the Rouge Plant, the automobile industry's most famous factory. After telling an aide he would like to walk through the plant and meet the employees, he was informed that "our executives don't talk directly to factory employees." With that, he insisted on going there immediately. Mulally's initial meetings convinced him that Ford's problems were far deeper than the staggering losses projected for the year. An intuitive leader who knows far more than he lets on, Mulally understood he was facing a broken culture requiring a massive overhaul.

Born in Kansas and true to his roots, Mulally lacks pretension and approaches people with a warm, "aw shucks" demeanor that immediately puts people at ease. At Ford, Mulally's style was low-key and down-to-earth—a marked contrast with the air of sophistication and palace court politics that preceded him. He wrote notes with smileys, engaged in casual conversations, popped into meetings unannounced, and often offered hugs. Many of Ford's executives underestimated him at first, describing his approach as corny. As Bryce Hoffman describes Mulally in *American Icon*, the definitive book on his turnaround of Ford, "Mulally's character was an odd mix of guilelessness and relentless determination that was born of an austere childhood and a lifelong desire to write his name across the sky."

Mulally joined Boeing in 1969 and worked his way up to head of its troubled commercial aviation division, leading a spectacular turnaround that positioned him to become Boeing's next CEO. Yet the forced resignations of CEOs Phil Condit and Harry

Stonecipher for misconduct caused the Boeing board to go outside its ranks to recruit 3M's CEO, Jim McNerney, as its new CEO.

Even then, Mulally bled Boeing blue. Only a personal telephone call from Bill Ford, great-grandson of Henry Ford, could have opened up his thinking to a career change. After extensive discussions with Ford and his board members, Mulally declined the Ford CEO role in favor of staying at Boeing. Eventually Ford board members persuaded him to accept the challenge of saving one of America's most iconic companies.

It didn't take Mulally long to realize the depth of Ford's problems. In spite of $12.7 billion in losses, the largest in Ford's history, nobody on Mulally's new executive team was willing to acknowledge its problems. Mulally told me that the company—along with its Detroit competitors, General Motors and Chrysler—had been going out of business for the prior 30 years, yet no one was willing to face that reality. Realizing decisive action was required to give Ford a cushion against further problems and economic downturns, Mulally approved a plan to borrow $23.5 billion, leveraging Ford's entire balance sheet and the iconic Ford oval as collateral.

Mulally then established a strategy of meeting customer needs with a complete lineup of superior cars and trucks—not just sport utility vehicles and trucks—while insisting that Ford's factory costs in its unionized U.S. facilities had to be equivalent to nonunion factories in the South. This required a landmark agreement with the United Automobile Workers involving half-wage positions to bring the production of midsize autos back to Michigan, which the company's unionized workforce ratified in 2007. Meanwhile, Mulally narrowed the company's brands to Ford and Lincoln while spinning off luxury brands, such as Jaguar and Land Rover.

At a weekly business performance review (BPR), Mulally brought together his direct reports for a full day of in-depth, fact-based reviews of Ford's business. During these meetings, he dove into the details several levels deeper than any senior executive had done previously and expected candid appraisals. He used a green, yellow, and red color coding system to assess the status of key projects. Given the depth of the company's problems, he was puzzled when every project was coded green.

At his fifth BPR, he confronted his team about the dichotomy between billions of losses and their consistent reports of positive progress. "Is there anything that's not going well here?" he asked. Nobody responded. The following week, Americas president Mark Fields faced reality with a red indication that a key new vehicle launch had to be held up. Although Fields's colleagues all thought he would be fired, instead Mulally clapped, saying, "Mark, that is great visibility." Mulally not only accepted problems but also consciously shifted the focus to problem solving. He echoed the same encouragement throughout his conversations: "You *have* a problem . . . *You* are not the problem."

Remarkably, Mulally made few personnel changes upon assuming the CEO position. Rather, he changed the culture by getting each leader immersed in the details of the business and working like a team to improve performance. One of those executives, International president Mark Schulz fiercely resisted Mulally's approaches, refusing to get into details and calling in sick for meetings, in part because he thought he could do an end run to chairman Bill Ford. It didn't work. Schulz was the first member of Mulally's team to go.

Turnarounds such as Ford's do not occur by happenstance. Leaders set the vision and then empower their teams to achieve it. Mulally rallied Ford employees with openness and candor. He never asked more of team members than he was willing to give himself. He had a unique ability to combine genuine caring for his people with real accountability for their results. His brand of tough love involved both toughness and caring: He was tough enough to transform Ford's executive suite and caring enough to empower senior leaders and rally Ford's employees around a new vision for global competitiveness.

What happened to Mark Fields, the executive who came clean about his problems? He became Mulally's successor in 2014.

Your Leadership Style

The topic of style has been saved for last because the style of an effective leader must come from an authentic place. That can happen only when you have a high level of self-awareness, are clear about your values, and understand your leadership purpose. Your style should be *the outward manifestation of your authentic leadership*. Style without authenticity makes you a persona. Without this clarity, your style will be shaped by the expectations of your organization or the outside world and will not be seen as authentic. Nor will it be empowering to people.

Many organizations work hard to get young leaders to embrace the company's normative leadership style, sending them to training programs to bring their styles into line. Therein lies the risk: Will you have to compromise who you are to succeed in the organization? If you do, you will feel like an imposter, trying to be something you are not.

One of the most important observations about the empowering leaders profiled in this chapter—Anne Mulcahy, Roy Vagelos, Marilyn Carlson Nelson, Kent Thiry, Tony Hsieh, and Alan Mulally—is that they all have unique styles that work effectively for them. None of us could ever succeed by emulating their styles.

In thinking about your leadership style, ask yourself these questions, and consider where you fit among the categories shown in Figure 11.1:

- Is your leadership style consistent with your leadership principles and values?
- How do you adapt your style to the circumstances facing you?
- Are you concerned whether your authentic style will be acceptable in your organization?
- Do you worry that you may have to modify your style to get ahead?

The directive style of leadership was common in the past, especially in military and manufacturing operations. It is still needed

Directive:	Demand compliance and obedience with rules
Engaged:	Mobilize people around shared purpose and values
Coaching:	Develop people for leadership roles
Consensus:	Build agreement through participation
Affiliative:	Create emotional bonds and harmony
Expert:	Expect competence and self-direction

Figure 11.1 Leadership Styles

during crises when time is of the essence. As more companies are built on knowledge workers, however, the directive style has proved ineffective in motivating people to take initiative or be creative.

The most common style to emerge in recent years is the engaged style. Leaders such as Anne Mulcahy and Alan Mulally are actively engaged with people at all levels of the organization—questioning, listening, motivating, and encouraging them to perform at a higher level—but always within the organization's shared purpose and values.

Coaching leaders, such as John Donahoe of eBay, bring out the best in people and develop them for future leadership roles. Usually such leaders are more concerned with people's development to achieve long-term results than they are with immediate outcomes.

Consensus leaders treat everyone on the team as equal and encourage everyone to participate in decision making. They are quite willing to take the time to reach conclusions, even to the point of postponing decisions, until a consensus emerges. Most nonprofit organizations need consensus leaders to motivate the various constituent groups.

Affiliative leaders build bonds of trust among people by keeping harmony among team members, even at the expense of near-term results. These leaders are often most effective at bringing out the best in their teammates by leading in subtle and restrained ways.

Expert leaders, such as Craig Venter, rely heavily on their own knowledge and expertise. They are often found in scientific organizations, consulting, and financial services, where individual stars rise to leadership positions. They tend to listen to other experts while demanding that their teammates exhibit equally high levels of knowledge and individual performance.

Within your authentic leadership, a range of styles is both effective and appropriate for the situation. You should adapt your leadership style to the capabilities of your teammates and their readiness to accept greater responsibility. For example, if your teammates need clear direction, they may not be ready to respond to a consensus style. Conversely, creative or independent thinkers will not respond positively to a directive style.

In leading, it is important to understand the situation in which you are operating, as well as the performance imperative, and have the flexibility to maximize your effectiveness *in that situation*. As Narayana Murthy said, "Leadership must always be put in a context. If you take the best corporate leaders and make them senators or president, they may not succeed because that is a different context." Once you understand the context, however, you can adjust your communication and leadership style to get results yet retain your authenticity.

Selecting Your Altitude

Kevin Sharer's experience at MCI taught him the value of a flexible leadership style, one that could vary with the needs of the business and the readiness of his team to operate autonomously. He describes style as the appropriate "altitude" for the level of specificity of the task at hand:

> At the highest altitude, you're asking the big questions: What are the company's mission and strategy? Do people understand and believe in these aims? At the lowest altitude, you're looking at on-the-ground operations: Did we make that sale? What was the yield on the last lot in the factory? In between, you ask questions like: Should we invest in a small biotechnology company that has a promising new drug? How many chemists should we hire this quarter?
>
> As a CEO, you've got to function at all of these levels simultaneously. I learned from Jack Welch the skill of rapidly shifting between levels, or even engaging several levels at once. Most CEOs tend to gravitate toward the altitude where they're most comfortable. Unfortunately, they get in trouble because they get stuck at a particular altitude.

Sharer acknowledged his own tendency to be preoccupied by the nitty-gritty details of a problem:

When I go into my submarine mode, I go very deep into a problem and think I can solve it myself. That's when I'm at risk of ignoring advice of experts and closing down debate. Moving nimbly in and out at different altitudes is crucial to leadership success, particularly in times of rapid growth and uncertainty.

As a leader, you should adopt a style that fits your personality but be flexible enough to adapt to the situation and the needs of your colleagues. Only in this way can you maintain your authenticity and empower people through a range of challenges.

Exercise: Empowering Other Leaders

1. Describe an example from your past where you have been effective in inspiring other leaders around a common purpose and shared values.

2. How effective are you today at empowering other people to step up and lead? How do you go about doing this? What are you doing to improve your effectiveness?

3. Recall a situation in which you faced a conflict between empowering other people and reaching your performance goals.

   a. How did you resolve the conflict?

   b. Did you give preference to reaching your goals or to your relationships?

   c. Would you act differently in the future when facing a conflict between relationships and performance?

12

GLOBAL LEADERSHIP

> The organization model of a global company by 2020
> is going to be very different than the traditional
> Western model. The culture that comes
> with it must be entirely different.
> —*Paul Polman, CEO, Unilever*

In this final chapter, we examine the challenges of leading in the global world. Corporate leaders recognize that today's interconnected and global world requires that they have new competencies. In global roles, you will be asked to demonstrate geopolitical savvy, reinvent business models for emerging markets, build diverse teams, and redesign organizational models. Thriving in this complex environment requires qualities above and beyond those of authentic leaders. To help you prepare for global leadership, we introduce the concept of global intelligence, or GQ, and explore how to develop the traits of GQ leadership.

Paul Polman: Transforming Unilever's Global Leadership

Under the leadership of CEO Paul Polman, Unilever has transformed itself into the leading global consumer products company. Polman was born and educated in the Netherlands. He spent 26 years with Unilever's archrival, Procter & Gamble, many of them in the United States and Europe, and then three years with Nestlé as CFO and head of the Americas. As the first Unilever chief executive recruited from outside the company, he faced a challenging turnaround when he became CEO in early 2009. For two decades, Unilever's revenues, profits, and market capitalization had been declining. In his interview for this book, Polman observed, "We had forgotten how to win in the marketplace."

Unilever was founded in 1929 through the merger of British soap maker Lever Brothers and Dutch margarine producer Margarine Unie. As an Anglo-Dutch company, Unilever historically had two boards of directors and rotated the CEO position between leaders of British and Dutch descent. This split, which led to internal struggles over the years, was resolved when Polman became CEO.

Shortly after Polman joined the company, a director told him, "You're a very nice guy, but you don't belong here because we always promote people internally." That comment energized him to study the company's history and to build on the legacy of Lord Leverhulme, who used Sunlight soap to help eliminate malaria in Britain. A unified Unilever board was established, with the company based in London. During Polman's tenure, Unilever's board has been diversified to include a Swedish chairman and directors from China, the United States, India, and South Africa.

In 2011, he startled the City of London, where most of Unilever's shares are traded, when he said, "My job is not to serve shareholders, but to serve Unilever's customers and consumers." In addition, he suspended guidance and reporting on quarterly earnings so that Unilever's executives could concentrate on its long-term strategy and transformation into the leading global consumer products company.

Polman understood Unilever's potential to help people throughout the world and build its mission around sustainability. He created the Unilever Sustainable Living Plan as the basis for Unilever's strategy. As Polman and his top 50 executives addressed these issues at a program we created for them, we concluded, "Sustainability *Is* Unilever's True North."

To transform Unilever's culture, Polman created the Compass, his internal set of mission, values, and strategy statements that emphasize growth and winning in the market. He simplified the company's product-geographic structure, reducing contact points from 200 to just 32, and created several global functions. "It is very clear that the organizational model of a global company by 2020 is going to be very different than the traditional Western model. The culture that comes with it must be entirely different," he noted.

At the outset he worried that Unilever's leadership team was too Eurocentric, because most executives came from the United Kingdom or the Netherlands. In his initial years, he changed 70 of Unilever's top 100 executives—half internally promoted and half recruited externally. He explained:

> We had to look for people with a growth mind-set who were externally focused and had passion for consumers and customers. I asked our leaders 10 questions focused on customers to see how much time they were spending with them. Their responses were embarrassing.

Yet he was impressed that the company already derived 41 percent of its revenues from emerging markets. He established the goal of generating 70 percent of revenues from emerging markets, a dramatic change in the company's geographic footprint. Six years into Polman's tenure, Unilever has 60 percent of its revenues from these markets.

> We want to create competitive advantage through the diversity of our people. Because the company's center of gravity is shifting to the East, we put our chief operating officer, a major business unit, and Four Acres Singapore, our new €44 million leadership development center, in Singapore. Today, we have more people there than in London.
>
> Unilever must have geographically distributed leaders, because I don't think the concept of head offices will be relevant in the future. You don't want product categories in a London-based, Anglo-Saxon model anymore, but rather dispersed globally. In addition, we put two big research centers in Bangalore and in China, and brought all of our engineering centers to India.

Unilever is working hard to develop more leaders from emerging markets. Polman said, "We are blessed to have many senior leaders from emerging markets compared to other companies, but we are still well underrepresented." COO Harish Manwani proposed, "If 70 percent of our business will be in emerging markets, ultimately 70 percent of our leaders must come from these markets." Added Polman: "We have to create new leadership cultures for the future, but do so with leaders who are running the business now."

> We need leaders who are more sensitive to the cultures of emerging markets, with higher levels of transparency, cooperation, and comfort with volatility. You have to expose your leadership team to crucible moments that make the lights go on for what their leadership must be.

Under Polman's leadership, Unilever has embarked on a visionary program for developing its global leaders—the Unilever Leadership Development Program (ULDP). Polman said, "ULDP prepares our future leaders for an increasingly volatile and uncertain world where the only true differentiation between companies is the quality of leadership."

Through the ULDP, Unilever has trained its top 600 global executives in authentic leadership. Participants build their EQ, discover their leadership purpose, and determine how they can integrate their purpose into Unilever's mission and strategy. As South African Gail Klintworth, Unilever's head of sustainability, explained:

> My participation in ULDP was transformational. It helped me understand that sustainability and improving people's lives are my driving strengths. I wanted a role that merged sustainability and business to prove that sustainable business is the only viable model. My new role is the perfect fit, but I wouldn't have been brave enough to take it had it not been for ULDP.

One of Polman's executive moves was to promote Leena Nair to global head of human resources. Nair, a career employee of Hindustan Unilever, was formerly head of human resources for South Asia and led global diversity. However, the move to London was a challenging one for her, as she noted:

> This was the moment I had always dreaded, as I had said I wasn't mobile because my husband runs a successful company in India. But Paul convinced me I needed to build networks and relationships with senior leaders and the board. Today, my two sons and I live in London and my husband splits his time.

Nair added:

> Unilever's leadership profile needs to reflect the world of 2020. We need more women in our leadership ranks, and a greater global footprint in our leaders. To transform the organization to compete for the future, we need people with a global mind-set and the ability to understand our complex global organization who can leverage its strengths.

Challenges of the Global Context

Over the long term, organizations run by leaders who are effective in operating globally will be more competitive, more productive, and more profitable. Taking advantage of the emerging markets in today's world of rapid-fire communication and global supply chains requires leaders who understand the rapidly changing global context in which they are operating.

Understanding Geopolitical Context

Today's world is far more uncertain than it was in the past, largely because of the rise of emerging markets with greater instability, speed of information technology, and interdependency of nations. To adapt to this rapidly changing world, companies need a clear understanding of the geopolitical context of their business and have a keen awareness of how geopolitical events can affect it. Will political unrest in Egypt delay a supplier? Will conflict in

Ukraine affect natural gas prices? Could a data center problem in India undermine your research center in Shanghai?

If your organization has a distributed global workforce with crossfunctional teams working across time zones, you can gain competitive advantage by accessing world-class talent, increasing productivity, and benefitting from comparative advantage in your organizational structure. When I was at Medtronic, software teams in Minneapolis uploaded their code each evening for continued development by their counterparts in India, which reduced product development cycles by 40 percent, cut costs, and increased quality. However, this global value chain also increased risk exposure to potential project delays and unexpected quality issues. What is the impact of a wild currency swing, a regional military conflict, or the passage of new adverse legal regulations? Navigating these challenges is not simple.

Reinventing Business Models

In mature markets, industry structures are often well defined. For example, the relationship between medical device makers and health care providers in the United States is a straightforward vendor-customer relationship in which doctors select devices for patients and maintain responsibility for the entire patient experience. In contrast, emerging markets offer the opportunity to create new business models and test them out.

When Omar Ishrak became CEO of Medtronic in 2011, he saw many opportunities for increased growth in emerging markets. Born in West Bengal (now Bangladesh) and educated in London, Ishrak exemplifies the new global leader. He worked for Dutch conglomerate Philips for eight years, eventually moving to ultrasound leader Diasonics and then to General Electric. "Since Philips was a Dutch company," he explained, "you couldn't advance unless you were Dutch. At an American company I felt I could have greater impact."

First, he broadened the company's predominantly American leadership team, adding six non-Americans to the company's executive committee. This immediately changed decision making at the top and placed increased emphasis on emerging markets. Next, his leadership team reenvisioned the medical technology ecosystem by introducing revolutionary new business models.

Ishrak explained, "What I learned at Medtronic caused me to think differently about globalization."

> Conventional wisdom is to make low-cost products in local product centers, cut prices, and you will globalize. Instead, I found our products were not being used by people who could afford them. So my priority shifted to education, training, patient and physician awareness, and building infrastructure.

This insight led to the creation of Medtronic University in Beijing to train physicians, as well as the establishment of patient centers throughout China to educate patients about their diseases. In India, diagnostic camps were created and guaranteed bank loans made to patients to finance their medical care. Even in Europe, Medtronic created new business models, such as building and operating catheterization labs that use Medtronic products.

Flipping the Headquarters Paradigm

Most multinational organizations deploy matrix structures that attempt to balance strategic business units with geographic organizations. In the past, multinationals sent talented expatriates from their home countries to lead regional and local units and to transfer headquarters standards, processes, control systems, and marketing approaches to local countries. It was the rare foreign national who made it to the decision-making table of these multinational organizations, much less ascended to the top of the corporation. For example, the bank HSBC had a long-standing practice of hiring 200 expatriates from the United Kingdom and sending them overseas to manage its local banks, mostly in Asia, in accordance with policies set in London.

During my years as president of Honeywell Europe in the 1980s, the corporation sent many American expatriates to regional and country operations to transfer U.S.-based marketing programs as well as engineering and manufacturing expertise. Too often U.S. colleagues seemed insensitive to the significant differences of the markets of Europe, the Middle East, and Africa and were intent on imposing U.S. practices on them. So I asked INSEAD professor Andre Laurent to create a leadership program for my American colleagues on cultural differences and how to bridge them. He proposed doing the first two days on American culture and the next two days on European cultures, saying, "Americans rarely understand their own cultural biases, and just assume their ways are superior if only others understood."

Companies are finding that imposing norms and marketing programs from headquarters does not work in emerging markets. In trying to sell food products globally, many consumer companies have learned the hard way that their products did not fit the tastes of local consumers. Thus, they were unable to compete head-to-head with skilled local companies in countries such as Japan, Korea, India, Brazil, and Russia that had a deeper understanding of local consumers' needs.

Building Diverse Leadership Teams

To maximize growth in emerging markets, companies are recognizing they require much greater diversity in their decision-making ranks. As Siemens CEO Peter Loescher said in 2008, "Siemens is not achieving its full potential on the international stage, because its management is too white, too German and too male. We are too one-dimensional." Arguing greater diversity was essential for Siemans's future, Loescher observed, "If your leadership does not reflect your global client base, you cannot achieve your full potential."

Consequently, companies are opening up their executive ranks to the best leaders from around the world, without regard to national origin. Coca-Cola, a longtime pioneer of this practice, paved the way by appointing five CEOs from outside the United States. Separately,

Daniel Vasella, the visionary who built Novartis from a Swiss-dominated company into a global one, initiated the move of Novartis's research headquarters from Basel, Switzerland, to Cambridge, Massachusetts, to tap into the top scientists at the Massachusetts Institute of Technology (MIT) and Harvard. Vasella also foresaw the need to move from a Swiss-dominated management team and board of directors to a global leadership team, without regard to nationality.

Despite their efforts, even progressive companies, such as Novartis, still struggle to develop top global leaders from emerging markets. CEO Joe Jimenez noted how difficult this process is: "You look around our executive committee and there's not one person from Brazil, China, or Russia. It's not because we don't look for them; it's because we haven't been able to develop them."

Developing Global Intelligence (GQ)

Succeeding in the new global context will require companies to cultivate a cadre of executives—as many as 500 per company—who have the capabilities of global leaders. Developing these new leaders requires unique leadership experiences, ideally in emerging markets, combined with leadership development programs that differ materially from today's corporate training programs. Traditionally, the latter have focused on managerial skills and building one's functional knowledge. Yet the shortcomings of leaders—and their subsequent failures—usually result from the lack of leadership capabilities that we call global intelligence, or GQ.

GQ consists of seven elements, all of which are essential for global leaders:

- Adaptability
- Awareness
- Curiosity
- Empathy
- Alignment

- Collaboration
- Integration

Several of these characteristics—such as awareness—seem very similar to parts of the process we've examined for discovering your True North. That's by design. Global interactions heighten the stress that leaders face. The more global the context, the more demanding leadership becomes. When leaders are placed in emerging market situations, the complexity increases exponentially because the differences in language, culture, customer preferences, negotiating tactics, business practices, laws, and ethical standards are so great. The same applies to the activities of daily living in these countries. That's why many otherwise solid leaders struggle with global assignments and working in emerging markets.

Let's examine each of these characteristics of global leaders.

Adaptability

Being a global leader requires the ability to understand today's volatile world and foresee changes coming in the years ahead. Global leaders must be able to adapt quickly to the rapidly changing global context by shifting resources to opportunity areas and developing contingency plans to cope with adverse geopolitical situations. This is particularly true in emerging markets, where frequent changes in government, currency movements, financial crises, ethnic conflicts, wars, and terrorism may literally change the business climate overnight. In recent years, we have seen this happen in Greece, Egypt, Iraq, Pakistan, Ukraine, Russia, and India, to mention just a few. Global leaders must be prepared to alter their tactics quickly to adjust to changes.

Awareness

Leaders need to understand the world around them, as well as themselves—their strengths, vulnerabilities, and biases—to perceive how they will react to the significant cultural differences they encounter. When people from developed countries live in emerging markets, they become much more aware of themselves and their insecurities as they begin to understand the complexities of other languages, being in the minority, and differences in cultures and norms.

Curiosity

Global leaders must have deep curiosity about the cultures they encounter. This includes a personal passion for diverse experiences and an insatiable desire to learn from other cultures. They also must be humble to recognize that different cultural norms and ways of doing things guiding other cultures may often be superior to their own. When you visit an emerging market, such as China or India, do you stay in a deluxe hotel and eat in Western restaurants, or do you get out into the country, meet the people, go to local markets and shops, and visit people's homes to see how they live? That marks the difference between domestic leaders traveling overseas and global leaders who are open to experiencing all the world has to offer.

Empathy

Empathy is the ability to walk in someone else's shoes. This requires humility and the capability to engage people from different cultures personally, rather than standing back and judging them. Empathy builds rapport and bonding and creates lasting relationships. Only with empathy are leaders able to draw the highest level of engagement from colleagues from different cultures and empower them to achieve exceptional performance.

Alignment

The challenge for global leaders is to align all employees around the company's mission and its values, a commitment that transcends national and cultural differences. Achieving alignment is far more difficult in a global context because the business practices and ethics in emerging markets often differ so dramatically from those of developed countries. Thus, global leaders are asking local employees to put the company's mission and values ahead of the business practices and values in countries where they have grown up and worked. It is no longer sufficient just to comply with the laws and ethics without regard for negative consequences their business practices may have on the countries in which they operate. However, this does *not* mean giving up their culture and the norms by which they live, because norms can vary widely from country to country.

Collaboration

In a global context, collaboration is the ability to create horizontal networks that cut across geographic lines, bring people together around common goals, and create a modus operandi that transcends geographic norms. In authentic global collaborations, participants put company and project goals first and work together in partnerships to achieve them. The most successful geographic collaborations are led by global leaders who know the strengths and weaknesses of each regional group and who make assignments within the team to take advantage of their relative strengths.

Integration

One of the greatest challenges global leaders face is incorporating local and global issues into an integrated corporate strategy. Such a strategy enables them to optimize their position in a wide array of local markets efficiently to create sustainable competitive advantage. Doing so requires deep understanding of local markets and the global vision to see how their companies can serve their customers' needs in a superior manner by leveraging their corporate strengths. That's the only way they can outcompete local companies, which often have a cost advantage because they operate in the region.

As Unilever's Manwani explained, "We have a globally distrib-uted organizational model that balances local relevance with global leverage."

We don't believe in "Think local; act global." Instead, we believe in "Act local; think global." The company starts by acting locally, creating relevance through an understanding of consumer needs and desires and their local cultures. Then we leverage Unilever's vast global resources to deliver superior products to meet those needs. This is how we gain competitive advantage over local producers. We are committed to bringing our expertise to local markets.

Increasing Your GQ

One of the best ways for aspiring leaders to increase their GQ is to live in an emerging country. The earlier in life you do so—when you are most open to learning about new cultures and taking risks—the greater your ability to understand emerging markets. If you are unable to move overseas, then at least visit developing countries and spend time in the countryside, where the culture can be more authentic and less international than in the metropolitan areas.

Novartis's Jimenez believes that physically living in different countries is critically important for the globalization of leaders. He explained:

When we take leaders out of their U.S. comfort zone and put them in a country like China or India, where they have to figure out how to buy groceries, go to the doctor, and exist in another country, we see powerful transformations in their self-awareness, empathy, and respect for other cultures. As a result, they figure out how to grow their business using different business models than the ones they are used to.

Operating in emerging markets where everything is different—the language, customs, culture, laws, and preferences—forces leaders to challenge assumptions about themselves. Global leaders must examine why they react in certain ways when confronted with extreme differences. If they are open to these entirely new experiences and approach them with a deep desire to learn, they will gain much higher levels of awareness.

Leading crosscultural task teams can also provide deeper understanding of cultural differences. It is also important to learn an area's languages to communicate more effectively with local people. Often the unique aspects of a culture are revealed through language, nuances that can be missed when locals have to shift to your language.

Interpersonally, global leaders must possess GQ to empower people throughout the world. If they lack GQ, their view of their colleagues and customers in emerging markets becomes more rigid and judgmental, and their learning is constrained. Instead of increasing their empathy for people's differences, discomfort may cause them to withdraw from intimate engagement.

When working with teams from many cultures, leaders without GQ skills try to force people into their company's dominant culture rather than create a collaborative environment that draws out the best of each of their teammates. Rather than enhancing learning, creativity and innovation, they stifle it. That's why it is so important to develop your GQ as a global leader early in your life while your mind is most receptive to new experiences.

Emerging Global Leaders

In many ways, the new generation of leaders is setting the standards for leading globally. To understand how they develop their GQ, let's look at some examples of younger leaders who have already developed as global leaders.

David Thai, the Serial Entrepreneur

David Thai was born in Vietnam in 1972. As the war wound down and Communists took over the country, his family was forced to flee to Vanuatu, a small island in the South Pacific. In his early years, Thai moved a dozen times before his family eventually settled in Redmond, Washington. Thai's entrepreneurial instincts showed up early. When he was only 12, he sold candy door-to-door, but soon realized more lucrative opportunities by selling to businesses. His success empowered him to create several more businesses in high school and at the University of Washington.

Wanting to explore his roots, yet with little comprehension of the language, he traveled to Vietnam against his parents' wishes. "Toward the end of my university education," he explained, "I felt a burning desire to discover myself. Returning to Vietnam not only helped me to understand who I am, but also ignited my desire to build a lasting legacy for the next generation in Vietnam and Southeast Asia."

Inspired by the success of Starbucks in his hometown, he created his first full-time business at age 25: the Highlands Coffee Company, which sold packaged local coffee through retailers. Its founding marked the first time a Vietnamese person living overseas was able to register a private company within Vietnam. With the success of his brand, he created a retail chain of Highlands Coffee stores around Ho Chi Minh City and Hanoi, all sourced from local coffee growers. Today, Vietnam ranks second only to Brazil in coffee production. Thai's success led to his creation of Viet Thai International, a holding company for several additional businesses, including Pho 24 Vietnamese noodles.

For his accomplishments, Thai was named a Young Global Leader of the World Economic Forum in 2009. Despite all his success, he remains remarkably humble—a serial entrepreneur committed to free enterprise within the auspices of Vietnam's Communist government.

Tamara Rogers, the Traveler

Unilever's Tamara Rogers was born in Zambia after her parents left England when they were 21 and 18. She said, "I've been traveling since the day I was born. By the age of 10, I had been to most African countries, Thailand, Singapore, the U.S., and many countries in Europe. I became comfortable with different languages, cultures, faces, colors, creeds, and I loved it." Rogers went to the United Kingdom for her high school education but took a year off to explore countries in Latin America, living from a backpack on three dollars per day.

Following a serious automobile accident that left her pelvis broken in five places, she returned to school with the desire to live every day to the fullest. After graduating from college, she took time to travel throughout Asia before joining Unilever. Within the company, her strength lies in bringing together leaders from diverse backgrounds, helping bring out the best in each of them, and getting them to collaborate to produce creative solutions.

Rogers's skills in leading people have made her a very effective senior vice president at Unilever, where she has been promoted several times in recent years. She explained, "In Asia, I learned to turn up the volume on listening and down on talking."

While Americans and Germans give clear and direct messages, in Asia you can miss what people are trying to tell you, so you have to turn up the amplifier to pick up the signals. I love that diversity. On my leadership team, we encourage everyone to express their point of view to be sure everyone is being heard. We develop people by encouraging them to move out of their comfort zones, as this is where they learn the most, yet give them a safety net.

Peilung Li, the Rebel

Peilung Li, who at only 39 is chair of SoftBank Investment China, faced many challenges in his early years. He learned he could thrive only by going his own way. Born in Taiwan, Li suffered loneliness at the age of five when his parents divorced. Life got even tougher when his mother married a strict disciplinarian he was afraid of. Because he saw the world so differently from his instructors, Li was bored in school and became known as a rebel and troublemaker. So he turned inward and used art to express his ideas.

When he was 15, he moved to California to live with his uncle, where he was forced to become independent. Speaking little English, he spent most of his time drawing. When his mother immigrated to the United States to start a restaurant, they moved to a lower-class neighborhood. There he had to confront robberies in her restaurant, and later he was assaulted at gunpoint in his school bathroom. "I was terrified that the robbers would attack me again because they saw me in court when I testified," he explained. "In order to protect myself, I decided to dress in disguise."

After graduating from the University of California, Santa Barbara, he won a scholarship to study in Japan, where once again he did not speak the language. Nevertheless, he excelled in his Japanese school and stayed in Japan to work in consulting. More than once, he had to challenge his superiors' ethics. Joining Daiwa Securities in Tokyo, he was sent to China to create a four-way joint venture, where he frequently got in disputes with the partners over misuse of funds.

After a brief stint in the United States, Li joined SoftBank Investments (SBI), first in Tokyo and then in Beijing, using his language fluency and cultural understanding to build SoftBank's business in China. He frequently found himself in opposition to the ethics of the Chinese joint venture partner, and had to resist being blackmailed. Winning the trust of SBI's chair, Li set up a series of joint ventures out of his Shanghai office and was rewarded with the promotion to chair of SBI China.

What has enabled Li to be so successful before turning 40? Quite likely, his early experiences forced him to be his own person and to venture into new situations where he knew no one and did not understand the language. These experiences helped develop his character, his values, and the courage to take on challenging situations, while confronting dishonesty. This independence of thought and spirit characterizes not only Li but also the new generation of emerging global leaders.

Rodrigo Mascarenhas, the Multiplier

Rodrigo Mascarenhas grew up in Brazil—a shy boy who dreamed of becoming an astrophysicist. When he gave a speech in his Dale Carnegie course, he said, "Something inside of me clicked, and I changed completely. I learned by telling my story that I could connect to people's hearts and to their experiences. My self-confidence exploded."

Unfulfilled by working in his father's tire business, Mascarenhas went through the Hoffman Process of self-discovery, where he learned how to align his emotional self with his intellectual self, his body, and his spirit. That gave him the courage to break away from his father's business and get his MBA degree from Case Western. Work experiences led him from Brazil to Spain, the Czech Republic, and eventually London.

What has distinguished him in each situation is his ability to be a multiplier for people's abilities. He explained, "I have the gift of creating a bridge of trust with people."

I connected with something deeper inside them and helped them see their potential and blossom. They did the same with people around them, and it became a multiplying effect. Every time, they blossomed and became strong leaders, full of self-confidence. It impacted their lives, their children, their view of life, and even their physical condition . . .

I was sitting on the greatest gift anyone can have—a treasure box—without understanding who I was. I had the keys to the box, but instead I was looking outside myself, when the gift was already within me.

Because we live in a complex world where there are so many choices, it is easy to sell your soul for fame, money, and status. But my purpose is to impact people's lives in positive ways. Throughout my career I have been catapulted because I am a multiplier. It's this gift I have to reach out to people and connect with them at a deeper level, regardless of their nationality. Life doesn't get much better than that. I feel a powerful spiritual calling, because I am part of something larger than myself.

Abby Falik, Developing Global Leaders

At 27, Abby Falik founded the nonprofit Global Citizen Year to create a gap year for high school graduates who want to live and serve in an emerging market before going to college. A polished and accomplished woman, Falik got her exposure to emerging markets at a young age. At 13, her parents took her to Indonesia, where she encountered extreme poverty. Emotions of confusion and guilt overwhelmed her. "In the words of one of my mentors, once the social justice nerve gets exposed," she said, "you cannot ignore it." Her interactions with young people left her deeply unsettled. "I was born in a time and place where I've been told I can be whatever I want. Talking to young people who were growing up in a dramatically different context, I realized they had none of the opportunities I had, just because of where they were born."

Global experiences continued to shape Falik. In high school, she spent a summer teaching in Nicaragua while living with a family. "That experience solidified my desire to use my leadership in a global context," she said, "but I also learned that leadership was about humility, listening, and patience." She left Nicaragua committed to developing herself to address these issues. During college, Falik took a year off from school and returned to the Nicaraguan community, determined to build a library. "The books I had brought when I was 16 were still being passed around the community because there were so few books. There was a long waiting list just to devour the books I brought five years before."

Falik's idealism hit obstacles. "This experience was the hardest and most humbling of my life. I had arrived with some resources, yet had no idea how to make things work." Community fissures slowed the library project. She explained, "I had no business being a forewoman on a construction project in a foreign language and culture," she said. "At the end of each day, I was deflated that more progress wasn't being made, but I also learned that failure can be constructive."

Before founding Global Citizen Year, Falik sought advice from Teach For America's Wendy Kopp. She dreamed of growth like that organization's rocketlike trajectory, but the market for donors and fellows for a gap-year program wasn't as large. Although the pace was slower than anticipated, she stayed focused on her purpose. As one of her board members observed, "I have never seen anyone as unwavering in commitment to her mission. She just kept pushing to sign up donors and students, believing we had to change the way we prepare young people for global leadership."

Falik's experiences living in emerging markets shaped the program she designed for Global Citizen Year. Her goal is for every high school graduate to consider a bridge year before going to college. In 2015, Falik sent 100 graduates on yearlong service fellowships in Brazil, Senegal, and Ecuador. She observed:

Early on, fellows face loneliness in living with their host families and undertaking service assignments in unfamiliar languages, which forces them to look inside themselves. My experiences in my gap year broke me down. When everything is new and uncomfortable, you see yourself through a fresh lens.

Today, the cohort of Global Fellows has grown tenfold. Increasingly, the organization is shaping a broader conversation on the role of service and global experience in higher education. Behind the scenes, Falik is advising government leaders and university presidents on how to give tomorrow's leaders global exposure. "It's an even bigger opportunity than I thought it could be," Falik said. "Within 10 years, I hope Global Citizen Year will influence all young people to live and serve abroad, become mindful, and grow into authentic global leaders."

The Future for Global Leaders

From Paul Polman to Peilung Li to Abby Falik, the new generation of authentic global leaders is changing the way business is done around the world. This new generation is much broader and worldly than my generation. These leaders recognize that in the future, businesses can thrive only by serving all the people of the world equitably while also contributing to their societies.

Exercise: Developing GQ

1. Have you immersed yourself in an unfamiliar environment and if so, what feelings did you experience—vulnerability, loneliness, uncertainty?

2. How will globalization change your organization's mix of customers and products? How will you need to grow and adapt to lead in the future state of the organization?

3. How high is your GQ? What concrete actions can you take to raise it?

Afterword

Stakeholders in Society

> I don't spend 15 minutes thinking about making money.
> What is important in my life is influencing many people as
> well as China's development.
> —Jack Ma, CEO, Alibaba

We conclude *Discover Your True North* by addressing the challenging, often controversial topic of the role of business in our twenty-first-century global society. We are at risk of losing sight of the purpose of business. It is not only to reward shareholders in the near term but also to build sustainable entities that create value for all their constituencies.

Jack Ma: China's First Global Leader

Alibaba's Jack Ma has emerged as China's first truly global leader, the face of the new China: a free-enterprise entrepreneur working within the confines of a Communist government to build a more equitable society.

Ma was on fire as we talked over lunch the day that Alibaba launched the largest initial public offering (IPO) in history. Its stock price makes Alibaba the eighteenth-largest global company by market capitalization. Ma's goal isn't making money. Because of Alibaba's success, he is already China's wealthiest citizen, with a $20 billion net worth. Yet when he asked his wife whether it was more important to be wealthy or have respect, they agreed upon respect.

In person, Ma is warm, affable, open, and authentic. For all his success, he is extremely humble, preferring to talk about building a great company that helps customers, creates jobs, and serves society. "I'm just a purist. I don't spend 15 minutes thinking about making money," he said. "What is important in my life is influencing many people as well as China's development. When I am by myself, I am relaxed and happy." He added, "They call me 'Crazy Jack.' I hope to stay crazy for the next 30 years."

China's large and growing economy has made it an increasing economic force the past two decades, but it has not produced global companies. Instead, Chinese businesses have focused domestically and engaged in low-cost production for international companies. Ma has a very different approach. He sees the Internet as a worldwide phenomenon that knows no borders. Today, the Alibaba companies serve 600 million customers in 240 countries. Ma intends to expand aggressively in the American, European, and emerging markets by linking 1 million small businesses with 2 billion Asian consumers. He also has plans to disrupt China's commercial banking and insurance sectors.

In the times I have been with him, Ma relishes telling his life story. Raised in humble origins in Hangzhou in the 1980s, he overcame one obstacle after another. He was rejected at virtually every school he applied to, even grade schools, because he didn't test well in math.

Yet he persevered. From ages 12 to 20, he rode his bicycle 40 minutes to a hotel where he could practice his English. "China was opening up, and a lot of foreign tourists went there," he said. "I showed them around as a free guide. Those eight years changed me deeply, as I became more globalized than most Chinese. What foreign visitors told us was different from what I learned from my teachers and books."

As a young man, Ma applied for jobs at 30 companies and was rejected at every one. He seemed most stung by his experience at Kentucky Fried Chicken where 24 people applied and 23 got jobs. Ma was the only applicant rejected. Consequently, he became an

English teacher at Hangzhou Electronics Technology College. When he visited America for the first time in 1999, he was stunned by the entrepreneurial culture he saw in California. "I got my dream from America," he said. "In the evenings in Silicon Valley, the roads were full of cars, and all the buildings had lights on. That's the vision of what I wanted to create [at home in China]."

Returning to Hangzhou, he and Joe Tsai (now executive vice chair) founded Alibaba in Ma's modest apartment. "We chose the name," he explained, "because people everywhere associate it with 'Open, Sesame,' the command Ali Baba used to open doors to hidden treasures in *One Thousand and One Nights*." Ma focused on applying his team's ideas to help businesses and consumers find their own hidden treasures. Yet he was unsuccessful in raising even $2 million from American venture capitalists, but, once again, he persevered. Eventually, he raised $5 million through Goldman Sachs, and later, Masayoshi Son of Japan's SoftBank invested $20 million.

Ma is passionate about building the Alibaba ecosystem in order to help people, a philosophy that he is trying to embed into the DNA of the company. At the company's founding, he issued generous stock option packages to early employees because he wanted to enrich their lives. The day of the IPO, he insisted Alibaba's six values—Customer First, Teamwork, Embrace Change, Integrity, Passion, Commitment—be placed on the pillars of the New York Stock Exchange.

Ma's commitment to a cause larger than himself has propelled him forward.

> My vision is to build an e-commerce ecosystem that allows consumers and businesses to do all aspects of business online. I want to create one million jobs, change China's social and economic environment, and make it the largest Internet market in the world.

American tech leaders, such as Larry Page of Google and Mark Zuckerberg of Facebook, have emphasized technology and product above everything. Not Ma. "I'm not a tech guy," he said. "I'm looking at technology with the eyes of my customers—normal people's eyes."

With his light-hearted nature, Ma participates in annual talent shows where he sings pop songs. He also practices Tai Chi and martial arts, which he calls "the most down-to-earth way of explaining Confucianism, Buddhism, and Taoism. These practices cherish brotherhood, morality, courage, emotion, and conscience."

Ma worries that China lost an entire generation when Mao Zedong phased out Confucianism and other forms of spirituality. His bold vision is to restore that sense of values and purpose to the next generation. "It's not policies we need, but genuine people," he said. Ma is highly ethical in his business practices. He noted, "I would rather shut down my company than pay a bribe."

For all his confidence, Ma is not without worries. He believes his biggest challenges are to create genuine value for his customers, to work cooperatively with the government, and to build his team of global leaders. He would like to use his wealth to found a university for entrepreneurs that can produce the next generation of Chinese entrepreneurs. "Our challenge," Ma said, "is to help more people to make money in a sustainable manner. That is not only good for them but also good for society."

The Purpose of Business

In recent years, short-term traders, including hedge funds, have steadily gained power. These active investors, compensated with high fees and earning 20 percent of the realized profits, have had an insidious effect on capitalism. Focused on driving short-term gains rather than investing in companies for long-term returns, they have created a frenzy to maximize short-term shareholder value. By forcing companies to cut research and other long-term investments, their pressure can destroy the economic value and the future viability of firms.

Nevertheless, the debate continues to rage about whether businesses are chartered to maximize value to their shareholders and owners, or whether they have broader obligations to all their stakeholders. In November 2014, as a guest lecturer for third-year students at the Harvard Law School, I posed the question: "Is the corporation an institution to be developed to serve society, or a collection of assets organized to maximize returns to investors?" I was both surprised and disappointed when all 30 students said it was the latter, to maximize returns to investors. They were so strong in their views that we had difficulty getting a good debate going on the topic.

In fact, the legal structure of publicly held corporations in most countries—a limited liability corporation—is chartered by society to serve society. Yet, the fierce pressures from shareholder groups over the past 30 years have convinced most investors and many business-people that their role is solely to manage assets to maximize near-term shareholder returns.

Sadly, many investors and companies take the legal freedom to operate as a given, not realizing the extreme remedies society can exact on companies when they misbehave. Therein lies the risk to capitalism. As we have seen since the fall of Enron in 2003 and the virtual collapse of the global financial system in 2008, unbounded capitalism is at risk of self-destructing. That's why the United States passed laws such as Sarbanes-Oxley in 2003 and Dodd-Frank in 2011 to restrain free markets. But laws alone are not the answer. What is required is that corporate and government leaders work together to restore capitalism to its original purpose of serving society through its mission to serve all its stakeholders.

Infosys founder Narayana Murthy believes the purpose of business must go beyond maximizing shareholder value. He said, "You cannot sustain long-term shareholder value unless you create sustainable value for your customers, while assuring fairness to all stakeholders: customers, employees, investors, vendor partners, governments, and society."

The best index of success is longevity. If you have existed for a long time, that means you have gone through thick and thin, learned to strengthen your character, focused on clients, and tightened your belt. That is what makes you stronger.

Murthy emerged from his experience in Paris in his twenties with four guiding principles that he calls "compassionate capitalism." First, the only way to remove poverty is to create new jobs and more wealth. Second, only a few people can lead the creation of these enterprises and create jobs and wealth. Third, these people need incentives to create wealth fairly. Finally, it is not the responsibility of the government to create jobs or wealth; the government's task is to create an environment where a fair incentive system encourages people to create more jobs and more wealth. He explained, "People need opportunities, incentives, and competition in order to better themselves. This is the essence of capitalism. If you combine the spirit of capitalism with fairness, decency, transparency, and honesty, the result is compassionate capitalism."

Whole Foods founder John Mackey addressed these issues directly in his 2013 book, *Conscious Capitalism*.

> *Our vision for Conscious Capitalism is to inspire the creation of more conscious businesses that are galvanized and aligned by higher purposes that serve the interests of all their stakeholders; with conscious leaders who exist in service to the company's purpose, the people it touches and the planet . . . Together, business leaders can liberate the extraordinary power of business and capitalism to create . . . a world of compassion, freedom, and prosperity.*

In my experience many proponents of maximizing shareholder value do not understand how companies create *sustainable* share-holder value—or they don't care because they are simply traders of stocks, not long-term investors in companies. Creating sustainable value must start with the alignment of all stakeholders around a shared mission and values in service to a corporation's customers and all those who have a stake in its success.

The mission provides the inspiration for employees to innovate and to give superior service to customers—and values are the glue that binds global companies together. In turn, innovation and superior service create revenue and profit growth, which creates sustainable

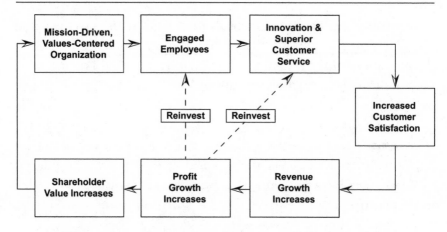

Figure A.1   Sustaining Growth and Performance

shareholder value, provided companies continue to make long-term investments to sustain their success (see Figure A.1). Thus, the interests of all stakeholders align, which puts the enterprise on a sustainable course.

Becoming Stakeholders in Society

At this point in history, when public trust in corporations and their leaders is so low, we need to move beyond the shareholder-versus-stakeholder debate and reframe it as: *How well are global corporations serving society through their business?*

Klaus Schwab, founder and CEO of the World Economic Forum, has long been a leading voice in advocating that corporate leaders must help address society's problems. His questions are even more pertinent now that global society is so closely intertwined. At dinner with a group that included me at Harvard, Schwab proposed the idea that instead of looking at society as one of their stakeholders, companies should consider themselves "stakeholders in society."

Professor Michael Porter and Mark Kramer addressed this issue in their seminal article in *Harvard Business Review* (January 2011), "Creating Shared Value." They proposed that the role of companies is to create value for society through their mainstream business, not just as a sidelight by using their philanthropic foundations.

In commenting on Porter's article, Unilever's Paul Polman said, "My philosophy goes one step further."

It's not enough anymore to say you contribute to a better world. You actually have to be part of the solution, and solve some of the issues to reverse what is happening. Instead of thinking how you can use society to be successful, you have to start thinking how you can contribute to society and the environment to be successful.

"To do these things, you must have a much higher level of transparency and a longer time frame than the stock markets try to impose on you," Polman explained.

Discovering my True North helps me because we are in a territory that nobody has walked. Frankly, the forces are against you until we have a drastic change in the way we measure externalities and the financial markets' success, which have brought us to the problems we have today.

Polman argued that being part of a socially responsible enterprise requires an even higher level of performance because the commitment you set to society is so much higher:

We need new business models led by a generation of leaders with the mind-set and courage to tackle the challenges of the future. Business must become part of the solution to those challenges. Issues like deforestation and food security cannot be tackled by just one company acting alone; they require collaboration within and across industry sectors. In a world of scarcity, there will be great pressure to ensure that wealth is created not just for the few, but that the benefits are spread to all.

Polman concluded by saying, "Unilever's purpose is having a sustainable business model that is put at the service of the greater good. It is as simple as that."

What if all companies reframed their purpose along these lines? Think of the impact that global companies and local enterprises—both for-profit and nonprofit—could have on addressing the world's most pressing problems: global health, food and water supplies, population control, energy and the environment, job creation, wealth distribution, and global peace.

Leaders can sustain the effectiveness of their organizations only if they empower employees around a shared purpose. As a leader, you must convey passion for the business every day while maintaining clarity about the mission of your organization. That's what Jack Ma, Ken Frazier, Indra Nooyi, and so many members of this new generation of global leaders are doing.

I hope that you, too, will commit to becoming an authentic leader who will Discover Your True North. The world faces important problems. Your leadership, teamed with that of other leaders who are similarly committed, is needed to build sustainable business, government, and nonprofit organizations that collectively make this world a better place to live for all the people who inhabit it.

New Leaders Featured in *Discover Your True North*

Name	Title	Organization
Abby Falik	Founder	Global Citizen Year
Alan Mulally	CEO	Ford Motor
Arianna Huffington	Founder	*Huffington Post*
Brad Garlinghouse	Founder	Hightail
Brian Cornell	CEO	Target
Chade-Meng Tan	Jolly Good Fellow	Google
David Thai	Founder	Viet Thai International
Donald Graham	CEO	Washington Post Company
Ellen Langer	Professor of Psychology	Harvard University
Erskine Bowles	Cochair	President's Commission on Fiscal Stability
Gail Klintworth	Senior Vice President of Sustainability	Unilever
Hank Paulson	Secretary of Treasury and former Chair and CEO	Goldman Sachs
Harish Manwani	Chief Operating Officer	Unilever
Indra Nooyi	CEO	PepsiCo
Jack Ma	Founder	Alibaba
Jes Lipson	Founder	ShareFile
Jim Wallis	Founder	Sojourners
Joe Jimenez	CEO	Novartis
John Hope Bryant	Founder	Operation Hope
John Mackey	Founder and Co-CEO	Whole Foods Market

(continued)

(*continued*)

Name	Title	Organization
Ken Frazier	CEO	Merck
Lance Armstrong	Cyclist	
Leena Nair	Vice President of Human Resources	Unilever
Lord John Browne	CEO	British Petroleum
Mark Zuckerberg	Founder and CEO	Facebook
Michael Bloomberg	Founder and CEO; former Mayor	Bloomberg; New York City
Nelson Mandela	President	South Africa
Omar Ishrak	CEO	Medtronic
Paul Polman	CEO	Unilever
Pedro Algorta	Survivor of Uruguayan rugby team's crash in the Andes	
Peilung Li	Chair	SoftBank China
Peter Loescher	CEO	Siemens
Rajat Gupta	Worldwide Managing Director	McKinsey
Richard Fuld	CEO	Lehman Brothers
Robert Greenleaf	Creator	Servant leadership
Rodrigo Mascarenhas	Managing Director	Bunzl
Sallie Krawcheck	Chief Financial Officer	Citigroup
Sam Palmisano	CEO	IBM
Seth Moulton	Representative	U.S. Congress
Sheryl Sandberg	Chief Operating Officer	Facebook
Steve Jobs	Founder	Apple
Tamara Rogers	Senior Vice President	Unilever
Taylor Carol	Student	Harvard University
Tim Cook	CEO	Apple
Tony Hsieh	CEO	Zappos
Tracy Britt	CEO	The Pampered Chef
Warren Buffett	CEO	Berkshire Hathaway
Zach Clayton	Founder	Three Ships

Note: The titles listed reflect the individuals' titles at the time of the interview or the story contained in this book.

Participants from the Original Research for *True North*

Name	Title	Organization
Addison "Tad" Piper	CEO	Piper Jaffray
Akshata Murthy	Student	Stanford Business School
Alan Horn	President	Warner Bros.
Ann Fudge	CEO	Young & Rubicam
Ann Moore	CEO	Time Inc.
Anne Mulcahy	CEO	Xerox
Bill Campbell	Chairman	Intuit
Brenda Barnes	CEO	Sara Lee
Bruce Chizen	CEO	Adobe Systems
Cesar Conde	Vice President	Univision
Charles Schwab	CEO	Charles Schwab
Chris O'Connell	Senior Vice President	Medtronic
Dave Cox	CEO	Cowles Media
David Pottruck	Co-CEO	Charles Schwab
David Gergen	Director	Center for Public Leadership, Harvard Kennedy School
Denise O'Leary	Venture capitalist	
Dick Kovacevich	CEO	Wells Fargo
Donna Dubinsky	CEO	Numenta
Doug Baker Jr.	CEO	Ecolab
Daniel Vasella	CEO	Novartis
Reatha Clark King	President	General Mills Foundation
Roy Vagelos	Former CEO	Merck
Gail McGovern	Professor	Harvard Business School

(*continued*)

(*continued*)

Name	Title	Organization
Howard Schultz	Chairman	Starbucks
Ian Chan	Founder	U.S. Genomics
Jack Brennan	CEO	Vanguard
Jaime Irick	Vice President	General Electric
Jean-Pierre Rosso	Chairman	World Economic Forum USA
Jeff Immelt	CEO	General Electric
John Donahoe	CEO	eBay
Jon Huntsman Sr.	Chairman	Huntsman
Judy Haberkorn	President, Consumer Sales	Verizon
Judy Vredenburgh	CEO	Big Brothers Big Sisters of America
Keith Krach	Former CEO	Ariba
Kent Thiry	CEO	DaVita
Kevin Sharer	CEO	Amgen
Lisa Dawe	Regional Operations Director	DaVita
Marilyn Carlson Nelson	CEO	Carlson Companies
Martha Goldberg Aronson	Vice President	Medtronic
Michele Hooper	Vice President	Baxter
Mike Baker	CEO	Arthrocare
Mike Sweeney	CEO	Steinway
Narayana Murthy	CEO	Infosys
Oprah Winfrey	Founder	Harpo
Paula Rosput Reynolds	CEO	Safeco
Per Lofberg	CEO	Merdo
Philip McCrea	Founder	Vitesse Learning
Randy Komisar	Partner	Kleiner Perkins Caufield & Byers
Sam Palmisano	CEO	IBM
Steve Rothschild	Founder	Twin Cities RISE!
Warren Bennis	Professor	University of Southern California
Warren Buffett	Chairman	Berkshire Hathaway
Wendy Kopp	Founder	Teach For America

Note: The titles listed reflect the individuals' titles at the time of their interview or the story contained in this book.

Where Are They Now?

A. G. Lafley   A. G. Lafley is chairman of the board, president, and CEO of Procter & Gamble. Lafley retired in 2010 and rejoined Procter & Gamble in May 2013.

Alan Horn   Alan Horn has been chairman of The Walt Disney Studios since June 2012.

Alice Woodwark   Alice Woodwark joined Compass Group as strategic development director in December 2013.

Andrea Jung   Andrea Jung is president and CEO of Grameen America, and a board member of Apple, General Electric, and Daimler AG.

Ann Fudge   Ann Fudge serves on the boards of General Electric, Novartis, Unilever, and Infosys.

Ann Moore   In February 2014, Ann Moore became founder of The Curator Gallery. She retired as CEO and chair of Time Inc. in 2011.

Anne Mulcahy   Anne Mulcahy is chair of Save the Children Federation. She retired as chair and CEO of Xerox in May 2010.

Bill Campbell   Bill Campbell is chairman of the board of Intuit.

Bill Gates   Bill Gates is founder and board member of Microsoft Corporation. He served as chairman of the board until February 2014. He is now focusing on the Gates Foundation.

Bob Fisher	Bob Fisher is director of The Gap, where he was previously CEO.
Bowen "Buzz" McCoy	Bowen "Buzz" McCoy is a real estate and business counselor with Buzz McCoy Associates.
Brenda Barnes	In 2010, Brenda Barnes resigned from her position as CEO of Sara Lee.
Bruce Chizen	Bruce Chizen is a venture partner at Voyager Capital, where he's served since 2009.
Cesar Conde	Cesar Conde is executive vice president at NBCUniversal.
Charles Schwab	Charles Schwab is chairman of The Charles Schwab Corporation.
Chris O'Connell	Chris O'Connell is executive vice president of Medtronic, where he has served since 2009.
Craig Venter	Craig Venter is founder and CEO of J. Craig Venter Institute and founder and CEO of Synthetic Genomics.
Dan Schulman	Dan Schulman is group president, Enterprise Growth, of American Express.
Dave Cox	In 1998, Dave Cox retired as CEO of Cowles Media.
David Darst	David Darst is a venture capitalist at OrbiMed Advisors.
David Dillon	Dave Dillon retired as chair and CEO of The Kroger Company at the end of 2013.
David Gergen	David Gergen is a professor of public service and codirector of the Center for Public Leadership at the Harvard Kennedy School, and is a regular commentator for CNN.
David Pottruck	David Pottruck serves as chair of HighTower Advisors.

Debra Dunn	Debra Dunn is a consulting associate professor at the Institute of Design at Stanford.
Denise O'Leary	Denise O'Leary is a private venture capital investor. She is a board member of Medtronic, US Airways, and Calpine Corporation.
Dermot Dunphy	Dermot Dunphy is CEO and executive chairman of Cryovac.
Dick Kovacevich	Dick Kovacevich serves as a member of the Federal Reserve's Federal Advisory Council. He was chair and CEO of Wells Fargo until 2009.
Don Carty	Don Carty is chairman of Virgin America and Porter Airlines.
Donna Dubinsky	Donna Dubinsky is CEO and cofounder of Numenta.
Douglas Baker Jr.	Douglas Baker Jr. is chairman of the board and CEO of Ecolab.
Daniel Vasella	Dr. Daniel Vasella served as CEO of Novartis from 1996 to 2010 and as board chair from 1999 to 2013. He is currently a board member of PepsiCo and American Express.
Reatha Clark King	Dr. Reatha Clark King is chairman of the National Association of Corporate directors, and former board member of Exxon Mobil, Wells Fargo, Minnesota Mutual, H. B. Fuller Company, and Lenox Group
Roy Vagelos	Dr. Roy Vagelos has served as chair of Regeneron Pharmaceuticals since 1995.
Durk Jager	Durk Jager served as director of Chiquita Brands International from December 2002 to November 2010.
Earl Bakken	Earl Bakken cofounded Medtronic and served as chairman and CEO from 1957 to 1976 and retired from the board in August 1994.

Ellen Breyer	Ellen Breyer is the former CEO of the Hazelden Foundation.
Ellen Marram	Ellen Marram serves on the board of directors for The New York Times Company, Ford Motor Company, and Eli Lilly and Company.
Fadi Ghandour	Fadi Ghandour is the president and vice chairman of Aramex International.
Gail McGovern	Gail McGovern has served as president and CEO of the American Red Cross since 2008.
George Shultz	George Shultz is a fellow at the Hoover Institution at Stanford University.
Howard Schultz	Howard Schultz is the chairman, president, and CEO of Starbucks Corporation.
Ian Chan	Ian Chan is founder and CEO of Abpro Corporation.
Jack Brennan	Jack Brennan serves on the board of General Electric and is chairman emeritus and senior advisor to Vanguard.
Jack Welch	Jack Welch is senior advisor to Clayton, Dubilier & Rice.
Jaime Irick	Jaime Irick is general manager for North America Professional Solutions at General Electric.
Jean-Pierre Rosso	Jean-Pierre Rosso is the chairman of the World Economic Forum USA.
Jeff Immelt	Jeff Immelt is the chairman and CEO of General Electric.
Jim Burke	In September 2012, Jim Burke passed away at the age of 87.
Jim Thompson	Jim Thompson teaches classes as part of Stanford University's Continuing Studies Program and has authored eight books.

Joe Rogers Jr.	Joe Rogers Jr. has served as chairman and CEO of Waffle House since 1973.
Joel Peterson	Joel Peterson is chairman of the board at JetBlue Airways and a faculty member at the Graduate School of Business at Stanford University.
John Browne	John Browne is managing director and managing partner (Europe) of Riverstone Holdings.
John Donahoe	John Donahoe has been president and CEO of eBay since 2008.
John Morgridge	John Morgridge is a trustee of Stanford University, where he teaches management at the Graduate School of Business.
John Thain	John Thain is chairman and CEO of CIT.
John Whitehead	In February 2015, John Whitehead passed away at the age of 92.
Jon Huntsman Sr.	Jon Huntsman Sr. is executive chairman of Huntsman Corporation.
Jonathan Doochin	Jonathan Doochin is CEO of Soligent Holdings.
Judy Haberkorn	Judy Haberkorn serves as a director for Computer Sciences Corporation.
Judy Vredenburgh	Judy Vredenburgh is the president and CEO of the Girl Scouts.
Julian Flannery	Julian Flannery is the cohead of Global Research at Gerson Lehrman Group.
Keith Krach	Keith Krach serves as chairman and CEO of DocuSign.
Kent Thiry	Kent Thiry is CEO of HealthCare Partners.
Kevin Sharer	Kevin Sharer is a senior lecturer of business administration at Harvard Business School.

Kris Johnson	Kris Johnson is president of Affinity Capital Management.
Lisa Dawe	Lisa Dawe is regional president, West Coast, of IntegraMed Fertility.
Lynn Forester de Rothschild	Lynn Forester de Rothschild serves on the boards of directors of the Economist Group, Weather Central, Christie's International, and the Estée Lauder Companies.
Marianne Toldalagi	Marianne Toldalagi is president of BTA-Partners.
Marilyn Carlson Nelson	Marilyn Carlson Nelson is former chairman and former CEO of Carlson.
Mark Reynoso	Mark Reynoso is CEO of EcoSense Lighting.
Martha Goldberg Aronson	Martha Goldberg Aronson is executive vice president of Ecolab.
Michele Hooper	Michele Hooper is CEO of MJH Consulting.
Mike Baker	Mike Baker was formerly CEO of Arthrocare.
Mike Sweeney	Michael Sweeney is CEO of Steinway.
Nancy Barry	Nancy Barry is founder and president of Enterprise Solutions to Poverty.
Narayana Murthy	Narayana Murthy is the founder of Infosys, where he served as CEO from 1981 to 2002 and as board chair until 2011. He is on the boards of HSBC, DBS Bank, Unilever, ICICI Bank, and NDTV.
Ned Barnholt	Ned Barnholt is chair of KLA-Tencor.
Nelson Mandela	In December 2013, Nelson Mandela passed away at the age of 95.
Oprah Winfrey	Oprah Winfrey is president of Harpo Productions.
Paula Rosput Reynolds	Paula Rosput Reynolds is president and CEO of PreferWest.

Penny George	Penny George is president of the George Family Foundation.
Phil McCrea	Philip McCrea is CEO of ClearPoint.
Randy Komisar	Randy Komisar is a partner at Kleiner Perkins Caufield & Byers.
Richard Grasso	From 1995 to 2003, Richard Grasso was chairman and CEO of the New York Stock Exchange.
Richard Tait	Richard Tait is CEO and cofounder of the sports drink company Golazo.
Rob Chess	Rob Chess is the chairman of OPX Biotechnologies.
Ryan Frederick	Ryan Frederick is the founder and president of Point Forward Solutions.
Sam Palmisano	Sam Palmisano was chair and CEO of IBM from 2002 until 2011.
Steve Rothschild	Steve Rothschild is the founder and chair of Twin Cities RISE!
Tad Piper	Tad Piper is a board member and former chair and CEO of Piper Jaffray.
Tom Tierney	Tom Tierney is the chairman and cofounder of the Bridgespan Group.
Warren Bennis	In July 2014, Warren Bennis passed away at the age of 89.
Warren Buffett	Warren Buffett is chairman and CEO of Berkshire Hathaway.
Wendy Kopp	Wendy Kopp is founder and CEO of Teach For America, and CEO of Teach For All.
Zyg Nagorski	In July 2011, Zyg Nagorski passed away at the age of 98.

References

Preface

Bennis, Warren. *Managing People Is Like Herding Cats: Warren Bennis on Leadership*. Provo: Executive Excellence Publishing, 1999, p. 163.

Bennis, Warren. *On Becoming a Leader*. New York: Perseus Books, 1989.

Bennis, Warren, and Patricia Ward Biederman. *Still Surprised: A Memoir of a Life in Leadership*. San Francisco: Jossey-Bass, 2010.

Bennis, Warren, and Joan Goldsmith. *Learning to Lead: A Workbook on Becoming a Leader*. 4th ed. New York: Basic Books, 2010.

George, Bill. *Authentic Leadership*. San Francisco: Jossey-Bass, 2003, p. xvi.

Longfellow, Henry Wadsworth. *A Psalm of Life*. New York: Cupples & Leon, 1900.

Introduction

George, Bill, and Andrew McLean. "Kevin Sharer at Amgen: Sustaining the High-Growth Company (A)." Boston: Harvard Business School, 2005, pp. 8–9.

James, William. *Letters of William James*. Vol. 1. 1878.

Medtronic. "One Company, One Mission." Accessed March 25, 2015. http://www.medtronic.com/us-en/about-3/mission-statement.html.

Werner Erhard Video. "Warren Bennis on the est Training." Video, 6:28. June 7, 2014. http://wernererhardvideo.com/warren-bennis-on-the-est-training/.

Chapter 1

Bennis, Warren, and Robert Thomas. *Geeks and Geezers: How Era, Values, and Defining Moments Shape Leaders*. Boston: Harvard Business School Press, 2002, p. 20.

Bloomberg, Michael, and Matthew Winkler. *Bloomberg by Bloomberg*. Hoboken, NJ: John Wiley & Sons, 2001.

Erikson, Erik. *Childhood and Society*. Reissue ed. New York: Norton, 1993.

George, Bill. *Authentic Leadership*. San Francisco: Jossey-Bass, 2003.

George, Bill, and Andrew McLean. "Howard Schultz: Building Starbucks Community." Boston: Harvard Business School, 2006, pp. 1–4.

John Barth quote from a conversation Barth had with Warren Bennis. Research interview with Warren Bennis, July 2005.

John Gardner quote from interview Gardner had with Warren Bennis. Research interview with Warren Bennis, July 2005.

Magee, David. *Jeff Immelt and the New GE Way: Innovation, Transformation, and Winning in the 21st Century*. New York: McGraw-Hill, 2009.

Sandberg, Sheryl. *Lean In: Women, Work, and the Will to Lead*. New York: Alfred A. Knopf, 2013, p. 53.

Chapter 2

George, Bill, and Andrew McLean. "Richard Grasso and the NYSE, Inc. (B)." Boston: Harvard Business School, 2005.

Gupta, Rajat. Speech at Columbia University, New York, 2005.

Hytha, Michael. "ArthroCare Ex-Chief Baker Gets 20-Year Term for Fraud." *Bloomberg*, August 30, 2014.

Jobs, Steve. Commencement address, Stanford University, Stanford, CA, June 12, 2005. http://news.stanford.edu/news/2005/june15/jobs-061505.html.

Lance Armstrong quote from a conversation Armstrong had with Oprah Winfrey. Interview with Oprah Winfrey, January 2013.

Mangalindan, J. P. "Why YouSendIt had to change its name." *Fortune*, July 10, 2013.

Paulson, Jr., Henry. *On the Brink: Inside the Race to Stop the Collapse of the Global Financial System*. New York: Business Plus, 2013, p. 138.

Raghavan, Anita. "Rajat Gupta's Lust for Zeros." *New York Times Magazine*, May 17, 2013.

Vasella, Daniel, and Clifton Leaf. "Daniel Vasella of Novartis Talks about Making the Numbers, Self-deception, and the Danger of Craving Success." *Fortune*, November 18, 2002.

Chapter 3

American Academy of Achievement. "Oprah Winfrey Interview." Last modified July 13, 2012. http://www.achievement.org/autodoc/page/win0int-1.

Bennis, Warren. *On Becoming a Leader*. New York: Perseus Books, 1989, p. xxiv.

Joseph, Stephen. *What Doesn't Kill Us: The New Psychology of Posttraumatic Growth*. New York: Basic Books, 2011.

Maslow, Abraham. "A Theory of Human Motivation." *Psychological Review*, 1943. Retrieved from http://psychclassics.yorku.ca/Maslow/motivation.htm.

Miller, Arthur. *The Crucible: A Play in Four Acts*. New York: Viking Press, 1953.

Pedro Algorta quote from a conversation Algorta had with Harvard Business School class, 2013.

Chapter 4

Browne, John. *The Glass Closet: Why Coming Out Is Good Business*. New York: HarperCollins, 2014, pp. 13, 21, and 182.

Bryant, John Hope. *How the Poor Can Save Capitalism: Rebuilding the Path to the Middle Class*. San Francisco: Berrett-Koehler Publishers, 2014.

Bryant, John Hope. *Love Leadership: The New Way to Lead in a Fear-Based World*. San Francisco: Jossey-Bass, 2009, p. 11.

Cook, Timothy. "Tim Cook Speaks Up." *Bloomberg Businessweek*, October 30, 2014.

Delphic Oracle. Inscription on the Oracle of Apollo at Delphi, Greece, sixth century BC, *The Columbia World of Quotations*, 1996. The words are traditionally ascribed to the "Seven Sages" or "Seven Wise Men" of ancient Greece, and specifically to Solon of Athens (c. 640–c. 558 BC).

Gelles, David. *Mindful Work: How Meditation Is Changing Business from the Inside Out*. New York: Houghton Mifflin Harcourt, 2015.

Goleman, Daniel. *Emotional Intelligence: Why It Can Matter More Than IQ*. New York: Bantam Books, 1995.

Kabat-Zinn, Jon. *Wherever You Go, There You Are: Mindfulness Meditation in Everyday Life*. New York: Hachette Books, 1994, pg. 3.

Langer, Ellen. *Mindfulness*. 2nd ed. A Merloyd Lawrence Book. Boston: Da Capo Lifelong Books, 2014.

Whyte, David. *Where Many Rivers Meet*. Langley, WA: Many Rivers Press, 1990.

Chapter 5

Jim Burke quotes from visit to Harvard Business School, 1994.

McLean, Andrew, Shailendra Singh, and Bill George."Narayana Murthy and Compassionate Capitalism." Boston: Harvard Business School, 2005, pp. 1, 6, and 8.

Sam Palmisano letter to IBM employees in "Our Values at Work: On Being An IBMer," November 2003.

Chapter 6

Berkshire Hathaway Annual Reports. Accessed March 25, 2015. http://www
.berkshirehathaway.com/reports.html.
George, Bill. "Truly Authentic Leadership." *US News and World Report*, October
30, 2006.
Lowenstein, Roger. *Buffett: The Making of an American Capitalist*. Reprint ed.
New York: Random House, 2008.
Schlender, Brent. "Gates and Buffett: The Bill and Warren Show." *Fortune*,
July 20, 1998.
Schroeder, Alice. *The Snowball: Warren Buffett and the Business of Life*. Updated
ed. New York: Bantam, 2009.
The concept of integrating one's motivations with one's abilities originated in
the System for Identifying Motivated Abilities. Accessed March 25,
2015. http://www.sima.co.uk.

Chapter 7

Kirkpatrick, David. *The Facebook Effect: The Inside Story of the Company That Is
Connecting the World*. New York: Simon & Schuster, 2010.
Stewart, Christopher, and Russell Adams. "When Zuckerberg Met Graham: A
Facebook Love Story." *Wall Street Journal*, January 5, 2012.

Chapter 8

Christensen, Clayton, James Allworth, and Karen Dillon. *How Will You
Measure Your Life?* New York: HarperCollins, 2012.
Langer, Ellen. "Ellen Langer—Science of Mindlessness and Mindfulness."
Interview by Krista Tippett. *On Being*, May 29, 2014. http://www
.onbeing.org/program/ellen-langer-science-of-mindlessness-and-
mindfulness/transcript/6335.
Sandberg, Sheryl. *Lean In: Women, Work, and the Will to Lead*. New York:
Alfred A. Knopf, 2013, pp. 122, 126, 129, 134, 138, and 139.

Chapter 9

Alighieri, Dante. *The Divine Comedy (The Inferno, The Purgatorio, and The
Paradiso)*. Translated by John Ciardi. New York: New American
Library, 2003.
Greenleaf, Robert. "The Servant as Leader." The Greenleaf Center for Servant
Leadership, 2008, p. 6.

Isaacson, Walter. *Steve Jobs*. New York: Simon & Schuster, 2011.

Jobs, Steve. Commencement address, Stanford University, Stanford, CA, June 12, 2005. http://news.stanford.edu/news/2005/june15/jobs-061505.html.

Mackey, John, and Rajendra Sisodia. *Conscious Capitalism: Liberating the Heroic Spirit of Business*. Boston: Harvard Business Review Press, 2014, p. 196.

Mandela, Nelson. *Long Walk to Freedom: The Autobiography of Nelson Mandela*. Boston: Little, Brown, 1994, pp. 563 and 568.

Chapter 10

Badaracco, Joseph, Jr., and Matthew Preble. "PepsiCo, Profits, and Food: The Belt Tightens." Boston: Harvard Business School, 2013.

Global Agenda Council on Values. "A New Social Covenant." Davos Kloster, Switzerland: World Economic Forum, 2013.

Stafford, William. *The Way It Is: New and Selected Poems*. Minneapolis: Graywolf Press, 1998.

Chapter 11

Brown, Daniel James. *The Boys in the Boat: Nine Americans and Their Epic Quest for Gold at the 1936 Berlin Olympics*. Reprint ed. New York: Penguin Books, 2014, p. 353.

George, Bill, and Andrew McLean. "Anne Mulcahy: Leading Xerox through the Perfect Storm (A)." Boston: Harvard Business School, 2005, pp. 5, 7, 8, 9, and 11.

George, Bill, and Andrew McLean. "Anne Mulcahy: Leading Xerox through the Perfect Storm (B)." Boston: Harvard Business School, 2005, pp. 2–3.

Gergen, David. *Eyewitness to Power: The Essence of Leadership: Nixon to Clinton*. New York: Touchstone, 2001, p. 177.

Hoffman, Bryce. *American Icon: Alan Mulally and the Fight to Save Ford Motor Company*. Reprint ed. New York: Crown Business, 2013, p. 58.

Hsieh, Tony. *Delivering Happiness: A Path to Profits, Passion, and Purpose*. Reprint ed. New York: Grand Central Publishing, 2013.

Goleman, Daniel. "Leadership That Gets Results," *Harvard Business Review*, March/April 2000.

Michelli, Joseph. *The Zappos Experience: 5 Principles to Inspire, Engage, and WOW*. New York: McGraw-Hill, 2011.

Chapter 12

George, Bill, and Natalie Kindred. "Omar Ishrak: Building Medtronic Globally." Boston: Harvard Business School, 2013.

Knoop, Carin-Isabel, Krishna Palepu, Matthew Preble, and Bill George.
"Unilever's Paul Polman: Developing Global Leaders." Boston:
Harvard Business School, 2013.

Milne, Richard. "Siemens 'Too White, German and Male.'" *Financial Times*,
June 24, 2008.

Palepu, Krishna, and Carin-Isabel Knoop. "Novartis' Sandoz." *Harvard Business
Review*, March 6, 2013.

Afterword

George, Bill. "Jack Ma on Alibaba, Entrepreneurs and the Role of Handstands."
New York Times, September 22, 2014.

Mackey, John, and Rajendra Sisodia. *Conscious Capitalism: Liberating the Heroic
Spirit of Business*. Boston: Harvard Business Review Press, 2014, p. 273.

Porter, Michael, and Mark Kramer. "Creating Shared Value." *Harvard Business
Review*, January 2011.

About the Author

Bill George is a senior fellow at Harvard Business School (HBS), where he teaches leadership in executive education programs. He was professor of management practice from 2004 to 2014. He is the author of four best-selling books: *Authentic Leadership*, *True North*, *Finding Your True North*, and *7 Lessons for Leading in Crisis*, and coauthor of *True North Groups* with Doug Baker Sr. He is faculty chair of HBS's executive education program Authentic Leadership Development and cochair of Leading Global Enterprises.

He was chair and CEO of Medtronic, the world's leading medical technology company. Under his leadership, Medtronic's market capitalization grew from $1.1 billion to $60 billion, averaging 35 percent a year. He joined Medtronic in 1989 as president and COO, was CEO from 1991 to 2001, and was chairman of the board from 1996 to 2002. Earlier in his career, he was an executive with Honeywell and Litton Industries and served in the U.S. Department of Defense.

He currently serves as a director of Goldman Sachs and the Mayo Clinic and recently served on the boards of ExxonMobil, Novartis, and Target. He is a director of Minnesota's Destination Medical Center Corporation and World Economic Forum USA.

He is the recipient of the 2014 Bower Award for Business Leadership from the Franklin Institute and the 2015 Lawrence A. Wein Award from CECP, and was elected to the National Academy of Engineering in 2012. He has been named one of the Top 25 Business Leaders of the Past 25 Years by PBS, Executive of the Year by the Academy of Management, and Director of the Year by the National Association of Corporate Directors.

He received his bachelor of science in industrial engineering with high honors from Georgia Tech and his MBA with high distinction from Harvard University, where he was a Baker Scholar. He has received honorary PhDs from Georgia Tech, Mayo Medical School, the University of St. Thomas, Augsburg College, and Bryant University. During 2002 to 2003, he was professor at the International Institute for Management Development and École Polytechnique in Lausanne, Switzerland, and executive-in-residence at Yale School of Management in 2003.

He and his wife, Penny, reside in Minneapolis, Minnesota.

Acknowledgments

I am deeply indebted to many people who contributed to *Discover Your True North* and to the ideas contained in these pages. First to Zach Clayton, who has been my partner throughout the process. Zach has added immeasurably to the quality of the text through his interviews of significant people in the book, his ideas, and his insightful editing. Additionally, he has helped me understand younger generations and especially their use of social media.

Next to Peter Sims, who coauthored the first edition of *True North*. Peter led the research process and interviews that provided the insights that still form the intellectual structure of this book, and is continuing his work as a thought leader—most recently with the publication of *Little Bets*. Diana Meyer contributed a great deal to the interviews and insights for the first edition and taught these ideas at New York University and Babson College.

The pioneering work on leadership by the late Warren Bennis, my mentor and dear friend, provided the intellectual basis for many of the ideas. He wisely guided me through the editing process in my first four books. David Gergen has been an invaluable partner and friend in advancing the new ideas on leadership throughout the past decade.

Without our leadership group at Harvard Business School (HBS), especially the research, leadership theories, and brilliant teaching of Dean Nitin Nohria, Scott Snook, and Tom DeLong, the new ideas in *Discover Your True North* would never have come together. I am also grateful to many other HBS colleagues for their insights, wisdom, and help in forming my ideas: most notably,

Michael Porter, Rob Kaplan, Jay Lorsch, Krishna Palepu, Clayton Christensen, Ranjay Gulati, Amy Edmondson, Joshua Margolis, Rosabeth Moss Kanter, Das Narayandas, Leslie Perlow, Lynn Paine, and Joe Bower.

I am grateful to the 47 new leaders whose stories find prominent roles in the ideas of *Discover Your True North*, and to the 125 leaders who offered their personal stories and perspectives on leadership for the first edition of *True North*. They are the role models for authentic leadership who provide evidence every day of the validity of these ideas as they practice them in the world.

Assistance from Shannon Vargo, Michael Friedberg, Tiffany Colon, Karen Murphy, and other John Wiley & Sons staff made the publication process smooth. Lauren Schwenk of Three Ships contributed edits and designs. Diane Weinhold and Stacy Walcheski of the George Family Office provided helpful support and project management.

Only with the insights, counsel, encouragement, and support of my wife, Penny, has this book been made possible. In discovering their True North and putting authentic leadership into practice, our sons, Jeff and Jon, and daughters-in-law, Renee Will and Jeannette Lager, have also helped these ideas come to life.

To all of you, I am deeply grateful for your support and for making this world a better place through your leadership.

Index

NOTE: Page references in *italics* refer to figures.

WELCOME TO YOUR JOURNEY TOWARD AUTHENTIC LEADERSHIP

WELCOME TO YOUR TRUE NORTH.

Whether you are just starting your leadership journey or are at the top of your organization, *The Discover Your True North Fieldbook* will help you become a better leader by learning to be an authentic one. Through reflective exercises, the *Fieldbook* helps you find the internal compass that guides you successfully through life — your True North.

With *The Discover Your True North Fieldbook* you will:

- Deepen your self-awareness
- Rediscover what motivates you to lead
- Learn how to lead from your values when it matters most
- Discover the purpose at the core of your leadership
- Grow as a global leader

The Discover Your True North Fieldbook is available at all online book retailers.

Work through the same lessons learned by MBA students at Harvard Business School and top leaders in many Fortune 100 companies!

START YOUR OWN JOURNEY TO DISCOVER YOUR TRUE NORTH AT
DISCOVERYOURTRUENORTH.ORG.